THE NEW NATURALIST
A SURVEY OF BRITISH NATURAL HISTORY

BRITISH SEALS

The aim of this series is to interest the general reader in the
wild life of Britain by recapturing the inquiring spirit of
the old naturalists. The Editors believe that the natural
pride of the British public in the native fauna and flora, to
which must be added concern for their conservation, is best
fostered by maintaining a high standard of accuracy combined with clarity of exposition in presenting the results of
modern scientific research.

BRITISH SEALS

H. R. HEWER
C.B.E., M.Sc., D.I.C.

Emeritus Professor in the
University of London

With 59 photographs in black and white
and 52 text figures

TAPLINGER PUBLISHING CO., INC.
NEW YORK

First published in the United States in 1974 by
TAPLINGER PUBLISHING CO., INC.
New York, New York

Library of Congress Catalog Card Number: 74-105
ISBN 0-8008-1056-2

CONTENTS

PLATES

FIGURES

EDITORS' PREFACE

SEALS are fascinating animals. Everyone knows what they look like, but most people, even some experienced naturalists, have only seen them alive in zoos, where the seals, and their relatives the sea lions, are such firm favourites with the crowds. It is not really difficult to see quite large numbers of both grey and common seals by visiting the correct coastal areas of Britain, but few casual visitors find themselves in the right place at the right time. The exception is the Farne Islands, where for many years great numbers of tourists have been able to see equally large numbers of grey seals, and to see the animals from boats without having to make the effort of walking long distances over sandy beaches and mud flats, or of scrambling energetically down steep and often treacherous cliffs.

Although seals are so well known, and are the subject of many fables and nursery tales, our knowledge of their life history and ecology was, until recently, very imperfect. We had little accurate knowledge of the size of their populations, and of whether they were increasing – as fishermen who believed they endangered their livelihood said – or whether they were in imminent danger of extinction – as some conservationists firmly insisted. Legislation on their protection, and efforts towards their control, were based on guesswork.

Professor Hewer would be the first to insist, as he does in several places in this book, that our knowledge is still imperfect and that much more research on these animals is still needed. But nevertheless our knowledge is now reasonably firmly based, and we are therefore glad to be able to publish this up to date and authoritative book at this time. We believe that, for the first time, it gives in one place the overall picture of these animals that many have been waiting for. It also enables the reader to understand the complex problems of seal conservation. Seals must be preserved, and this may sometimes include killing seals where (as in the Farne Islands) their numbers are too great for the habitat to support.

Professor Hewer modestly plays down his own contribution to our vastly increased knowledge of seals. He has himself, for over twenty years, been closely involved in all the major research in Britain. He has combined the careful laboratory investigations of the trained scientist with detailed studies of the animals, alive, in their natural habitats. As one fully employed as a university teacher (where his many students will testify to his conscientiousness) he has not always had the time or the opportunity to do, himself, all the experimental or observational work he would clearly have enjoyed, but all other workers in this field have gained so much from his freely given help and advice that his contribution to the whole subject has been unique. All other workers on British seals will readily acknowledge Professor Hewer as their spokesman.

Scientific knowledge of a subject is one thing, and this is the basis of this book, but its value is immensely enhanced by the fact that Professor Hewer really 'knows' seals. He has watched and lived alongside his subjects, and has come to know them as only one who is a skilled observer and a field naturalist can. These genuine observations on the living animals give this book a quality rarely found in works which also satisfy the most rigid canons of scientific accuracy.

AUTHOR'S PREFACE

THIS book has taken an unconscionable time being born. The usual excuses can be given but basically the subject has been a particularly active field of research over the past ten years, not only for myself but for the number of workers who have been drawn into it and whose contributions have been constantly filling in gaps in our knowledge. It has always been tempting to put off the day so that something interesting and useful might be included. The present moment is apt, not because there is a lull in research work, but because several events have combined to give research an added impetus and considerable advances can be anticipated in the near future. A stock-taking is therefore appropriate and this I have attempted to do.

Public opinion during this time has been aroused and the whole question of our seal populations has become over-heated largely in inverse ratio to the information available. While such debate is not conducive in itself to the elucidation of facts, it does create a political atmosphere in which funds become available for research. While my own work in the laboratory has been covered by the usual university finance, the collection of material and the field observations could only have been possible with the aid of official support, in this case through the Nature Conservancy. As the problems grew in number and scope, the appointment of special workers in seal biology became possible and I have not suffered the undue frustration of seeing interesting aspects neglected because they were beyond the capabilities of myself.

When I became involved in this work (1951) Mr J. L. Davies had already given some account of grey seal breeding on Ramsey Island and this had been followed up by Dr L. Harrison Matthews and others in 1950. Apart from Fraser Darling (now Sir Frank Darling) these were the only zoologists to interest themselves actively in research on British seals this century. Yet there were a number who had experience in Antarctica such as Dr Matthews himself and much is owed to their interest and encouragement over the last twenty years. It is very fitting that the head of the newly formed Seals Research Unit at Lowestoft, Nigel Bonner, served his apprenticeship in the antarctic.

For two things, and two things only, I take some credit; the first, a matter of priority, was that I decided that no further advance could be made in the understanding of the biology of the seals without having a completely reliable method of determining the age of a specimen. When in 1960 it was first possible to obtain specimens of breeding cows and bulls (in the otherwise 'protected season') the rapid formulation of a provisional life-table, which appeared as a breakthrough in understanding the life of the grey seal, was really due to the finding of a reliable method of age-determination some 5 years earlier.

The second, a matter of method, was that I believed that advances could best be made by keeping laboratory findings and field observations in close contact, each feeding back information or suggestion to the other for further research. For this reason I have spent much time in the field at all times of the year as well as using laboratory techniques to unravel the yearly sexual cycles.

This book is about seals and not about the people who study seals. I have therefore not introduced a lot of extraneous matter about the difficulties of field work other than as explanations as to why certain information is not available. Those of us, professional and amateur alike, who have observed seals in the 'field' have done so because we like the work no matter that occasionally conditions are somewhat inclement. Such do not last for long and modern types of transport and facilities really make things much easier than heretofore. When Dr Gorvett and I went to Shillay in 1954–55 no suitable portable radio equipment was available. In 1959 for the first North Rona expedition we had a receiver-transmitter capable of covering 100 miles. True it needed two people to carry the two parts and the massive batteries, while a 12 ft. aerial had to be erected (and dismantled each time in case it blew away). By 1962 the several parties working in Orkney each had two-way radio to each other (and the coastguard) in apparatus easily portable by one person. Parallel advances were made in sound apparatus for recording vocalisations. But perhaps the greatest benefit has been in the use of plastic containers and insulating material for the collection of material for later laboratory examination. By the mid-1960's I was able to obtain specimens of tissues and blood in Shetland, keep them at the low temperature necessary and send them to Oxford, where they arrived in perfect condition, for electron-microscopy and biochemical analyses. The advent of the high-speed inflatable dinghy has also contributed much towards landing parties obtaining material just as the helicopter and small plane have aided observation and censusing. One marvels at the work of early investigators such as Prof. W. Turner of Edinburgh who contributed much to our knowledge of seal and whale anatomy by the dissection of bodies many days old cast up on the beaches of Scotland. Nowadays it is possible to live among the seals in comfort and safety thanks to the advances in camping equipment, desiccated and tinned foods and weatherproof clothing. Although as Dr Backhouse has said there comes a time when we exclaim, 'What we suffer in the cause of science!', it is soon over and success is an ample reward.

It remains for me to thank the very large number of people without whose co-operation both the research and this book would have been impossible. First come the field-workers: J. L. Davies who started the 'seal movement' after the second war; the members of the Northumberland, Durham and

Newcastle-upon-Tyne Natural History Society ably inspired and led by Mrs Grace Hickling assisted by Dr J. Coulson of Durham University, A. W. Jones, I. M. Telfer and others; Prof. J. D. Craggs, N. F. Ellison and others who have recorded on the West Hoyle Bank for 15 years; U. M. and L. S. V. Venables whose work on common seals has been outstanding; Dr J. Morton Boyd who has maintained the grey seal work in the Nature Conservancy (Scotland) over the past 15 years, assisted by numerous other workers on the annual visits to North Rona. Among these must also be counted those who collected material: Dr J. D. Lockie who sent me the first from carcases in the Berwick-on-Tweed area, E. A. Smith who contributed so much from Orkney, Jack Landscail of Orkney and William Laurenson of Shetland whose marksmanship and skill in reclaiming bodies made collection as humane and as least wasteful as possible. My thanks go especially to those who have accompanied me on trips to uninhabited islands and have had to put up with my eccentricities: Dr Gorvett and the late J. W. Siddorn, both of Imperial College, Drs J. D. Boyd and J. D. Lockie and the late James MacGeogh, all of Nature Conservancy (Scotland) and most of all Dr K. M. Backhouse, who has been with me so often and to so many places and whose cheerfulness and resourcefulness have meant so much to me. I must also thank those who have encouraged me from time to time in the work: Dr L. Harrison Matthews F.R.S., Prof. E. C. Amoroso F.R.S., Prof. R. J. Harrison F.R.S., Dr R. M. Laws and other members of the Joint Committee.

Lastly I come to those who have read the manuscript and whose comments have been of great value to me: W. N. Bonner for the grey seal and W. Vaughan for the common seal. Nevertheless I must emphasise that all errors and omissions together with expressions of opinion are my sole responsibility. I do not mind sticking my neck out if it stimulates someone to find out the true facts.

CHAPTER I

THE PINNIPEDIA, THEIR MODE OF LIFE AND RELATIONS WITH OTHER MAMMALS

THERE are only two truly British species of seal, although a number of others may occasionally be seen in our water, usually in the north. Before these are considered in detail it is necessary to see how they fit into the group (Order) to which they belong, the Pinnipedia. These comprise the hair or true seals, (Phocidae), the fur-seals and sea-lions (Otariidae) and walruses (Odobaenidae). Collectively they may be found in all the oceans of the world although they are certainly most numerous, both in species and in individuals, in the cooler waters of the arctic and antarctic regions. A systematic list of all species of Pinnipedia with their common names and rough distributions will be found in Appendix A. However they are not the only group of marine mammals and a glimpse at the other forms which have reverted to an aquatic existence is an aid in recognising the special features which are the basic adaptations to life in the sea for warm-blooded air-breathing vertebrates such as the mammals.

Two other groups have forsaken their ancestral methods of living on land and taken to a wholly marine existence. These are the Cetacea, or whales, porpoises and dolphins, and the Sirenia, or sea-cows. All three groups are of great antiquity (in terms of mammals) and it is not altogether easy to be certain of their ancestral connections in any detail, since fossil forms are scarce and fragmentary. On the whole it may be stated that the Sirenia have connections with forms which are also related to the elephants (Proboscidea) while both Cetacea and Pinnipedia are related to carnivoran stock. It is not surprising therefore to find that the Sirenia are vegetarians, feeding on sea-weed, the Cetacea and Pinnipedia carnivorous, feeding on fish, squids and crustacea and other marine animals. The Cetacea broke away at a very early date long before the present carnivora became a defined Order of mammals. The Pinnipedia on the other hand have more recent connections and are directly related to the Carnivora. Indeed until recently they were always included as a Sub-order, and some systematists still so regard them.

The members of these three orders have features in common which have been evolved independently as essential adaptations to marine life. The most conspicuous of these is the streamlining of the animal by the production of a thick layer of blubber under the skin which not only smoothes out angularities but also provides an insulating layer against the low temperature of the water.

In addition the limbs are reduced in all, the long bones of the fore-limbs are shortened and in the Cetacea and Sirenia the hind-limbs are lost altogether, while in the Pinnipedia these hind-limbs are much modified. The body too is elongated and roughly spindle-shaped in its proportions. These modifications deal with two problems connected with water, namely its low temperature and its greater density. There remains a third which is in some ways more serious, namely, that these animals being mammals are firmly committed to air breathing, possessing lungs, so that access to the air is essential and a means of preventing the entry of water into the trachea and lungs equally so. All therefore have nostrils which are normally closed and are opened only by voluntary muscles when the head is above the surface of the water. The provision of oxygen to maintain activities when the animal is submerged is made in different ways in the different groups. For example Cetaceans dive with full lungs, pinnipedes with empty ones, but the details of respiration are complex and will be dealt with later. Propulsion through the dense medium of water has also led to another convergent feature, the fusing of the digits by webbing, either thin or thick, thus forming a flipper or fin out of the normal mammalian hand or foot. There is also a tendency for the hair to be reduced in length although this is not universal in the groups. In Cetacea and Sirenia the body is almost naked, but the vibrissae or moustachial hairs are retained either as normal tactile organs as in the Sirenia or much reduced in the Cetacea. In neither of these groups does the hair contribute to insulation. Nor does it do so in the hair-seals and other pinnipedes where the hair is short and easily wetted so that the water comes into direct contact with the skin. Only in the fur-seals is the hair dense so that on immersion a layer of air is trapped among the hairs of the undercoat and direct water to skin contact is prevented. Here the hair is accessory to the blubber as an insulating structure.

We are now beginning to deal with features in which there are considerable and obvious divergences between the groups and these can best be described by noting them in the pinnipedes and then briefly contrasting them with what appears in the other two orders. Unlike the Cetacea and Sirenia which are entirely aquatic throughout life, the Pinnipedia have not lost all contact with the land. Some spend more time in the water than others, but all come to land (or ice) for breeding and for basking between feeding bouts and therefore have retained an ability to move on land. This is achieved by two different methods, one found in the true seals and the other in the fur-seals, sea-lions and walruses (Fig. 1). In these latter the hind-limbs are still capable of being directed forwards and acting as a foot, albeit on an extremely short leg which is buried in blubber down to the ankle. Thus with the associated flexure of the trunk in the lumbar region they can move rapidly over a land surface. The true seals, however, have hind-limbs which are directed backwards and can only trail on land. Movement is therefore much more laboured in a terrestrial habitat. A comparison between the limbs of a fur-seal or sea-lion and those of a true seal shows clearly the very considerable differences not only in structure and posture, but also in use.

The fore-limbs of a fur-seal are long and on land are capable of reflexion between the wrist and palmar surface. The forearm and wrist form a vertical

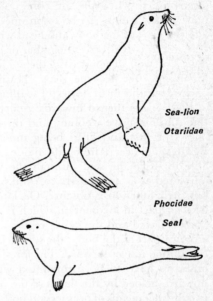

FIG. 1. External features of seal and sea-lion. Note the differences in the external ear, the longer fore-limb of the sea-lion and the way the hind-limbs of the sea-lion can turn forward compared with the trailing position in the seal. The sea-lion can raise the forepart of the body into an almost erect position.. The claws of the sea-lion are small and set back from the edge of the flippers. (*See also Plate 1*)

Sea-lion

Otariidae

Phocidae

Seal

prop as it were, while the hand, supported by the meta-carpal and digital bones, lies flat on the ground (Fig. 2a). The web between the digits is thin, in fact the whole of the distal part is much thinner and longer than in the true seals. This is associated with the much greater use which the fur-seals make of their fore-limbs in swimming. The claws are quite rudimentary and in some almost missing altogether. In the true seals the fore-arm is buried in blubber, and only the wrist and palmar surface with short digits protrude as short flaps (Fig. 1). The webbing cannot be distinguished as such for the digits are united by thick tissue so that the separate digital lines are not visible externally. The claws are strong and used for grooming the surface of the body. In the water these limbs are used principally for changing direction or for slow paddling, never for rapid movement, when they are held tightly pressed against the flanks. The digits still retain, as Backhouse has shown, an ability to flex with considerable power so that the animal can haul itself up over boulders and rocks and to some extent compensates for the loss of power of the hind-limbs. At any rate this is true for the northern true seals. In the antarctic species this ability if present is not used, so far as observations made by a number of observers appear to confirm (O'Gorman).

The hind-limbs of a fur-seal are also long but can be directed forwards for movement on land. They are also used on land during basking as fans. When fur-seals are hauled-out for breeding the bulls have to remain on their territories for a long time and they soon dry out. Their layer of blubber and the thick undercoat of fur, which keeps them warm in water, is now a disadvantage when the sun comes out. They then use the hind flippers as huge fans, turning the body on one side so that both flippers can fan the anterior part of the body and head which has less fur on it (Pl. 1). The claws here are usually absent altogether or quite rudimentary on the first and fifth digit but well developed in the middle three which can thus be used for grooming. In the true seals the hind-limbs are permanently directed backwards and form powerful sculling organs (Fig. 2). The palmar surfaces of the feet are turned inwards to face each other. The digits are united by thin and extensive webbing and the digits themselves are strong, the outer ones (the first and fifth) being much longer and thicker than the others. By alternate sweeps from side to side in a sculling movement these flippers are able to drive the seal through the water at great speed which has been estimated at as much as 12 to 15 m.p.h. Claws are retained on all the digits but their function is obscure. On land these hind flippers trail behind and take no part in locomotion which is achieved by a 'humping' motion. The body is flexed and the pelvic region advanced to give a forward push to the anterior part of the body, the stomach and the chest taking the main load as the animal moves forward. The fore-limbs are not used in this motion unless obstacles have to be surmounted when they assist in dragging the body upward, helped by the thrust of the pelvis. Thus in the Pinnipedia there are two distinct means of progression both on land and in water.

In the Cetacea the principal locomotor organ is the tail, flattened dorso-ventrally into a triangular fluke, and moved up and down in a sort of 'crawl' action. The hind-limbs are missing and the fore-limbs are well developed into flippers. Not only are the digits joined by thick webbing but the number of phalangeal bones is greatly increased so that the flipper becomes extremely flexible in its use as a propulsive organ and also in causing change in direction. The Sirenia are rather lethargic and movement is obtained by the action of the flattened tail and by the broad, short fore flippers. The latter are peculiar in having a great power of rotation so that their direction of action can vary over a wide angle. This is of considerable advantage when used as a paddle, the animal being able to turn almost in its own length, or when erect in the water, in little more than its own breadth.

A feature associated with streamlining is the reduction of the pinna or external ear flap. In the Pinnipedia all variations are found; among the fur-seals and sea-lions it is still fairly well developed but narrow (furled) and elongate, lying back alongside the head. For this reason they are often called the 'eared' seals. In the true seals it is much reduced and does not extend beyond the dried hair. When the hair is wet it can just be seen, if the light is right, as a circular rim round the earhole (Pl. 1). In the walrus it is

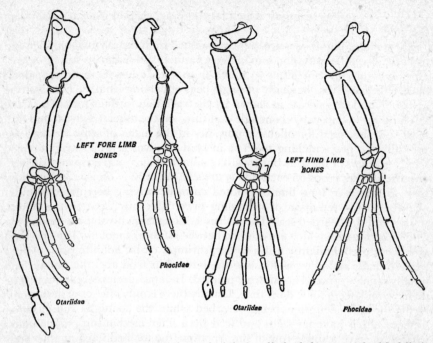

FIG. 2. Limb bones of seal and fur-seal: *left*, fore-limb skeletons; *right*, hind-limb skeletons. Note particularly the relatively small fore-limb of the seal (Phocidae) and the almost equal size of the 'big' and 'little' toes in the hind-limbs. In the Otariidae the 'thumb' and 'big' toe are much larger than the other digits, indicating the driving use made of *both* limbs. Notice too the very short thigh (femur) and upper arm (humerus) bones in both seal and fur-seal. For comparisons the hind-limbs of both are drawn to the same length and the fore-limbs to the same scale. *c.* $\times \frac{1}{10}$

equally inconspicuous. In both Cetaceans and Sirenia it is completely absent and in the former the earhole is plugged. (Only recently has the extraordinary hearing mechanism of whales and porpoises been demonstrated by Drs Fraser and Purves.)

The normal resting closed position of the nostrils has already been mentioned as common to all three groups. It remains to point out that the pinnipedes retain a 'rhinarium' external to the nostrils. This is the equivalent of the 'wet nose' of the dog and must constitute an important sense organ for the reception of chemical stimuli (scent). That it has to operate in water is no drawback because the molecules of the 'scent' must be dissolved before they can stimulate a receptor nerve ending, for which reason the rhinarium of land mammals is always kept moist with secreted mucus. In the pinnipedes it is possibly the sense organ which locates prey, such as shoals of fish at a distance.

The teeth of pinnipedes are greatly modified from the normal mammalian pattern. The differentiation into incisors, canines and molars is still recognisable, but they do not differ so much from each other as in other (land) mammals, consisting basically of single pegs of varying lengths. The incisors are small and degenerate as shown by the variation in their number. (It is not unusual to find two on one side and three on the other.) The canines are massive cones, used for offensive purposes in the males of some species but basically the prey-catching tooth as in land carnivores. The molars are no longer grinders or mashers but consist of a single major cusp or spike with one or more smaller cusps on each side *in line with the length of the jaw*. In this way there is formed a long line of pointed cusps of varying heights admirably adapted to the retention of struggling prey. The only exceptions are the walrus and the bearded seal. The walrus feeds on large bivalve molluscs, like clams and mussels, which are crushed between stub-like molars. The bearded seal is not predominantly a fish feeder, shrimps, crabs, holothurians, clams, whelks, snails and octopus forming the bulk of its food and the molars are usually much worn and not sharply pointed. In some species of seal the young do have milk teeth for a short time. Usually there is only one set of functional teeth, the milk dentition being resorbed while the foetus is still *in utero*. Cetacea either have no teeth and feed by a filter mechanism (whale-bone whales) or have a single row of simple cusps (the toothed whales, porpoises and dolphins), all alike, which are far more numerous than in any other mammal. This is a high specialisation for fish-eating, much greater than the pinnipede condition. The Sirenia have flattened grinders of degenerate form since the seaweeds on which they feed hardly require munching.

The skulls of most pinnipedes show traces of slow and incomplete ossification. This is particularly true of the region on a level with the eyes so that the front part can be easily detached from the hinder brainbox in even old animals. The fur-seals and seals differ considerably in the general appearance of their skulls thus lending support to the view that they are derived from different sections of the land carnivores (Fig. 3). The walrus is again an exception since there is massive ossification to provide support for the huge tusks. Cetacea have evolved quite differently since many of the cranial bones contain spaces filled with air or occasionally with oil. The Sirenia have massive skulls although the bone itself is not dense.

We now come to the respiratory modifications and it is impossible to separate these from peculiarities of the blood system since the oxygen required by the tissues is transported by the haemoglobin in the red cells of the blood. The modifications of the nostrils have already been mentioned, but there are others equally significant. Many pinnipedes have cartilaginous rings in the trachea which are incomplete on the upper side but some, and both of our British species are among them, have complete rings which thus prevent any collapse of the trachea when the seal is under pressure in diving. These rings are continued into the bronchi and bronchioles and cartilage continues to be found in the connective tissue of the lungs lying between the respiratory lobules. In addition there are, in the bronchi, valves of muscle

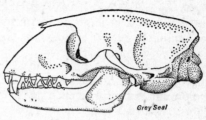

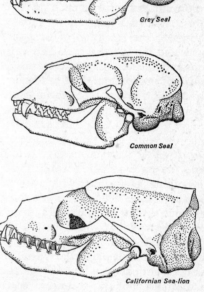

FIG. 3. Skulls of seals and sea-lion. All the skulls are of adult males. For comparisons the grey seal skull is drawn to the same length as that of the Californian sea-lion and the common seal skull to the same scale as that of the grey seal. Note the general similarities, particularly of the dentition, but also the differences which are most marked in the region behind the articulation of the lower jaw. c. × $\frac{1}{5}$

Grey Seal

Common Seal

Californian Sea-lion

and connective tissue which are able to form air-locks in the lungs and so prevent the residual air in the larger (and non-respiratory) tubes being forced under pressure into the respiratory alveoli. This appears to be a device to prevent nitrogen, which forms four-fifths of the air, being absorbed under pressure into the blood stream. If it were so absorbed, on return to the surface it would come out of solution in the blood under the reduced pressure to form gas bubbles in the smaller blood vessels and so cause 'bends' which can easily prove fatal, as it does when it occurs in man when diving.

The lungs themselves are not abnormally large and all pinnipedes *exhale* before or on diving so that there is literally little or no oxygen in the lungs to provide for tissue respiration during the activities of swimming and catching prey below the surface. The thorax, which also contains the heart and great

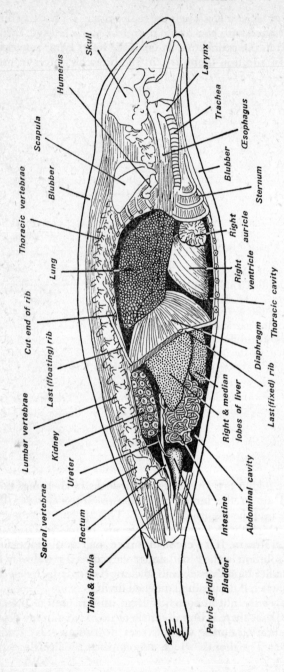

FIG. 4. Side view of the pinnipede body, to show the principal organs. The right side of the body is diagrammatically opened by removing the skin, blubber and outer muscle layers. The right fore-limb has also been removed as far as the 'elbow'. The genitalia are omitted. The œsophagus is indicated as passing above the heart and between the right and left lungs.

vessels besides the lungs, is more elongate than normal in mammals and the diaphragm, which separates its cavity from that of the abdomen, is set much more obliquely, its upper attachment to the body wall being set farther back than normal and the sternal support of the lower margin is shorter than usual (Fig. 4). This means that the cavity can be more completely compressed and a greater proportion of the air in the lungs exhaled than in normal land carnivores and other mammals. The small residium is driven into the non-respiratory trachea and bronchi. When the seal returns to the surface breathing recommences and a series of deep inhalations and expirations takes place. From my own observations on a southern elephant seal the number of such breaths is roughly proportional to the length of time that the nostrils have been closed. Even when on land and hauled-out seals will continue to remain with closed nostrils for considerable periods separated by series of breathings.

By way of contrast Cetaceans dive with full lungs and all the modifications are towards the prevention of collapse and the transmission of the external pressure to the air contained in the lungs; another 'anti-bends' device.

In the pinnipedes we are still left with the puzzle of how they obtain and maintain sufficient oxygen for their activities below the surface, and we must turn to the blood system for further information.

First it must be clear that if there is little or no air in the lungs there is no profit in circulating the blood from the lungs for there is no oxygen to pass on to the active tissues. It is therefore not altogether surprising to find that seals exhibit a phenomenon known as 'bradycardia'. This is a reduction in the heart beat both in the number per minute and in the strength of the beat. In fact it is reduced to little more than an occasional flutter by which some blood is circulated along the carotid artery to the brain. This has been shown to arise almost immediately the seal has dived, and in this it differs from the bradycardia of Cetaceans in which the rate and strength of the heart beat is *gradually* reduced to a low level. This difference must be associated with the difference of lung contents, the gradual bradycardia of Cetaceans keeping pace with the gradual exhaustion of the oxygen in the lungs (Fig. 5).

To prevent the 'used' blood from the tissues of the body being circulated even to a very minor degree in the pinnipedes, they have evolved a powerful sphincter muscle which closes the huge venous blood vessel leading to the heart and which draws blood from the hinder part of the body, the viscera and liver. This large blood vessel (*posterior vena cava*) is disproportionately large (usually double and enlarged) and so can act as a reservoir for the non-circulating blood. In addition there is a large vein lying below and up the sides of the spinal cord (*extradural vein*) which is enormously enlarged in pinnipedes. From it only a little blood can find its way back to the heart in the front region. Elsewhere this vein is connected by special large veins both directly to the *posterior vena cava* (at the hinder end where it is double) and indirectly round the kidneys in huge blood sinuses (Fig. 6). All these

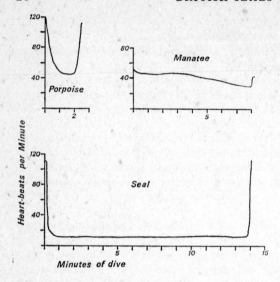

FIG. 5. Bradycardia in seal, porpoise and manatee. These are representatives of the three groups of truly marine mammals, the manatee, a surface feeder on seaweeds, being the least modified for diving. The seal immediately responds to diving by reducing heart activity, having expelled all the air from the lungs, while the porpoise, retaining air in the lungs, reduces the heart-beat rate only slowly. (*Redrawn from Irving, Scholander and Grinell, 1941*)

peculiarities increase the storage capacity of the venous system when bradycardia is in action. Some idea of the size of the veins will be conveyed by saying that in the grey seal the *posterior vena cava* in its posterior part is 'nearly as thick as your wrist' and King (1964) refers to their size in the walrus 'by the often quoted reference that they can be "pulled on like a pair of trousers" '.

But all these modifications tend to show that the blood is *not* the continuing source of oxygen during active diving. This is confirmed by two other facts; firstly the red blood cell count (the number of red blood cells per unit volume) is nothing out of the way, about 5–6 million (cf. human 4–5 million), and secondly that the amount of haemoglobin in a unit volume is not very high either, about 1.2 compared to the standard in man of 1.0. If this is all true, then how do seals manage to respire in their tissues during diving?

Part of the answer lies in another pigment known as myoglobin because it is present in muscle. Here we find an enormous difference from the normal and we hardly need figures to show it. Myoglobin is also coloured though not so deeply as haemoglobin and it gives the normal pink colour to muscle meat. In the Pinnipedia the muscle is almost black in colour, certainly very deep red. Those who remember the whale meat which was available after the second world war will recognise that Cetaceans too have a very high myoglobin content. To both of these groups then part of the answer is the ability to store oxygen attached to the myoglobin on the site where it is required for the respiration of the active muscle cells.

There is also evidence that these animals can run into oxygen debt, particularly in respect of metabolising the waste products, which are normally

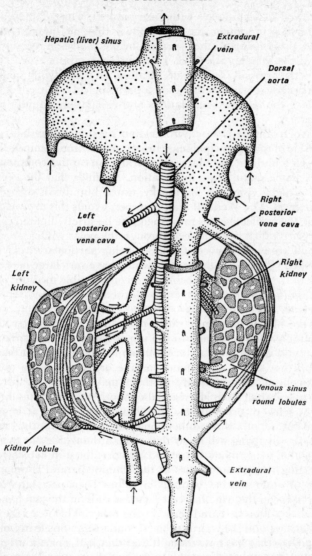

FIG. 6. Kidneys and *posterior vena cava*, showing the extra storage space in the blood sinuses. This is a view from above, the vertebral column and nerve cord being omitted. Part of the extradural vein is also omitted so as to allow the junction of the right and left branches of the *posterior vena cava* to be seen, with its continuation into the huge hepatic (liver) sinus. Arrows indicate the direction of the blood flow. (*Redrawn and somewhat modified from Harrison and Tomlinson, 1956*) × ¼

toxic if allowed to accumulate without treatment. This adaptation is not so extraordinary as it sounds, for it is known that, in humans, when slow starvation is prolonged and the organism begins to live on its muscle protein (autolysis of the muscle) a level of waste nitrogen products can build up to many times the normally *lethal* concentration. In these diving mammals this ability has become normal rather than a pathological occurrence. On return to the surface the repeated inhalations and exhalations rapidly restore the oxygen balance.

So atypic of mammals is the environment of the pinnipedes that speculation as to the value of their principal sense organs must come to mind. Not a great deal has been found out but Harrison, working on captive common seals, has contributed some useful basic information. He finds that the eyes are well adapted for night vision or for murky water but this is associated with short-sightedness. The Weddell seal, however, avoids this myopia by having a slit pupil. Their effectiveness must therefore be strictly limited particularly in those species which live and feed through the polar winter. Auditory and touch stimuli are well received, the latter being particularly relevant to the well-developed vibrissae on the muzzle which have very large nerves running from them to the brain. Water being an incompressible medium is excellent for the transmission of sound waves, so that sensitivity to auditory stimuli is to be expected. My own impression is that grey seals are more sensitive to sounds in the higher frequency range than those in the lower. *Phoca* and *Zalopus* both have good hearing in the upper range. It is possible that they can hear sounds which, to man, are ultrasonic but this has not been proved. Recent work has shown that many marine organisms make use of these higher frequencies and sensitivity to them may well be an advantage to carnivores in search of food. Harrison also found that the common seals have an excellent sense of orientation. This is obviously of great benefit to an animal making use of a three dimensional medium such as the sea. Anyone who has done any flying will know that man, although he has the necessary sense organs, has to learn how to use and interpret the stimuli received.

In discussing the characteristics of the Pinnipedia and comparing them with those of other marine mammalia it has been necessary to draw a distinction between the true, haired or earless seals on the one hand and the fur-seals and sea-lions or eared seals on the other. This is a very profound demarcation if we add the walrus to the second group. So clearly marked are these two groups that it is now thought that they had separate origins among the land carnivora, the true seals being derived from otter-like ancestors and the fur-seals and their relatives from bear-like forms. This can be expressed as shown at the top of p. 29.

The Otariidae are the least modified for marine existence. They retain a prominent external ear flap, there is an obvious neck region between the head and trunk, so that the body form is not perfectly streamlined or bobbin shaped, and their hind-limbs can be turned forward and used on land as feet.

Canoid (Dog-like) ancestral form

Ancestral otter-like forms (Lutrine)		Ancestral bear-like form (Ursine)	
↓		↓	
Phocoidea	(Super-families)	Otaroidea	
↓			
Phocidae	(Families)	*Otariidae*	*Odobaenidae*
(true seals)		(fur-seals &	(walrus)
		sea-lions)	

The pelvic region is also very obvious when they are on land. On the other hand the claws are much reduced either in numbers or size, and the flippers of both hind- and fore-limbs large and very well developed.

Their distribution is remarkable in that they are completely missing from the north Atlantic while present in all other oceans. Moreover, of the 12 species, 9 occur in the southern waters of the Atlantic, Indian and Pacific Oceans (including the circumpolar antarctic seas), 1 in sub-tropical Pacific waters and 2 in northern waters of the Pacific. Although this suggests that the family is southern in origin, palaeozoogeographical evidence (McLaren 1960) points to a north Pacific origin and that they evolved from a littoral canoid of bear-like appearance along the north-western coasts of North America, some time before the upper middle Miocene when their first fossils appear. Weight is given to this by the presence of the other ursine derivative, the walrus, in the circumpolar seas of the arctic. There are two sub-families: the Otariinae or sea-lions (with 5 species) and the Arcto-cephalinae or fur-seals (with 7 species). (See Appendix A, page 212.)

The Odobaenidae contain two species,* one Pacific and one Atlantic, both in arctic waters. It is probably better to consider them as sub-species of the one species: *Odobenus rosmarus*. Like the Otariidae they still retain hind flippers which can be used as feet, but they have become greatly modified in other respects. They are specialised feeders on shell fish; the tusks are used for digging the bivalves out of sand or mud and then the flattened molars crush them†. In the males the tusks are particularly well developed and used for fighting as well. Unlike the members of both the other families the walrus is almost hairless although the vibrissae on the muzzle are well developed as tactile organs. Although they have been hunted for many years and almost exterminated, they are now protected and some study is being made of their habits. The Atlantic form breeds on some of the Canadian islands and occasionally an immature individual is reported on the British coast.

The Phocidae have an inconspicuous external ear, concealed by dry hair

* Some would add a third, the Laptev walrus of the northern coast of eastern Siberia, but the numbers still surviving are small (4,000).

† But see p. 195.

but usually visible when wet. The neck is short and thick, smoothing the body outline into that of the head. The fore limbs are small and used for grooming, with well developed claws. Their use in swimming is small, usually only for changing direction or 'treading water'. On land they are not much employed in locomotion, although in the sub-family Phocinae the digital flexure enables them to clamber over rocks and broken ice. The hind flippers are the principal locomotor organs in water but trail on land. The movement of seals on land appears clumsy, but they can move faster for short distances than would be supposed. They occur in all the oceans of the world including the Mediterranean and Baltic Seas and several inland lakes which have had connection with the sea in glacial or post-glacial times. Until recently three sub-families have been recognised: Phocinae (with 8 species), Monachinae (with 7 species) and the Cystophorinae (with 3 species). Miss King (1966) however, has shown that the characters uniting the species of Cystophorinae are only superficial and differ in fundamentals, while many other characters show that the hooded seal is really a member of the Phocinae while the two elephant seals are closer to the Monachinae. Each of the two Sub-families are divided into two Tribes thus:

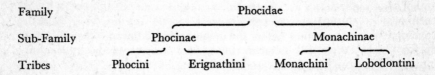

Family		Phocidae		
Sub-Family	Phocinae		Monachinae	
Tribes	Phocini	Erignathini	Monachini	Lobodontini

All the Phocinae are northern in both Atlantic and Pacific waters and their presently or recently connected seas and lakes. The Monachini or monk seals are tropical or sub-tropical while the Lobodontini are antarctic or sub-antarctic and circumpolar. The recent reallotting of the Cystophorinae species solves their equivocal position for the hooded seal as northern Atlantic and Pacific like the other Phocinae, while the elephant seals are brought more into line geographically with the southern distribution of the Lobodontini.

Despite the present wide distribution of the Phocidae the fossil evidence suggests their origin is Palaearctic from lutrine (otter-like) ancestors somewhere between early Oligocene and lower middle Miocene times.

Thus we can now say that the two seals which breed in British waters belong to the Phocinae, the two species, *Phoca vitulina* and *Halichoerus grypus* falling into the tribe Phocini.

Until recently much more had been discovered by British workers about the antarctic species of Lobodontini (and about the southern elephant seal) than about our own British species. How little was known until recently will become apparent when we consider each species separately, but something must be said about the reason for this neglect of our pinnipedes. Basically our ignorance has been due to the physical difficulties of obtaining information. Here we are dealing with animals which are amphibious. While they are on land we can watch them from the land but the slightest shift of the wind to send our scent towards them and they are away to sea where we cannot follow them. Extending this example to the period when they leave their breeding grounds on land, the problem becomes even greater. Antarctic forms, both mammals and birds, do not have a built-in fear of man and even the experiences of man's culling them over the last century and a half have not induced such a timidity as we find in the northern Atlantic species. Consequently there has been no easy way in which naturalists and zoologists could become interested in seals or, even if interested, pursue the study of them without a great deal of trouble, preparation and expense. It has, of course, been easier to kill them than to study them alive, but even then the difficulties involved have been sufficient to enable both species to survive under as great a pressure of persecution as man has found it possible and economical to mount. Had they been solely terrestrial they would have disappeared long ago. Had they been marine and social they may well have been as reduced in numbers as their fellow mammals the Cetacea. Only in modern times with greatly increased resources of powered boats, helicopters and of camping facilities in remote and uninhabited islands and coasts has it been possible to pursue a planned scheme of research on the grey seal. Investigation on the same scale for the common seal is yet to come, in fact it may not be necessary as its habits do not appear to be quite so complex, but it may be almost equally difficult to prove it.

Undoubtedly the species of pinnipede about which most is known is the northern fur-seal (*Callorhinus ursinus*). Its value as a fur-bearing animal made it essential that the main breeding colonies should be saved and during this century the United States Fish and Wildlife Service has carried out a series of investigations of the greatest importance. As a result of the knowledge gained it is now possible to 'manage' the population so as to obtain a maximum return of seal skins, consistent with the maintenance of the population at the necessary level of numbers and condition, at the same time preventing too great an excess which would adversely affect the important fishing interests of the north Pacific. While giving every credit to the ingenuity and skill of the research workers, it must be admitted that several factors have greatly assisted them. The first and obvious one is the economic value of the fur-seal which not only sanctioned the expenditure of money in research, but also provided considerable man-power (non-scientific) for major operations of tagging tens of thousands of the seal pups. The second factor involved is the behaviour of the immature groups which assemble on sites near to the breeding rookeries, segregated into the sexes. The adult bulls and cows too are markedly different in size and pelage and so can easily be distinguished at a distance without the aid of binoculars. Even in the non-breeding season help was available in an extensive pelagic sealing industry over the north

Pacific. Nothing comparable is available in the north Atlantic. For all the information available from ships in the North Sea, it might have no seals in it at all, yet we know now that young grey seals cross it regularly and that at certain times of the year the majority of grey seal cows are not in coastal waters. Consequently the pattern set out in detail for the northern fur-seal is of the greatest importance for purposes of comparison wherever possible.

British workers have been responsible for a great deal of work on antarctic pinnipedes such as the Weddell, crabeater and southern elephant seals (Phocidae), the southern sea-lion and southern fur-seal (Otariidae) in the course of the 'Discovery' investigations of the inter-war period and of the Falkland Islands Dependencies Survey after the second world war. These researches were undertaken in an attempt to save the natural resources of the southern whale and pinnipede populations. The latter had already been brought to a point of near extinction and the former could easily follow. As a matter of history the pinnipedes have been saved, while the whales have been brought near their end. We were probably right to put our energies into this exercise when we did for not only did it have a happy result for the seals, but we have acquired a national expertise in seals and sealing which is only equalled by that of the United States Fish and Wildlife Service who were responsible not only for the work in the Pribilov Islands, but also for research on the northern elephant seal and other pinnipedes off the Californian coast.

More recently the Canadian Arctic Biological Unit has been formed and is doing good work on seals and walrus off the western north Atlantic seaboard. In the Soviet Union attention has also been turned to this natural resource and work has been done on several species in the north western Pacific Ocean.

In the next chapter we shall see how in the last thirty years or so there has been a considerable growth in the interest shown by both professional and amateur zoologists in Britain in our own species. There has also been expressed a great deal of public concern over the status of our seals but much of this has been ill-informed. The problems are complex and over simplification can lead, as it has done in the past, to harmful action when only good is meant. Intentions are not enough; knowledge is essential.

PLATE I. *above:* Northern fur-seals, Pribilov Islands. The two bulls nearest the camera are using their hind flippers as fans to cool themselves in the bright sunlight.

below left: Bull grey seal, Shillay, Outer Hebrides. The external ear is a short tube caught by the light.

below right: Californian sea-lion. The external ear is a long narrow flap and very conspicuous.

PLATE 2. *above:* Porth Laoug, Ramsey Island, Pembrokeshire, typical of the narrow deeply shadowed coves on which only a few pups are born.

below: Eilean nan Ron, off Oronsay, Inner Hebrides. One of the small but crowded beaches, covered in dead seaweed used as rookeries. The surf can be seen breaking at the edge of the 'lowered' beach of rock, which surrounds the island. Easily accessible grass sward extends inland behind the beach, but is not used for pupping.

CHAPTER 2

THE GREY SEAL – INTRODUCTORY

THE relationships of the grey seal, *Halichoerus grypus* (Fab.) have been discussed in the previous chapter. It clearly emerges that this species occupies a unique position being the only species of the genus.

The world distribution of the grey seal is peculiar and unlike that of any other seal species. There appear to be three distinct populations (Fig. 7). To prove that there is *never* any interchange of individuals is practically impossible, but all the available evidence suggests that no real exchange takes place. The three populations are centred on the Baltic Sea, on the eastern north Atlantic and in the western north Atlantic. Davies (1957), in a very interesting paper which dealt with the possible geographical and historical reasons for this separation, suggested that these three populations should be called the Baltic, eastern Atlantic and western Atlantic respectively. There are also very good biological reasons for the separation. The eastern Atlantic grey seals, most of which are present in British waters, breed in the autumn;* the other two populations breed in late winter to early spring. Similarly the eastern Atlantic seals breed on land, either on beaches or on the landward slopes; the others tend to breed on ice and only if it is an exceptional year and there is little ice do the western Atlantic ones breed on the adjacent shore. Consequent upon these differences the social structure of the breeding seals is different. The eastern Atlantic seals tend to form large rookeries in which the cows outnumber the bulls by 5 to 10 times; in the ice-breeding forms a much closer approximation to equality is found in the western Atlantic region and such information as is available for the Baltic seems to suggest that the same applies there – isolated cows with their pups with attendant bulls over a wide area of ice floe.

Davies points out that all three populations must have been united during the last Inter-glacial period, occupying the seas from northern Labrador to Greenland, Iceland, Norway and the White Sea, on the average about 15° north of the present range (Fig. 8). As the species is a land-breeder as opposed to an ice-breeder the succeeding Glacial period would have forced the grey seals to separate into two populations, one occupying the seas from Newfoundland to Florida and the other the seas from the 'British Isles' (which were not separated from the continent at that time) to the Moroccan coast. With the first retreat of the ice and glacial conditions covering the 'British Isles' and northern Europe, the North Sea and Baltic Sea came into

* A few pups are born in Pembrokeshire and Cornwall in the spring. This anomaly will be discussed later.

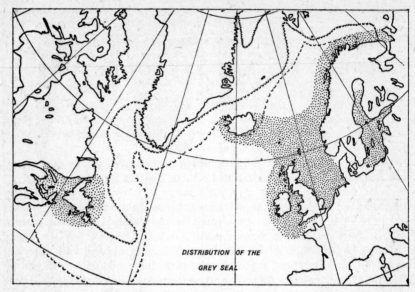

FIG. 7. World distribution of the grey seal. There are three distinct populations in: 1. the Western Atlantic, 2. the Eastern Atlantic and 3. the Baltic.

existence again broadly joined in the region now known as southern Sweden and Denmark. The grey seals of the eastern Atlantic had meanwhile moved northward again occupying the seas from the Bay of Biscay round the 'British Isles' and into the Baltic. However after this changes in the land and sea levels caused a land connection to appear between Sweden and north Germany (Pomerania) thus cutting off a lake comprising the area of the present Baltic, including the Gulf of Bothnia and most of present-day Finland. This is known as the Ancylus Lake and in it were isolated grey seals which formed the origin of the present Baltic population. Much more recently the North Sea and the Baltic have again been joined but only by very narrow channels at the southern end of the Kattegat. As we shall see later there is evidence that only the very northern end of the Kattegat is entered very occasionally by young grey seals. The main eastern Atlantic population of grey seals no longer use the southern shores of the North Sea which are sand and mud only, quite unlike the preferred rocky situations in Britain and Norway.

Until recently there has been a paucity of museum material. While this has been largely overcome for the eastern Atlantic form and some is being collected in Canada of the western Atlantic seals, practically nothing is yet available from the Baltic. In any case no one has yet brought what material

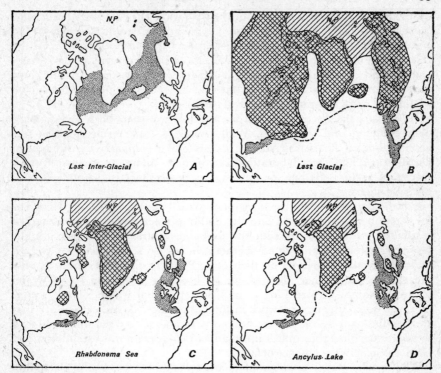

FIG. 8. The origin of the three populations of grey seals. Cross-hatched areas = glacial ice; diagonal lines = permanent sea (polar) ice; dotted line = approximate limit of seasonal drift ice; dotted areas = distribution of grey seals. A. shows the grey seals in *one* population close to the Arctic Circle in the Last Inter-glacial Period. B. shows the grey seals split into *two* populations, east and west Atlantic, by the maximum glaciation of the Last Glacial Period. C. shows the northward movement of the eastern Atlantic grey Seals following the retreating ice. The Baltic Sea is open to the North Sea across Denmark and southern Sweden, allowing entry of the grey seal. D. shows further northward movement of both ice and both populations of grey seals. England is still united to the continent but a bridge of land from Denmark to southern Sweden has locked off the Baltic population of grey seals. Since the period of the Ancylus Lake, Denmark has become separated from Sweden and England from the continent. (*Redrawn from Davies 1957*)

there is together for comparison. When this is done it is quite likely that sufficient difference will be found to warrant the recognition of 3 sub-species. The geographical isolation, which is normally required for such a recognition, appears to be complete and biologically reinforced. The Baltic grey seals occur in the Baltic itself and in the Gulf of Finland, but do not penetrate westward into the Bornholm area or the Kattegat. The eastern Atlantic seals occur from the west coast of Brittany, all round the British Isles and on the Norwegian coast, but few records exist of their appearance as adults on the Dutch coast or Frisian shores. Grey seals are certainly present in the Faeroes and Iceland region and it is thought that these are eastern Atlantic from their autumnal breeding season, but it is a far cry from Iceland to the western Atlantic breeding grounds off Nova Scotia.

In Canada the Arctic Unit has for a number of years been investigating both common and grey seals. While some of their results parallel our observations for the eastern Atlantic, others tend to emphasise the differences. Dr Mansfield and his collaborators have of course an interest in several other species of arctic seals but for our two species contact is maintained with British workers.

For the Baltic grey seal the story is not so satisfactory. Mr Oliver Hook has for a number of years been into the Baltic to track down the pups and to relate the ice movements with the probable centres of breeding. So far, however, except for willing co-operation in his work, the Swedes have not undertaken much research on their own. Political difficulties are probably the cause since further investigation of breeding areas and so on would almost certainly involve Finnish and Soviet coastal waters. There seems, however, some urgency for work in the Baltic since the indications are that the population is decreasing considerably. In an enclosed sea this could lead to near extermination, unless international co-operation is established and this is difficult in the absence of facts.

The species has a number of characteristics not normally taken into account by systematists which emphasise its uniqueness. All the other members of the Phocinae are either much more aquatic in their normal behaviour, or are confined to colder waters and associated with ice, or both. In British waters *Halichoerus grypus* is a truly temperate seal and always breeds on land. Both physical and behavioural (or ecological) characteristics tend to show that *Halichoerus grypus* diverged from the main Phocine stock early on. Its habit of breeding on land with the establishment of a social system may thus have evolved quite separately and does not indicate connecting links with other Pinnipede species in the Otariidae.

For many years the grey seal of Britain was thought to be the bearded seal, *Erignathus barbatus*, and it was not until 1825 that it was firmly established that it was *Halichoerus grypus*. This may appear to the layman as either merely a matter of words or else plainly stupid. But there is some excuse for this confusion. Normally when a species is named and described its name and description are tied to a specimen which is located in a museum, and any more specimens which might belong to that species can be compared with it. Unfortunately this is not the case with most species of seal and there has been an enormous amount of confusion, because everything depended on a verbal description. Consequently although it could confidently be asserted that

Halichoerus grypus existed (it could easily be seen in the Baltic) and that *Erignathus barbatus* was clearly different and occurred, widespread, in the north Atlantic, it was not known to which the grey seal of Britain belonged. The earlier descriptions of it were too vague, although several of the early workers thought they corresponded more nearly with those of the bearded seal. The really astounding thing was that there was such a paucity of material for comparison. Hundreds of grey seals were killed each year for blubber or hide, yet until very recently the British Museum (Natural History) had only *one* adult skull, and many international museums had none. No complete skeleton existed in any museum except the National Museum of Wales in Cardiff where that of a cow was mounted.* If the hard parts were not preserved then certainly the soft parts were not. No account of the general disposition of the viscera can be found in the literature and the information about most of the anatomy of soft parts contained in this book has been specially obtained by first-hand dissection.

An equal ignorance was displayed about the general behaviour and life-history of the animal. The principal account is given by Millais (1905) who collected together what previous writers had said and added a great many observations of his own. But all of this was anecdotal and largely based on occasional visits to rookeries lasting a few hours or at most a day or two. The basic difficulty was one of accessibility for, as we shall see, even the breeding sites are isolated and situated in some of the stormiest waters round the British Isles. When the seals are no longer on these rookeries they may be hauled-out on any of dozens of islets or skerries spread over many square miles of sea and can only be found by meticulous searching. We know now that these sites can alter with the seasons and may, to a lesser degree, alter from day to day depending on wind and tide or even, one feels, on the idiosyncrasies of the seals themselves. It is no wonder, therefore, that earlier workers found difficulties in establishing even the basic facts of the yearly cycles and life-histories of this seal, without the aid of modern means of transport.

The first serious attempt to come to grips with the problems posed by this species was made by F. Fraser Darling in the late 1930's. He decided to live with the grey seals and nearly all subsequent workers have done the same. This involves some difficulties and dangers, for all the islands involved are uninhabited and some are without fresh water. Consequently all supplies and a form of habitation must be taken ashore to cover not only the intended stay but for a much longer period, since return to the mainland is entirely dependent on weather and an enforced stay of up to a week tacked on to a planned three weeks is not unusual. Darling began his studies in small rookeries where each individual could be recognised and the progress of its behaviour related from day to day. Only in this way could the correct

* It had been obtained from a specimen which had lived in captivity in Cathay Park for over a quarter of a century.

succession or pattern of behaviour become firmly established. To plunge into a large rookery with hundreds or even thousands of individuals, more arriving and others departing, makes it impossible for the observer to understand what is happening unless prior experience has shown him the correct sequence of activities. Darling's observations in the Treshnish and Summer Isles therefore prepared him for North Rona, and his accounts of the breeding season are remarkably accurate.

In a book published in 1936 (*A Beast Book for the Pocket*) some 27 statements are made concerning the biology of the grey seal. Of these 22 are wrong; not slightly wrong but completely and utterly so. Darling's work altered all that for the autumnal period and for much of the summer.

After the second world war our knowledge increased rapidly. Mr J. L. Davies began in 1947 by investigating the breeding season in the comparatively small group found off the Pembrokeshire coast, notably on Ramsey Island. In two subsequent years, 1950–51 a small group from London led by Dr L. Harrison Matthews F.R.S. continued the work there and enlarged it to cover the nutrition of the pup and some basic aspects of reproduction. Quite independently in 1951 a group from the Northumberland, Durham and Newcastle-upon-Tyne Natural History Society led by Mrs Grace Hickling began to weigh and tag pups in the hope of tracing the movements of the moulters when once they had left the Farne Islands. Their success was immediate and the idea caught on. I had been with the group on Ramsey Island in 1951 and in the next two years tagged as many pups as I could. In the last of these years I was joined by Dr K. M. Backhouse who had taken part in the Farne Island work and who has continued to work with me both in the field and the laboratory ever since.

In 1954 and 1955 I went to Shillay in the Outer Hebrides to follow up a report of a disproportionate number of bull seals seen there by Dr J. Morton Boyd (who afterwards became Director of the Scottish Nature Conservancy). This led to interesting observations in pre-breeding behaviour, a field which is still largely open for the investigator. In 1956–57 Dr Backhouse joined me in observations in the Inner Hebrides, on islets off Oronsay, again to cover the pre-breeding period and the establishment of a breeding community on the rookery.

All these observations were connected with the breeding season, as, in fact, had been all the pre-war observations. In 1954 Dr Backhouse and myself decided to begin investigations during the winter and spring using the Ramsey Island group as our base as being within reasonable touch of London, travelling down over Friday night and back on Sunday night. This was dictated by our teaching duties during term time, but could be altered and ameliorated during the Christmas or Easter vacations. Our success was very limited since only two weekends a month were suitable on account of tides, and winter gales, either before or during the weekend, prevented us or the seals from reaching the island on many occasions.

Three very significant results emerged however; first that there was a delay in the development of the embryo (January 1956) and secondly that there was a small but quite significant number of births of spring pups (April 1956) and thirdly that this was associated in the Pembrokeshire group with large haul-outs of moulting bulls in the spring (April 1957).

Meanwhile quite unknown to us Prof. J. D. Craggs, an electronics engineer in the University of Liverpool, and N. F. Ellison, both active members of the Liverpool Natural History Society, turned their attention from the birds of Hilbre Island, off the Wirral peninsula, to the seals which gathered at low-water on the West Hoyle Bank a mile or so farther out to sea. These had previously not been very numerous and had always been thought to be common seals. They turned out to be grey seals and a series of observations made almost every fortnight throughout the year over five years (1952–57) showed not only that the numbers were increasing, but that they fluctuated regularly during the year. They were observing the obverse of those investigating the breeding grounds and thereby made a most valuable contribution.

To estimate the numbers of grey seals on and around the breeding grounds has always been an objective of observers and one of the difficulties has been the tendency of the seals to use small islands and skerries within a considerable radius from the breeding centre itself. Thus it was physically impossible to make a simultaneous count over the whole area, and this was imperative if the count was to have any significance. The use of an aeroplane had been tried during the breeding season in 1947 when J. L. Davies knew the numbers of seals from a 'ground count' in Pembrokeshire. It showed that little reliance could be placed on such observations unless the ground was fairly clear or only pups were being counted. Adults and moulters are too cryptically coloured to be easily recognisable. The only group which showed a promise of success was that of the Farne Islands where the haul-out points are necessarily limited to the outermost of the Outer Farnes and are not in fact far from the breeding islands of the Outer Farnes. From 1958 onwards monthly ground counts were made there by Mrs Hickling and Dr J. Coulson and so gave a picture the converse of Craggs and Ellison's.

In 1958 breeding of grey seals was discovered on Scroby Sands off Great Yarmouth and appeared to point to an increase and spread of the Farne Island group. In this year, too, North Rona became a National Nature Reserve so that in 1959 an expedition comprising Dr J. Morton Boyd and Dr J. Lockie of Nature Conservancy (Scotland), Mr J. MacGeogh, the honorary warden of North Rona and Sula Sgeir and myself (the only Sassenach!) landed there on October 1st to stay for at least three weeks and make periodic censuses of the pups and other observations. Similar expeditions have gone almost every year since with varying personnel to keep a check on the numbers. Dr Boyd also organised over several years observations from scattered points over the west coast of Scotland to see whether data could be collected indicating movements of seals to or from the breeding centres. Some interesting facts have emerged from this too and from aerial photographs of some islands to which access is extremely difficult and rarely possible.

But all this was field work and without a background of knowledge based on the examination of material in the laboratory many of the deductions which one would like to have made could only be very tentative. One of the outstanding problems related to the time-scale of the grey seal's life. Several views had been put forward in the past without any firm basis. This is very dangerous because such ideas are often repeated as though they were well established facts. Here was such an instance. Davies accepted the view that a 12-year life span was normal for the female grey seal and had based his calculations of the total south-western group population on this. There neither was then, nor is now, any way of determining the age of a seal in the field. At that time there was not any way of doing so even if the carcase of the animal was available for examination. 'How long do they live?' or 'How old is it?' are two of the commonest questions asked about animals and they are almost the most difficult to answer. To find a method was, therefore, of first priority.

Researches on the Pribilov fur-seal and several other mammals had shown during the post-war years that the deposition of some of the hard parts of the teeth was periodic and could be interpreted in terms of years, just as one can determine the age of some fish from their scales. By the late 1950's I had satisfied myself that the layers of cement on the outside of the root of the teeth could, after some practice, be so used in the grey seal with reasonable accuracy. All that was now wanted was more material.

During these years complaints from the salmon fishers, both rod and net, had been growing. Also from the white fish industry came reports that the occurrence of cod-worm was very much on the increase and the grey seal was blamed as the vector of this parasite while the Farne Island group were thought to be the centre of the culprits. Consequently the grey seal became of economic importance. The carcases of seals killed at the salmon nets along the east coast of Scotland were then made available and a great deal of material began to come in. It was not very well preserved of course and it was highly selective consisting only of those seals whose bodies could be recovered; if they were too heavy to handle they were not brought ashore. However, it was a start. Added to this an investigator, Mr E. A. Smith, was appointed in 1959 jointly by the Development Commission (on the Fisheries side) and by Nature Conservancy; he soon found that there was a group of grey seals (as well as common seals) in Orkney. Tagging soon showed that they were as guilty as the Farne Islands ones for depredations on the salmon of the Scottish east coast. Moreover the group was a very large one and could supply material in sufficient quantity for research without fear of seriously depleting the stocks. Of the other two known large groups, Farne Islands and North

Rona, one was a sanctuary under the National Trust and the other a National Nature Reserve. Orkney and later Shetland then supplied most of the really valuable material. Further, when some degree of cull was decided upon during the breeding season, the statutory protection afforded the grey seal since the early 1930's was lifted and for the first time we were able to obtain a sample of a breeding population in October 1960. Using the already discovered method of age determination an entirely new light was thrown on the age structure of the population, on the sexual life of both bulls and cows and many of the field observations previously made began to fall into place and to make sense.

Many more minor problems have been worked on since, particularly by Mr Smith in the field and by Dr Backhouse and myself in the laboratory. None of us however has failed to take part in the other type of work involved, since cross-fertilisation of ideas between field and laboratory is essential for orderly progress to be made. There remained of course a number of outstanding puzzles which will be mentioned in the pages which follow.

Within the last few years however, there have been developments which promise a continuation of systematic and sophisticated research, not only on the grey seal, but also on the common. The establishment of the 'Seals Research Unit' at Lowestoft under the National Environment Research Council with Mr Nigel Bonner in charge assisted by a small team of very active and resourceful zoologists has already shown what can be done using more modern equipment and the importance of prolonged co-ordination in work which must of necessity be scattered over a wide geographical area. Some of these results will be referred to later on.

It is now necessary to define certain words which will be used to describe collections of grey seals when found on land. In the past the term 'colony' has been used in so many different senses that it has become almost meaningless and I shall not employ it. Before appropriate alternative words could be found it was necessary to know something about the seals and how the world population was organised. Already it has been shown that there are three major units and I propose to refer to these as 'forms'. This term does not have the precise meaning taxonomically that 'sub-species' would carry but it does suggest that we are dealing with sub-units of the world population which are distinct on biological grounds as well as geographical. So little is known as yet of the break-down of the Baltic and western Atlantic forms that it is only possible to supply terms to describe the composition of the eastern Atlantic. Here first we must distinguish between the centre of breeding and places where, in the non-breeding season, the seals may haul out. The breeding centre will consist of 'rookeries' where pups are born and mating takes place. In addition there are collections of seals associated with the rookeries to which reference will be made later. The important biological fact of the rookery in relation to seal populations is that it is the *origin* of the population. If therefore the females may use one of several adjacent rookeries, the

products of these rookeries must be considered as a single population arising
from a 'group' of breeding centres. Here I propose the use of the word 'group'
to describe a subdivision of the eastern Atlantic population which appears to
behave as an entity and to possess some definable characteristics, either
geographical or biological or both, which separate them from other 'groups'.

In some instances we still do not know enough to be certain whether we are
dealing with one or two groups. For example, a number of grey seals breed
on the north Cornish coast, there is an occasional birth on the Isle of Lundy
and many more breed on the islands and coast of Pembrokeshire and
Cardiganshire. Are we justified in thinking of these as a single working unit
or 'group', or are there two? To add to the difficulty, just across the
St George's Channel, grey seals breed on the Irish islands of the Saltees and
farther north on Lambay Island off Dublin. Should these be separated or
included? What sort of evidence is there? We know that there are no
breeding sites in the northern part of the Irish Sea but in the area of the
Mersey Bight many can be seen in the non-breeding period of the year as
well as on Bardsey Island off the Caernarvonshire coast and around Holyhead
Island. Their numbers wane during the period when the Pembrokeshire
seals are breeding but some, instead of going south, might well go west or
south-west and breed on the Irish coast. Many a young seal in its first grey
coat, only a month or so old, marked in Pembrokeshire, has turned up on the
coast of Ireland even as far west as Galway Bay. Do they come back to the
Welsh coast when they are mature, or do they join the Irish breeding seals?
So far we have no definite answer and I prefer to think of a *south-western*
group which would include all those I have already mentioned on the west
and south coasts of Ireland, the Irish Sea, west Wales and Cornwall, the
Isles of Scilly and Ushant off the Brittany coast.

Other 'groups' for which there is some evidence are: *Southern Hebridean*,
comprising breeding areas on the Treshnish Isles (off Mull), in the islands
around Oronsay such as Eilean nan Ron and Ghaoidmeal and the occasional
birth recorded on Rathsay Island off Antrim, Northern Ireland; *Outer
Hebridean*, covering Gaskeir, Shillay, Coppay, Haskeir, Causamell, St Kilda
and North Rona, including Sula Sgeir; *Orkney and Shetland*; *North Sea*
comprising the Farne Islands, Isle of May and Scroby Sands (Figs. 9 and 10).

The islands detailed here are noted for the presence in the breeding season
of rookeries but there are other kinds of collections of grey seals particularly
in the non-breeding season to which descriptive names have been given.
Where the character of the collection is unknown it may simply be called a
'haul-out'. This may be qualified by the addition of an adjective as in a
'fishing haul-out'. Such a haul-out is temporary in the sense that although it
may be regularly used the number of the individuals may vary from day to
day and no one seal will necessarily remain there for very long. A fishing
haul-out is one where there are collected a sample of the grey seal population
using that area for fishing, as a temporary resting or basking site. The West

Hoyle Bank off the Wirral peninsula is a good example (Pl. 22). The seals there may vary from a very few (less than a dozen) to upwards of 200 depending on weather and tide. When not hauled-out they are probably feeding in the northern part of the Irish Sea. In some groups the absence of

Grey Seal

Recorded Sightings

FIG. 9. Distribution of the grey seal in British waters. Coasts where sightings have been recorded are shown in thick black line.

widely distributed haul-out sites often results in the same islands or groups of islands being used both as rookeries and for fishing haul-outs. It is rare however for exactly the same site to be used for the two purposes.

Another type of haul-out is the 'moulting haul-out'. These occur only in the later part of winter or early spring and consist predominantly of one sex or the other (Pl. 14). Such sites may be also used at other times as fishing haul-outs, but during the moult the numbers are often very great amounting to several thousand in the larger groups such as Orkney and Shetland. The number of these sites appears to be quite small, one or two alternative sites for use in different weather conditions sufficing.

As the breeding season approaches there are pre-breeding 'assemblages', not on the actual 'rookeries' or breeding sites, but usually adjacent. The number of seals there diminishes as the breeding season gets under way, but are replaced often on different skerries or islands by 'reservoirs' of grey seals. More will be said about the characteristics of these haul-outs later.

It cannot be too strongly emphasised that *all* of these haul-outs, including even the breeding rookeries, are biased samples of the population of the group. Never are all the members of a group collected together even within the land area covered by a number of breeding rookeries and reservoirs. Consequently there is no easy way to estimate the *total* number of grey seals in a group even if it were possible to carry out a simultaneous census on all land sites. The question 'How many grey seals are there?' is often asked by the layman. It is one of the most difficult to be answered by the scientist.

Some description of the geography involved is now desirable. Fraser Darling drew attention to the very variable conditions in which the grey seal breeds and considered that the land rookeries of North Rona represented the ancestral habit. Davies, who was a geographer as well as a zoologist, believed that the various breeding behaviours were forced on to the grey seal by the geographical features. Certainly it must be admitted that since the last glacial period the grey seal will have spread northward and that the most southern localities now used would have been the first to be occupied in these islands, if in fact they were ever entirely deserted. On the whole the evidence supports Davies. Certainly to understand the differences in behaviour the geography must be taken into account (Fig. 10).

SOUTH-WESTERN GROUP

This is the most widely dispersed group and although a considerable amount is known about the Welsh section, little information is available about either the Cornish or Irish sections apart from the barest outlines of the breeding localities. Throughout this group there is a tendency for the breeding sites to be small and contained in sea caves; they can hardly be dignified by the term rookeries as rarely more than a dozen cows pup in any one of the caves. Towards the middle of the breeding season pupping spreads to the beaches. These are either rocky or stony and backed by steep cliffs. Generally they are narrow so that at high water the sea may be lapping the base of the cliffs (Pl. 2). If this is not true at neap tides, it certainly is at springs. Several authors have referred to this group as the 'cave breeding seals'. Throughout the area will be found 'seal caves', the name may be used locally or may be 'official' and appear on Ordnance Survey maps. In many of the caves there are beaches only towards the back of the caves so that investigation can only be made from the sea. This feature has added to the difficulties of investigation for few, if any, of the local boatmen are willing to risk their craft close in among the rocks and currents of such exposed coasts. The steep cliffs also present problems if only of time in making a descent and return. However, they do provide vantage points for observation and counts of white coated pups can be made from the cliff-tops above the narrow beaches. At the sea caves observation can only be made of the cows bobbing about in the water. Observations over open beaches indicate that for every six pups on the beach about five cows can be seen as a maximum at any one time with their heads above water. One or more are usually off on a swim. This ratio can be

Grey Seal
Breeding Areas

FIG. 10. Distribution of the grey seal in British waters. The areas where breeding rookeries are known to occur are shown by black circles. On the Irish coast the exact localities are not known but possible sites are indicated by black spots. The size of the circle is *not* indicative of the numbers of seals involved in breeding.

applied to the caves to arrive at an approximate count of pups. Neither method allows one to make an accurate assessment of the age of the pup or its sex. This can only be done by ground investigation at close quarters. It is not surprising, therefore, that there is less accurate numerical information about the grey seals of this area than of any of the other groups. Another feature which adds to the difficulties of obtaining even the basic information is the length of the coastline involved. The island sites off the Welsh and Irish coasts are comparatively easy. As long ago as 1910 when the Clare Island survey was undertaken off Galway a reasonably complete account was given by Barrett-Hamilton of the breeding sites there. Similarly Lord Revelstoke (1907) describes the cave sites on Lambay Island, while more recently Davies gave an excellent record of the breeding season on Ramsey Island off Pembrokeshire. But the small widely distributed coastal beaches of Cornwall, the Welsh mainland and south-west Ireland have only been cursorily surveyed within the last few years.*

The narrow entrances to the caves and the shallow beaches both militate against the building of a social structure on shore during the breeding season. In this group the organisation takes its form in the sea and consequently the behaviour of both bulls and cows is very different from that found in the more northern groups. Over many weeks of observation maintained during the hours of daylight, I have only seen bulls ashore on four occasions and on two of these they were at the water's edge. Only in the most secluded coves can more than a few cows be seen at any one time, and then most will be seen to be suckling their pups and will have newly come ashore.

Little is known in the area occupied by this group of the use made of skerries and islands for non-breeding purposes. Haul-outs, presumably fishing ones, are usual on Lundy, the exact site being dictated by the weather. Skokholm and other Pembrokeshire islands and skerries have records of non-breeding haul-outs. Ramsey Island which provides one of the principal centres of breeding sites also has a moulting haul-out site in the late winter and spring. This beach, Aber Foel Fawr, which is inaccessible except by boat, but can be fully observed from a neighbouring cliff, is also used as a 'reservoir' during the breeding season as Davies has pointed out. Lockley has published a photograph of a beach with a similar moulting haul-out, but does not mention where it is. Since upwards of 200 seals, mostly of one sex, have been seen on each of these two beaches, it is possible that these are the only moulting sites for the Cornish-Pembroke-Wexford section of the group.

From what has been said about the difficulties of obtaining an accurate count of the pups and also from the absence of precise information about parts of the area occupied by this group, it will be readily appreciated that an estimate of the total number of grey seals in the group is very difficult to make. Estimates of the Welsh section made by Davies and, independently, by myself suggest that there were about 1,000 of all ages and both sexes connected with the breeding grounds of west Wales and the southern Irish Sea. This may now be exceeded. For Cornwall, the Scilly Isles and the west of Ireland the estimates cannot be much more than inspired guesses and would possibly add a total of 1,000+, making 2,000+ in all.

Despite the vagueness of this total it can be confidently said that the numbers are on the increase. Reference has already been made to the fishing haul-out on the West Hoyle Bank, off the Wirral peninsula, where Craggs and Ellison made counts of the grey seals. Quite apart from the seasonal variations, which were reported annually, their figures showed a steady increase year by year. Since the publication of their paper (1960) the number continued to increase but has levelled off in the last five years. This could, of course, mean that the Mersey Bight has become a more popular fishing ground, but independent observations, without however the

* A list of all known 'rookeries' and 'haul-outs' is given in Appendix B.

numerical precision of Craggs and Ellison's data, show an increase on Bardsey Island and on the west Wales breeding sites.

SOUTHERN HEBRIDEAN GROUP

This group is centred around the southern Inner Hebrides, more correctly known as The Ebudes. The group is a small one but of considerable geographical interest. The breeding rookeries are on the Treshnish Isles (west of Mull) and the islands of Ghaoidmeal and Eilean nan Ron, off Oronsay. Occasional pups are born on beaches on Colonsay. The skerries adjoining Ghaoidmeal called Eilean an Eoin, Sgeir Leathan and Cearn Riobha may also have a few pups born on them but also provide the sites of the 'reservoirs', while the pre-breeding assembly occurs on the skerries which lie between Oronsay and Eilean nan Ron. Nothing is yet known about the haul-outs during the non-breeding period.

The geographical peculiarity of these islands is that all are surrounded by erosion platforms which are exposed at low water. These platforms are very extensive and riven by channels so that, although the tides are very small (8–12 feet), within a very short time the area of exposed 'land' is vastly increased but cut across by deep water channels which thus connect the true beaches with the open sea. Only in the Treshnish Isles are the platforms narrow.

As will be seen later, this geography has a profound effect on the social organisation and behaviour of the bulls and cows (Pl. 2). The pups are born on the small beaches and, although none have insuperable barriers separating them from the grass-covered tops of the islands, they do not move inland until they have become moulters. The cows make frequent visits to the open sea along the channels and the bulls hold territory along these channels and on the platform to intercept the cows and mate with them. The group is not large numerically, but has certainly increased under the total protection afforded by the late Lord Strathcona and Mount Royal. It is probably limited by the number of available breeding sites. The total population based on these islands is probably about 2,000.

OUTER HEBRIDEAN GROUP

This may well have been more extensive in the past although one of the largest collection of rookeries, on North Rona, must be of comparatively recent date since there is no record of grey seals using that island during the time of human habitation up to the mid-19th century. Breeding on Canna and a few other islands has taken place until the last century but now all rookeries occur on islands in the open Atlantic. Chief of these is North Rona (Pl. 4), but Gaskeir has about 700–800 pups annually (Pl. 6). Shillay (Pl. 3), Coppay, Haskeir, Causamell and St Kilda have small breeding sites and there is some evidence that while the numbers on Haskeir were larger in the past, Coppay and St Kilda are new sites and increasingly used.

All these islands are largely rock-bound, several with precipitous sides which in many places can be dignified by the term cliff. All however have some point (a geo) or points of access to the vegetation-covered top of the island. This is necessary because, situated where they are, they are subjected to continual Atlantic swell. Thus on none are there any beaches in the normal meaning of the word except on the east or leeward side if the geology permits it. Shillay and St Kilda have such easterly bays and, as Shillay is uninhabited, full use is made of it both as a site for pre-breeding assembly and for a rookery (Pl. 3). On all these islands, the main rookeries are developed well above sea-level where the swell cannot reach, and we find a completely terrestrial set-up as opposed to the almost marine one of Pembrokeshire.

Reservoir sites are known for North Rona on Loba Sgeir, the northern skerries of Fianuis such as Lisgear Mòire and Lice Mhor and on Gealldruig Mhor to the south-east of the island. Reports of seals on Sula Sgeir and on Sule Skerry point to these being used as fishing haul-outs, but moulting haul-outs have not yet been seen because no one has been there at the right time of year. Elsewhere nothing is known of the reservoir and non-breeding haul-outs, although the Flannen Isles are likely to be so used to the west of Lewis.

This group is a large one comprising probably about 15,000+ seals of all ages. There is little evidence as to whether the numbers are increasing or not. The population based on North Rona appears to be fairly stable, although there seems to be room for the expansion of the existing rookeries. However, the recent establishment of breeding rookeries on St Kilda and Coppay may indicate a small increase.

ORKNEY AND SHETLAND GROUP

Until about ten years ago virtually nothing was known about the seal population in this area. Darling writing in 1947 said that 'this seal occurs in Orkney and Shetland in relatively small numbers'. We know now that this is very far from the truth and that a population of 8,000 or more are based on these two groups of islands. They have, since 1960, been subjected to a great deal of research. All the main and most of the minor rookeries are known and several moulting sites and other types of haul-out places have been identified. The task has not been made easier because common seals are also present in the area so that records and reports are often not clear as to which species is referred to.

The types of rookeries are rather variable. Perhaps this is because, being an archipelago, the Atlantic swell, already somewhat broken by the north coast of Scotland particularly in Orkney, is not an overwhelming factor. In South Ronaldsay, for example, wide and deep beaches are used as rookeries much

PLATE 3. *above:* Shell-sand beach, Shillay, Outer Hebrides. The beach is occupied by the pre-breeding assembly of bulls and cows in the centre; the older bulls are segregated at the far end (arrowed), and a cow and two pups are seen in the foreground. (September 1954.)

below: The wallows, Shillay. By mid-October breeding has spread over onto the wallows inland and numerous cows with their pups are found there. Three territorial bulls are seen (arrowed).

PLATE 4. *above:* North Rona: the breeding rookery in the central part of the Fianuis peninsula. Note the pounding of the ground into a mud wallow. Toa Rona is seen in the background. A small group of grey seals breed in the saddle to its right, just over 200 feet above sea-level.

below: North Rona: ring-marking a moulter with a modified cattle ear tag. The rookery in the background is a small one in a gully on the east side of the island. The tendency to keep near to pools is clearly shown.

as the narrower ones of Pembrokeshire are. The bulls however are stationed *on* the beaches and not offshore. Elsewhere, such as on the Greenholms, the rookeries, beginning on the rocky foreshore (Pl. 5) stretch inland on the grassland in a very Hebridean manner. Perhaps here more than anywhere else one is driven to concede that the grey seal is extremely adaptable and much of an opportunist.

About half the annual pup production was accounted for in the Muckle and Little Greenholms (1,100–1,500).* Several other islands in this central area of the archipelago, such as Wart Holm, Rusk Holm, Holm of Fara, Fara, Holms of Spurness, Little Linga and Gairsay provide another total of about 1,000. North Ronaldsay probably has only about 100 pups a year, but south of Mainland on South Ronaldsay, Swona and Little Skerry (in the Pentlands) another 250–300 are born. The research work and a local intensification of sealing has recently reduced the population a little and disturbance in one breeding season has been reflected by a change of site or a redistribution of numbers in the next.

Many other skerries, such as Auskerry, Taing Skerry, Wyre Skerry, Eynhallow, Boray Holm, Holm of Birsay, Damsay, the Barrel of Butter and others are used as haul-out sites during the non-breeding period, some of the breeding islands such as Rusk Holm, Holms of Spurness and Little Greenholm are also used in the early months of the year. It is, however, very noticeable that non-breeding haul-outs are *never* seen on the major breeding rookeries. This differentiation of site use is particularly well shown on Rusk Holm where the two southern skerries are used as reservoir haul-outs during the breeding season, the rookery is on the eastern pebble beach and north-eastern rocks, while the moulting haul-outs are either on the north-western rocks or on the south or south-eastern rocks according to wind and tide.

The numbers in Shetland are much fewer. This must be attributed as much to the rock-bound nature of the coast-line as to the scarcity of small uninhabited islands. In the southern part Lady Holm, Horse Holm and the geos or narrow beaches under Fitful Head provide small rookeries. Only in the north does the lie of the islands provide any lee so that small rookeries are found around Yell and Fetlar. The beaches under Ronas Hill are important breeding sites. In total there are probably only 200–300 pups each year.

In the non-breeding season the major haul-outs in the south and west are on Horse Holm, Lady Holm, around Fitful Head and on the Ve Skerries, west of Papa Stour. Small though these last are they sometimes hold up to 2,000 seals not all of which can be considered as Shetland grey seals in the sense that in the breeding season they will be found on the Shetland rookeries. Fair Isle, halfway between Orkney and Shetland, also has haul-outs and as a number of young seals marked in Orkney have been found in Shetland there is little doubt that the adults move freely between the two groups of islands.

---

* This is now reduced to about 850, almost certainly due to human disturbance, the cows using other islands.

The picture here too is somewhat complicated by the presence of common seals and there is no doubt that much more is to be learnt about their distribution here, particularly in the northern islands.

In Orkney and Shetland there has persisted a tradition of sealing which has never been so strong in the Hebrides, possibly by reason of the Norse connections. The grey seal population here, therefore, appears to be fairly stable, fluctuating largely as a result of variations in sealing effort dependent, in turn, on the market price of seal-skins.

NORTH SEA GROUP

There is little difficulty in deciding that the centre of this group is the Farne Islands (Pl. 5). The North Sea is peculiarly free of islands and it may as well be stated straight away that only on the Island of May in the Firth of Forth and on Scroby Sands off Great Yarmouth are there any breeding rookeries other than on the Outer Farnes. Elsewhere there is evidence of their fishing inshore along the east as far south as the Wash, and the coast of Holland, and as far north as the Moray Firth. Fishing haul-outs have been recorded from the Abertay Sands to the Wash, but there is always a haul-out on the outermost islands of the Outer Farnes. At certain times of the year, notably the spring, they consist of very large numbers indeed. The population has been rising steadily in recent years. Annual counts of pup production have been made with considerable accuracy over the past fifteen years or so and an annual increase of about 7% has been calculated. Undoubtedly at the turn of the century the population was at a very low ebb. The islands at present involved as rookeries are the North and South Walmses, Staple and Brownsman, but in the more distant past others were used as rookery sites such as the Wide Opens and other islands of the Inner Farnes. At times of the year, other than the breeding, haul-outs are found on the Longstone and Longstone End, the Harcars and on other skerries of the Outer Farnes. All of these islands are low with at least one or two shelving rock beaches so that access is easy and sheltered within the archipelago. The interiors of the islands are used as well as the 'beaches' for rookery sites, but usually only after the more shoreward zones have become congested.

At the time of writing the number of pups produced annually had reached 2,011 (1971) making the Farne Islands group the third largest known in the British Isles with an estimated total population of almost 6,500–7,000.

Before going into the details of the life history of the grey seal, it is necessary to give a brief description of the yearly cycle of both adult males and females. Until recently it was really quite unknown. Even worse, statements appeared in the literature which cannot have been founded on observation because they were so wildly wrong. Until the early 1950's this species had only been studied during the breeding season. It is not difficult to find the reasons for this. During the late autumn and winter months the weather makes visits to the islands a very chancy affair and few people feel inclined to camp on these isolated spots during this time of year. Yet these are the only ways in which information can be gathered. During the summer months the weather is generally good but on the other hand very few seals will be seen. For the spring however, there is no excuse and it is a very important season indeed. Dr K. M. Backhouse and myself started visiting the Ramsey Island sites in 1952 and soon every month except December and July had been covered. Later all months in Orkney had been covered by Mr E. A. Smith and in the Farnes by Dr J. C. Coulson and Mrs Hickling. The work of Craggs and Ellison throughout the year on West Hoyle Bank has already been referred to. (Oddly enough it was undertaken quite independently of the other work in Pembrokeshire, Orkney and Farnes on which there was considerable interchange of knowledge and information. An example of this interchange will be given below when dealing with the annual moult.)

The best time to start describing the annual cycle is during the summer months of June, July and August. This is a very active feeding period for both bulls and cows. The bulls have to put on sufficient blubber to sustain them during their period of starvation, while they are maintaining territory. The cows also have to put on blubber to provide the fat for the rich milk suckled by the pups, but in addition, must eat sufficient to permit the foetus within to grow. (During the summer the foetus may increase by more than a pound a week.) Towards the end of August there is a tendency for both bulls and cows to move towards their breeding areas. This has been shown by J. Morton Boyd by the ingenious analysis of observations made at a number of points along the coastline of north-west Scotland. In the south-western group this drift is probably a little earlier, but newly arrived cows have been seen by me in early September on Ramsey Island. It is difficult to be precise in an animal whose breeding period extends over at least 2 months. The most that can be done is to note when such a tendency is at its peak and therefore most conspicuous. Other individual seals will still be at sea feeding, others still may already have arrived at the breeding rookeries and have pupped.

Bulls and cows must now be studied separately because the purpose of their assembling in the rookeries is quite different and consequently their behaviour and timing is different. Put very briefly and perhaps in an over simplified way, bulls assemble for mating, cows for pupping and only secondarily for mating.

Bulls seem to predominate at the beginning of the breeding season on or near the rookeries. Here they appear to sort themselves into a dominance order, those having previously bred clearly taking precedence over the younger ones. Gradually they take up station on a territory which they defend against all comers (Pl. 7). Although they immediately approach an invading cow, their agonistic behaviour dies down as soon as they recognise her sex. Invasion by new and younger bulls (Pl. 6) continues for a considerable time and for at least a fortnight or so defence is the dominant activity of each bull holding territory.

Meanwhile cows begin to arrive at the rookeries (Pl. 7) and shortly give birth to their pups. Suckling commences within the hour and is repeated several times a day for at least a fortnight, sometimes for nearly three weeks. During this period the cows resent any approaches by the bull, who is repelled by hooting and rapid waving of the fore flippers ('flippering'). Eventually, some time in the third week after giving birth, the cow accepts the bull in mating. Mating is often repeated several times at intervals. The cows desert their pups and leave the rookeries. Whether they go immediately to sea or remain in nearby waters is not yet certain, although I am inclined to believe the former is more likely.

The deserted pups moult their first or 'puppy' coat of white hair and appear in their 'moulter' coat which is similar to the adult pelage. In a healthy pup this process takes about a week; the fourth week of their life. When moulted the pups may, as in the south-west, immediately leave their natal beach, or as in the north and north-west remain on land and in fact move farther inland. Hunger will however eventually drive them to sea within a week or two.

The bulls remain on station for five to six weeks before becoming exhausted. They then move away from the rookeries to sea and recommence feeding to restore the blubber they have used during their enforced fast.

While this is the time-table of individual cows and bulls, it must be remembered that the time-table of the rookery is more extended. Thus a fortnight after the first pups have been born matings will begin, but this will probably be before the peak of the pupping. Consequently while the *peaks* of the various processes, pupping, mating, moulting, desertion by cows and leaving by bulls will be separated by periods corresponding to the normal time-table of individuals, this central period will be preceded by two or three weeks when arrivals of bulls and cows and some pupping are the only phenomena and will be followed by several weeks in which mating and desertions will predominate. The overall period will be about $2-2\frac{1}{2}$ months.

Now follows a period about which not so much is known. The nearby haul-out sites are used but not to a great extent. Probably the answer is that both bulls and cows are feeding as much as possible to replace their lost blubber, to fit themselves for the rigours of the winter. One of the most remarkable facts of this period, which covers about $3\frac{1}{2}-4$ months, is that among the cows found on the haul-outs, non-pregnant ones predominate. A high proportion of these non-pregnant cows are comparatively young and virgin or nulliparous. The differential behaviour of pregnant and non-pregnant cows is very remarkable, the more so because very little development of the embryo takes place for the first hundred days after conception (about $3\frac{1}{2}$ months). (See Chapter 4.) Towards the end of this period most of the cows go into the annual moult.

PLATE 5. *above:* Muckle Greenholm, Orkney. Part of the breeding rookery near the sea. It extends inland on to the grass to cover much of the island. Three territorial bulls can be identified (arrowed).

below: Staple Island, Farne Islands. The dense concentration of the seals in the centre of a breeding rookery is particularly well shown. Brownsman, in the background, is also thickly covered. Three territorial bulls are arrowed.

PLATE 6. *above:* Aerial view of Gasker, Outer Hebrides. Many adults can be made out but the pups stand out more clearly and can be counted. (18 October 1956.)

below: Bull and cow grey seals near a peat pool at the edge of the Braeside rookery on North Rona. The sexual difference in colouration is marked and also the breadth of the muzzles. The bull is a late arrival and occupies a peripheral territory. (October 1959.)

I have not mentioned the actual dates through this breeding and post-breeding period because there are differences between the geographical groups and generalisation is therefore difficult. What makes precision even more difficult is that the full story is not known in detail for all of the groups. However, some attempt may be made to give an overall picture if we omit the Farne Islands group. In the south-western group the peak of pupping is probably in the first week in October, and by mid-November all the beaches are completely deserted. In the Hebrides and North Rona the dates are about 10–14 days later, although the much larger size of the rookeries results in more early and late puppings so that the season *appears* to be longer and a few adults may still be found in the breeding grounds in early December. In Orkney and Shetland a further 7–10 days should be allowed, so that mid-December would be a reasonable date to compare with mid-November in the south-west. January to March may be counted as the months of the cow moult, although few Orcadian cows will have begun in January and few, if any, Pembrokeshire ones will remain unmoulted in March.

For the Farne Islands group all these dates must be delayed by about a further month. There the first pups are in late October and the peak about 3–4 weeks later in November, pupping continuing actively well into December.

Our knowledge of the growth of the foetus is derived solely from northern material from Orkney. The mean date of the recommencement of the growth of the embryo is the middle of February. Thereafter the foetus grows apace in about 80% of the cows, the others are non-pregnant. So far as can be made out they continue to fish in the adjacent seas periodically coming ashore in fishing haul-outs for short periods at low tide. In the summer months the haul-outs must be both few and short because the numbers seen are very few indeed compared to those at other times of the year.

We have left the bulls at sea after the breeding season and it is not until mid-February that we have any evidence that large numbers come ashore. Their annual moult appears to be timed about two months after that of the cows. It was first observed in April in Pembrokeshire, but by then many were completely moulted and few remained unmoulted early in May. Dr Backhouse and myself, having found the comparatively large moulting haul-outs of bulls in Pembrokeshire, were able to direct attention to this in other groups, such as the Farne Islands, where the same phenomenon was then seen by other observers. These moulting haul-outs of the bulls are very remarkable and often number thousands at a time in the large northern groups. The bulls, like the cows, largely disappear in the summer months from all the inshore sites and we can only conclude that they too are feeding at sea to prepare themselves for the breeding season.

We can now turn to some of the distinguishing characteristics of this species, both in structure and habits.

It is always extremely difficult, if not impossible, to estimate the length or size of seals in the field since there is rarely, if ever, any standard for comparison. Measurements therefore, while of use on a carcase, cannot really be used by an observer in the field. Any deductions based on claims to be able to 'age' seals in the field must therefore be regarded as highly dubious and probably very misleading. The pup is born at a length of about 33 ins. and 32–33 lbs. Bull pups appear to be very slightly heavier, but the difference is not truly significant having regard to the numbers which have been weighed. In any case it could only amount to a few ounces. It is very difficult indeed to speak about moulters since by that time all the differences in nutrition have taken effect and weights can vary between 100 lbs. or more and little more than the birth weight, if the moulter has been starved and is likely soon to die. The growth in length is quite small so that few moulters reach 40 inches until well after they have left their natal beaches however great their weight. Some of these very heavy moulters (over 100 lbs.) are so bloated with blubber that they can hardly turn their heads and movements are quite lethargic. There is some evidence that pups which do not reach the weight of 90 lbs. before being deserted by their mothers and moulting, have little or no chance of surviving their first year of life. Certainly all those below 60 lbs. appear to die before the first six months is out and *all* the recorded weights of grey seals in their first year of life are about 90 lbs. or less. Further, yearlings which have been weighed on the Farne Islands appear to fall more or less within the limits shown by the largest moulters. In other words there is little, if any, increase in weight in the first year of life.

These conclusions appear to be confirmed by the known weights of older bulls and cows. 3–4 year old bulls only weigh 170–190 lbs. while the same age group of cows weigh 130–150 lbs.; 5–6 year old cows may reach 170–180 lbs. but records for bulls are very few, although they suggest that by that age they may attain 2 cwt. There are practically no weights of fully mature bulls or cows to justify generalisations. All that can be said is that probably the older well-established breeding cows are over 2 cwt. and the older territorial bulls probably top 3 cwt. or even reach 4 cwt. In any case the bulls vary much more than the cows and in both sexes changes in weight amounting to $\frac{1}{2}$–$\frac{3}{4}$ cwt. are usual during the yearly cycle.

Much more data is available about lengths. Although little, if any, weight is acquired during the first year, the moulters grow considerably in length, an average of 55–60 ins. being normal at the end of the first year for both sexes. Thereafter some differences can be considered significant between the two sexes. The rate of growth is fairly steady until puberty at 5–6 years when cows will average about 6 ft. and bulls 6 ft. 6 ins. During the following 3 or 4 years the rate of growth of cows declines so that at 10 years of age they have attained their near maximum of 80–84 ins. (7 ft.). Some growth appears to continue throughout life but it is very small in the cows.

The years following puberty in the bulls account for the great difference between the older bulls and cows, for their rate of growth falls off much more slowly and is continued at the higher rate for a longer period. By 10 years of age the average is 90 ins. and 96 ins. is reached about 2 years later. Thus in round figures mature cows are about 7 ft. long and territorial bulls average about 8 ft. but may vary about 6 ins. more or less.

Turning now to the pelage we find very useful characters to distinguish bulls and cows in the field. These features are, in fact, visible in the pigmentation of the skin of the foetus at a comparatively early age, namely at 110–120 days of active gestation. Growth of the white pup hair coat however obscures this pigmentation by the 150th day of foetal growth. This puppy coat is uniformly unpigmented except occasionally in the region of the muzzle and top of the head. The hair is very long and creamy white on the newly born pup. The occurrence of the greyish areas around muzzle and crown has been interpreted as part of the moult which has taken place before birth and only resumed later at about 3 weeks of age. The excuse for this belief lies in the peculiar hormonal situation existing in the pup at birth, but examination of the hair from these areas shows that the pigment is confined to the tops of the hair and that the hairs themselves are quite unlike those of the later moulter coat. No explanation of these greyish areas is yet available, and their occurrence is very odd. Some groups, notably Pembrokeshire, show a much higher incidence than others, such as the Farnes. Further, these areas are the first to show any hair in the foetus and the time of their eruption makes it clear that the tops must have been formed in the follicles *before* the appearance of any general pigmentation in the skin.

The pup may begin to moult as early as the 10th day, but this is most unusual and it is generally the 18th day before the first signs appear on the fore and hind flippers and on the head. If the pup belongs to a group such as the Pembrokeshire where entering the sea is a common occurrence, much of the moulting hair is washed off and, as the puppy coat becomes thinner, the pattern of the moulter coat shows through. Even here, however, many of the pups do not enter the sea during the moult and in the northern groups, of course, this is the usual pattern of behaviour. Under these conditions the puppy coat is rubbed off in patches and often the moulter can be found lying on a carpet of its old hair.

This moulter coat is to all intents and purposes the same as all the subsequent coats, heavily pigmented on the back and sides at least and marked by even darker spots and blotches. It is in the abundance and distribution of the darker spots that the difference between bulls and cows can be seen. In cows the lighter pattern consists of a medium grey back shading to a lighter belly, the darker spots are comparatively few and only rarely run together. In the bulls the darker pattern is so extensive that the lighter one is seen only as small triangular patches between the dark spots and blotches which have run together over most of the body.

There is, however, considerable variation in both sexes. In the cows the pale underside may be any colour from pale cream to tawny yellow and the upperside may vary from grey or blue-grey to brown. Some cows may have very considerable blotching, but never to the extent shown in the bulls. In bulls the chief variation is in the overall tone of the darker pattern which may be dark brown to black in colour. A number of older bulls too show a markedly lighter head and sometimes the blotches unite so much as to give the impression of uniform black or dark brown.

These remarks of course apply to the new coat which is grown each year. As the time of moult approaches the whole pelage becomes duller, browner and more uniform in appearance due to the splitting of the hairs so that it is only in the wet pelt that the patterns can be distinguished. It should always be borne in mind when observing grey seals on shore that the appearance of the pelage alters considerably as it dries and that the change is more marked as the moulting season approaches.

The disparate growth of the bulls and cows is well seen in the skull and reflected in their profiles. The skull of the grey seal has a long flat vault which clearly distinguishes it from that of the common seal where the shorter, rounder vault gives rise to the dome-like head. The nasal bones too are differently placed so that the grey seal has, in the bull, a 'roman' nose profile and in the cow a straight or 'grecian' profile, while the common seal in both sexes shows a slight depression or 'retroussé' nose (Fig. 11). The young grey seal however has a skull very similar in appearance to that of the common seal and to that it owes its puppyish look. Within the first year the specific elongation and flattening of the skull takes place and there is little difficulty in distinguishing the two species in the field.

As grey seals grow older these characteristics are accentuated. At 5–6 years of age the sutures between the frontals, parietals, squamosals and occipitals fuse but the anterior sutures between frontals, nasals and premaxillae remain free throughout life and some increase in both length and breadth of the skull continues. In some of the oldest of the cows the profile may begin to take on a 'roman' bend, just as the young bulls approaching puberty still have such a straight profile that their identification by this character alone is by no means sure.

The teeth of the grey seal are very distinctive and unlike those of any other phocid. The formula is normally $\frac{\text{i.c.p.m.}}{}$ $\frac{3.1.2.3.}{2.1.2.3.}$ and the dentition which erupts during puppyhood is the adult or definitive one. The milk dentition, in which the molars are not represented, is formed and resorbed in the foetal stages. The molars and premolars possess one large cusp and two others so small that often they appear to be missing (Fig. 12a) (cf. common seal with three well developed cusps). Wear of the teeth is no criterion of age. Normally the teeth of the upper jaw fit between and behind those of the lower jaw but occasionally the jaws are relatively misplaced (prognathous) and the teeth meet over part

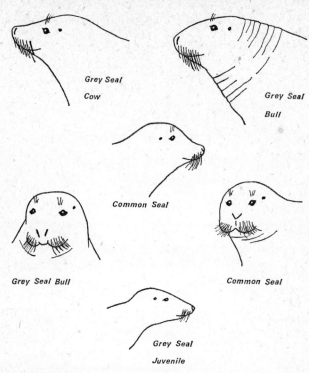

FIG. 11. External differences between common and grey seals and between grey seal bulls and cows. Between grey and common seals the position of the nostrils is diagnostic and also the domed and rounded head of the common. Between grey seal bulls and cows the profile is the most certain distinguishing feature when only the head is visible above water. Common seal bulls and cows are almost impossible to separate by head features alone.

or all of their basal area. In an extreme case the teeth of both jaws then become worn down to flattened stumps. One such has been recorded at only 11 years of age. Very few instances of diseased teeth have been found, although deformed and diseased conditions of the jaws are a little more frequent. It must be assumed that in such vital structures any major deficiency rapidly leads to semi-starvation, loss of condition and death.

In the bulls the canines are much larger than in the cows. Not only are they heavier, but the root is more bulbous. It is quite possible to sex an isolated lower jaw of any animal over the age of 5 years by the shape of the canine tooth. In the bulls the upper incisors are also broader and this results in a greater width between the canines. Externally these features unite in producing a broader muzzle and a greater gap between the nostrils in the

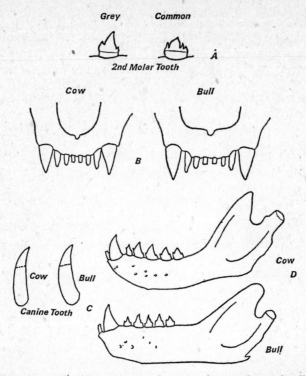

FIG. 12. Jaws and teeth in the common and grey seals. A. shows the differences in the molar teeth of common and grey seals. B. shows the markedly broader muzzle in the bulls. C. shows the greater curvature in the canine teeth of bull grey seals. D. shows the greater depth in the lower jaw of bull grey seals. Both jaws are drawn to the same *length*. A, B & C, c. × ½; D, c. × ⅓

male. The breadth of the male muzzle is further accentuated by the massive pads on which the vibrissae are mounted (Fig. 12).

The position and arrangement of the nostrils are also diagnostic features distinguishing grey from common seals. In the latter the two nostrils almost meet at their most anterior and ventral point and diverge above this at a distinct angle. In the grey seal the nostrils are almost parallel and their anterior ventral points are separated by a large pad of skin (Fig. 11).

The grey seal is highly vocal, particularly the cow. All aggression by cows, if only jostling for position in a haul-out, is accompanied by high-pitched hooting which has a peculiar quavering quality, partly of pitch and partly of volume. This hooting often carried out by several cows at once produces a weird sound which has been called 'singing' but it is far from singing at its best! The bulls are capable of a snarling hiss which also has a guttural quality. However, often in mild aggression they do no more than open their mouths and emit an exhalation which is almost soundless. The high pitched voice of the pup is described later (p. 121).

There are many parts of Britain where the species of seal present can be almost certainly determined by the habitat. Thus, as Fraser Darling has said, the common seal on the west coast of Scotland is a sea-loch seal, the grey a seal of the outer islands and the strong Atlantic seas. And again on the Essex coast the mud and sand flats are typical haul-out sites for common seals, while the rock-bound coasts of west Wales provide typical grounds for the grey. Nevertheless it is not possible to generalise completely. Certainly the grey seal uses habitats which would rarely be used by common seals, isolated skerries and islands swept by Atlantic gales and surrounded by tidal rips which throw the sea into tumultuous heaps. The common seal will use estuarine waters and the mud and sand banks associated with them where the grey would never go. Yet between these extremes there are many habitats which both use. Many of the haul-outs in Orkney and Shetland are mixed, although of course the breeding grounds never are.

It must also be remembered that the choice of the grey seal of breeding rookery sites is very variable. Taking the broadest view of the world population we have the ice-floe breeding of the Baltic portion and the fast-ice positions of the western Atlantic to set against the shore or land breeding habits of the eastern Atlantic seals. Within this the sites vary from cave and cove breeding in the south-western group to the truly land breeding of those on North Rona and some of the Hebridean and Orcadian Islands. Yet in Shetland with its cliff-bound shores cove breeding is again the rule in the Fitful Head region. And finally we find a sandbank rookery on Scroby Sands off the Norfolk coast. Davies has suggested that much of this variation is dictated by geographical features. But this cannot be the whole answer because there exist many sites which provide adequate terrain for rookeries which are not occupied. Almost certainly this is due to the extremely conservative attitude of the grey seal in respect of these rookeries. Only at intervals during their past history have they come to colonise new sites either through their evacuation by man as at North Rona and St Kilda or by pressure of population increase and spread as in the North Sea with the occupation of the Wash and Norfolk coasts.

There is perhaps a greater uniformity in the character of fishing and moulting haul-outs. Here a flat shelving approach is all that is necessary; sometimes of rock, sometimes of pebbles and rarely of sand. So long as the skerry or sandbank is within range of the feeding grounds, easy of access and free from human interference it will serve, whether it is the rocky Ve Skerries of Shetland and elsewhere, the pebbles and boulders of some of the Orcadian islands and Pembrokeshire, the shell-sand beaches of the Outer Hebrides or the sandbanks of the Wirral or Scroby.

CHAPTER 3

THE GREY SEAL – AGE DETERMINATION, LONGEVITY AND MATURITY

UNTIL the early 1950's nearly all field observations had centred on the breeding period. All observers agreed that there were many more cows than bulls present. Just how many differed in different parts of the rookery if it was a large one, but that was also true for other species of seal and for the northern fur-seal. Darling thought that the discrepancy in numbers must be accounted for in part by a slight differential mortality, since the sex-ratio of pups was roughly 1 : 1. Another feature which he had also noticed was the absence of obviously young seals. One might have expected to see many more young seals since their age groups should be more numerous than the later ones. This paucity of young non-breeding seals may have led to the view expressed by Davies that sexual maturity came early.

I posed to myself two questions: the first, and more fundamental, was how does one determine the age of a seal? And secondly, are the missing seals, the 'young' and the 'other bulls', not dead but somewhere else? The latter question is dealt with in later chapters as far as our present knowledge will allow. The determination of age is the subject of this chapter and its solution is of vital importance in understanding the overall biology of the animal. It also occurred to me that there might be some differential mortality among the bulls but not necessarily *before* they became territorial; and further that their length of life was considerably shorter than that of the cows. A combination of these two factors might account for the discrepancy in the cow to bull ratio.

But how did one tell the age of a seal? By its length, or size, or were such measurements so variable that they could not be relied on? And anyway, how could you measure the dimensions of a seal or even estimate it accurately with nothing apart from rocks and sand to compare it with? Davies tried to separate them into year groups in the field but, as we shall see, his conclusions were not correct. In the past, museum workers on other species of seal had noted that some skulls had several of the bones fused together along the sutures while others, smaller in size as a rule still had the sutures open. So they had been able to establish two groups of older and younger animals, but could not talk about age in years. Then came the work of the United States Fish and Wildlife Service on the northern fur-seal of the Pribilov Islands. The task here was to find out the structure of the population of fur-seals so as to be able to determine how many of the bulls could be culled for their skins

PLATE 7. *above:* A massive grey seal bull holding territory on Brownsman, Farne Islands. The wet pelt shows the prevalent darker colour pattern of the male. His tail has clearly been damaged earlier, probably in territorial fights. (December 1955.)

below: A very typical grey seal cow newly landed on Brownsman. Contrast her colour pattern with that of the bull (*above*). Her straight profile suggests a moderate age (10 to 20 years). (December 1955.)

PLATE 8.   *above:* Longitudinal section of the root of a canine tooth of a grey seal. The pulp cavity runs down the middle and the narrow canal through the base has been largely missed by the section. The dentine shows some indication of banding in the outer parts but the inner part is dense and obscure. Outside the dentine is the *cementum*, clearly showing many layers, each representing one year. This grey seal cow was in her 24th year. × 5.7

below: (a) Two whole canine teeth from 1st year grey seals. They are widely open at the base and show circular ridges which have nothing to do with the age of the animal. × 1.0

below (b) Two whole canine teeth; that on the right is of a cow and that on the left from a bull, showing the greater thickness and curvature of the bull's. × 1.0

below (c–d): Highly magnified sections of *cementum* to show the annual layers.

c. from an 8-year-old grey seal bull. × c. 30
d. from an 18-year-old grey seal bull. × c. 30

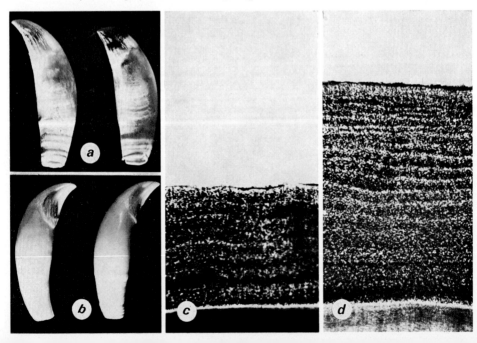

and still keep the colony healthy and numerous. The workers there knew that the determination of age was essential. Some of the seals had been branded many years before so they had some animals of known age and the marking by tags, which was started later, increased this number considerably. Certain hard parts of the body may be laid down periodically throughout life, perhaps once every year, perhaps twice. The obvious thing to do was to look at some of these parts and find if there was any correlation between the known ages of the animal and the layers laid down. To cut a long story short, Dr Scheffer and his co-workers found the canine teeth were the most suitable because consecutive cones of dentine were laid down, one a year, inside the pulp cavity which remained open. Thus the age of an untagged fur-seal could be found. It is true the animal had to be dead, but this was better than nothing. Dr Laws who worked on the southern elephant seal in the Antarctic found a similar method useful there. In fact he looked at the teeth of several species of other seal and found that the age of some could be determined by this method. However, he found that the grey seal's canine did not remain open at the base except for a narrow tube through which the blood vessels to the 'pulp' passed, and by the time 5 or 6 years of dentine had been deposited there was no more room. Moreover, the lines between the layers of dentine were not very distinct in this species.

This was the state of knowledge in 1956 when I came into the picture. I found that another material, known as 'cementum' which is laid down *outside* the root of the tooth and cements it into the socket of the jawbone, was also deposited in layers (Pl. 8). A specimen in the National Museum of Wales from a cow grey seal which had lived in captivity for 27 years, gave the chance to see whether these layers were annual. Thanks to the generosity of the Curator I was able to show that this was so. Shortly afterwards a cow of the known age of 6 years died in the London Zoo and was used to confirm the method. At last there was a means of determining the age of a grey seal when dead. Unfortunately, from the research point of view, at that time grey seals were protected all through the breeding season and as at other times of the year they are not all easy to shoot and recover, there was very little material on which to use this newly acquired technique.

Meanwhile some seals had been received which had been shot while marauding the salmon nets on the east coast of Scotland. Some of these were a bit stale by the time they came into competent hands, but nevertheless information was being slowly collected particularly about young or immature grey seals. (Most of the mature ones were too heavy to be collected.) All sorts of data were recorded, not only the age as determined by the cement of the teeth, but weights and sizes of the teeth, measurements of the jaw bones, weights and measurements of some of the 'soft parts' such as the ovaries and testes. Gradually a picture was being built up about the earlier years. In 1960 an Order was made permitting the killing off of a limited number in the Orkney breeding colony and for the first time material was available from sexually mature animals in a rookery. The data collected then and in subsequent years has filled in the older age groups.

Everything of course depended on an *accurate* determination of age and it was some time before this could be relied on confidently. The reason for this difficulty is obvious if you think of the reason for being able to count the layers of cement at all. The layers are distinct because at some time during the year there is a change in the way the cement is put down and consequently it looks different (Pl. 8). The question is when does this change occur, because the years counted in layers of cement may not be the years of the animal's life dating from its birthday. In the grey seal it was found that the layer was completed by September, that is by the onset of the breeding season, and that new deposition did not begin until after the moult in the late winter or spring. As the moult in cows and bulls occurs at different times of the year and extends over a considerable period it was necessary to be extremely careful about determining the age of animals killed during the months of January to March for cows and of February to April for bulls. In the majority of instances a mistake of one year would not be very significant, but for the determination of the age of puberty and also, for bulls, the age of entry into the breeding rookeries, it was essential to be accurate. This accuracy has been achieved since the results do not show abnormalities or inconsistencies beyond what might be reasonably expected as the result of individual variations in several hundred specimens.

The first problem to be tackled was that of sexual maturity. It was not possible simply to link age with the condition of the gonads. Examination of both male and female organs clearly indicated a yearly cycle in which very profound changes could be seen almost month by month, which tended to obscure age differences, particularly in the male.

The cows were not so difficult to deal with, but nevertheless did present problems. (For a fuller account, see Chapter 4.) A mature cow liberates an egg from a large well-developed follicle shortly after giving birth to a pup, or, in a virgin cow, ovulates some time during the breeding season. The follicle then thickens its wall considerably and produces a *corpus luteum* which is an easily recognisable body of some size. If the cow is mated an embryo forms and becomes attached in the uterus. Thus at any time of the year it should be possible to say if a female is mature. The only exception to this is if the cow is not mated; then the *corpus luteum* only persists for a few months and special techniques have to be used to make the degenerating *corpus* visible. When in 1963 I made a first attempt to come to some conclusions regarding maturity in the cow, I had examined 93 cows; 39 in their first to fourth years were immature; 46 in their sixth to thirty-fourth years were mature. The remaining eight in their fifth year were equally divided, four immature and four mature. Examination of many more cows since then has confirmed the impression that cows tend to ovulate first at the end of their fifth year. This conclusion was confirmed by other observations. During the years of immaturity the ovary remains small and hard. At maturity several eggs begin to mature within enlarging follicles, although only one of them will be released in the breeding season. The ovary therefore becomes considerably larger and softer since the follicles are filled with a gelatinous fluid. The ovaries continue to increase in size throughout life as remnants of the *corpora lutea* and resorbed follicles remain behind. Generally speaking the ovarian size corresponds with the determined age.

The difficulty of determining the age of puberty in the bulls arises from the fact that each year, after breeding, the testes of a mature bull return to an almost passive condition. During the years of immaturity the testes grow very little in size and attain an average weight of about 40 grammes before puberty occurs. Some, however, may weigh as much as 50 grammes or slightly over. If therefore a bull is found with a testis of 60 grammes, in a mature condition in, say, February, is it one which is coming into puberty that year to produce sperm in the following autumn, or is it one which has already been marginally active the previous autumn? The age of puberty in the bull is therefore less easy to define precisely; there is some evidence too that bulls may begin puberty rather earlier than usual but fail to produce active sperm in the breeding season of that year. The result is that one can only say that all bulls of 6 years and over are potentially breeders, but that many do produce some sperm when they are 5 years of age. Only a few appear to 'have a go' at sperm production when 4, failing to achieve the final stages.

As soon as this conclusion was available and attention was directed to these particular years of life another feature of bull anatomy was noticed. Many mammals, particularly carnivores and pinnipedes, have evolved a peculiar bone known as the *baculum* or *os penis* to support the penis in copulation. This bone grows during the life of the bull, but it soon became apparent that its growth was not regular (Fig. 13). Two measurements made this clear; the length and the weight. During the latter years of life the *os penis* becomes heavier without increasing in length, partly by increasing its thickness and partly perhaps by making the bone more compact and dense. The best way of combining these two measurements into one factor for comparison with the age of the animal is to divide the weight by the length, the weight being expressed in grammes, the length in centimetres. The result is an *Index* and by plotting the index against the age of about 200 bulls two remarkable features appeared (Fig. 14). For the years of immaturity the index increases steadily, that is to say the *os penis* becomes heavier (thicker) relative to its length, but at puberty and for several years afterwards there is a disproportionate growth in length with comparatively little increase in weight. This sudden *change* is a confirmation of the onset of puberty. But round about the age of 8–9–10 years, growth in length again becomes slow but the weight increases considerably. What can be the significance of this? Mention has already been made of the occasion in 1960 when material from a breeding rookery was available for the first time. This not only confirmed what had been suspected about the maturity of the cows, but brought to light a quite unexpected fact. This was that the bulls holding territory in the rookery were, with one exception, 10 years old or more. The exception was 9 years. Since that time many more specimens have become available and it

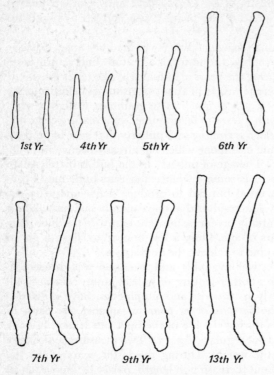

1st Yr   4th Yr   5th Yr   6th Yr

7th Yr   9th Yr   13th Yr

FIG. 13. Growth and maturation of the *os penis*. Front and side views of the developing *os penis*. The considerable increase in size etween the 4th and 5th years is indicative of the onset of puberty. × ⅓

is now quite firmly established that the bulls, although sexually mature and potent during the breeding season from the age of 6 years onwards, do not achieve the status of Territory Holders usually until the age of 10 years, rarely at 9. Even if the exact significance of the 'maturing' of the *os penis* at 9–10 years of age is not certain, the coincidence is certainly of interest.

The most probable explanation is that there is a natural selection value in postponing the maintenance of territory to as late an age as possible since the holding of territory places a very severe physical strain upon the bulls. The same minimum age of 'beach-masters' was found for the northern fur-seal. There is also evidence suggesting that the sexually mature but non-territory holding bulls (6–9 year old age groups) have a special part to play in the reproductive activity of the species *which could not be undertaken by the territorial bulls*. This will be discussed later.

Before leaving the subject of sexual maturity one other point may be made.

Examination of the layers of cement on the canine teeth showed that the layers formed in later years were much thinner than those formed earlier. In the majority examined this decrease in thickness is not gradual; there appears a sudden decrease in thickness after 5 or 6 layers in cows and after 6 or 7 in bulls (Pl. 8). It almost looks as though this too marks puberty.

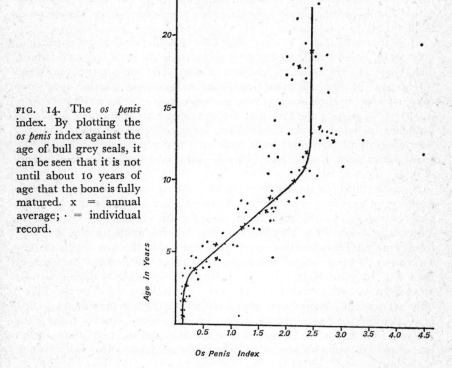

FIG. 14. The *os penis* index. By plotting the *os penis* index against the age of bull grey seals, it can be seen that it is not until about 10 years of age that the bone is fully matured. x = annual average; · = individual record.

Confirmation of the ages of maturity and of territory holding has come within the last few years. A system of marking by brands indicating the year of birth was used in the Farne Islands in 1960. The first breeding cow to be recognised by her brand was in 1966, at the age of 6 years, and the first bull was seen also in 1966, but in the month of June in an ordinary haul-out. Not until 1970 was the first bull holding territory seen at the age of 10 years, another, the same age, was still in a non-breeding part of the rookery. Also in that year there were at least four breeding cows of 10 years of age. However sure we may be from laboratory evidence it is always satisfactory to have the conclusions confirmed by actual observations in the field (Table 11).

During the years 1956 to 1966 specimens were collected, some from the normal practice of fishery protection, some specially shot for research purposes. Generally speaking there has been no attempt at selective collection so that, other things being equal, the collection is a fair sample of the population available. By determining the age of all these (c. 240 cows and c. 250 bulls) it has been possible to obtain some idea of the length of life of the grey seal. In Table 1 these have been distributed according to their ages. There is probably a disproportionate number of yearlings since, although they are naturally the largest single age group, they form a high proportion of those killed and collected on the salmon grounds of the east coast of Scotland.

From these figures it is clear that only a few cows live to more than 30 years of age in nature and that 35 seems to be the limit in round figures. The longevity of bulls is quite a different story. The oldest records are those of three, two of whose skeletons were found on breeding rookeries, at 23 years of age. The proportion however who live more than 15 years is comparatively small (12%) despite the fact that a disproportionate number of territorial bulls are included in the total. (They were collected for other reasons.) The majority of territorial bulls have ages between 10 and 15 years, the more robust ones survive from 15 to 20 and a very occasional 20+ occurs (Fig. 15).

A consideration of these figures for longevity in bulls and cows begins to produce an answer to one of the questions asked at the beginning of the chapter, namely, what explanation is there for the relatively few bulls seen in a breeding rookery. The breeding cow population is made up of year-groups from 5 to 35. Probably the first 2 or 3 years and the last 5 contain few individuals because not all newly matured cows will become pregnant in their first or even second year of maturity. Nevertheless there are over 20 year-groups well represented. The territorial bulls on the other hand have only 5 fairly fully represented with another 5 poorly represented, say the equivalent of 7 or 8 year-groups. Thus a ratio of about 3 cows to 1 bull is the *minimum* to be expected. Observation in the field and mortality data suggest that there are other factors to be taken into account. These will be dealt with later.

Some mention must be made now of possible reasons for this great difference in the longevity of cows and bulls. The longevity of the cows does not require an 'explanation'. There are two records of grey seals in captivity having lived for a considerable time. One, in Cardiff, has already been mentioned; a cow which lived for just over 27 years. The other is of a bull which lived in Skansen Zoo, Stockholm for 41 years and was probably 42 years old when he died. The normal span of a cow grey seal in nature is therefore not very different from the known potential life span. It is the very brief life of so many of the bulls and indeed the comparatively short life of even the most long-lived which requires explaining. To produce such an effect in the bull population it is necessary to postulate an annual mortality of between 40% and 50% among territorial bulls, assuming that their

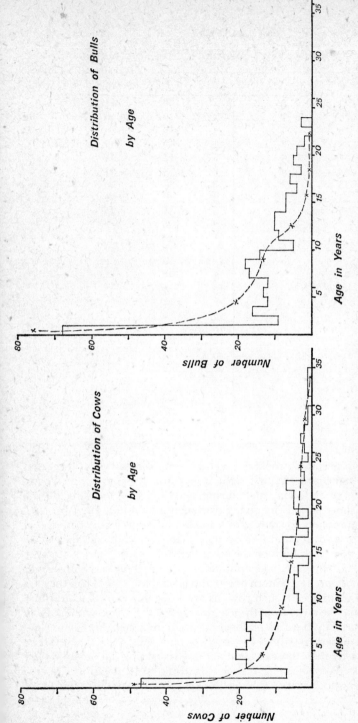

FIG. 15. Distribution by age of cow and bull grey seals. The block histograms are of cows and bulls collected for research in as random a manner as possible. The broken line shows the expected number based on the life-table. Although true random collection is impossible the agreement is not bad, particularly for the cows.

Table 1. Distribution of Cows and Bulls in Years of Age

	Cows				Bulls		
1	47	27	3	1	68	27	—
2	7	28	2	2	9	28	—
3	18	29	1	3	16	29	—
4	21	30	1	4	12	30	—
5	18	31	—	5	13	31	—
6	17	32	1	6	12	32	—
7	18	33	1	7	17	33	—
8	14	34	1	8	18	34	—
9	3	35	—	9	14	35	—
10	4		239	10	5		254
11	5			11	9		
12	5			12	10		
13	4			13	10		
14	1			14	7		
15	8			15	7		
16	8			16	4		
17	1			17	6		
18	4			18	3		
19	1			19	5		
20	5			20	4		
21	5			21	2		
22	7			22	—		
23	2			23	3		
24	3			24	—		
25	1			25	—		
26	2			26	—		

mortality prior to becoming rookery breeders is not very different from that of cows of the same age. At first sight it would seem that the cows are subjected to a greater strain, first during gestation and secondly during suckling over a short period (by giving extremely rich milk). However they are ashore in the rookery for only 2 to 3 weeks and many make trips to the sea, some very frequently, and feeding may take place although there is no evidence that it does. The bulls on the other hand come ashore soon after the first of the cows, if not before, take up station and have to fight off other bulls for several weeks before the pattern of territories is established. Then they are concerned with mating with such cows as are to be found in their territory and in all they may be away from the sea for as much as 6 weeks without food. During that time they have to perform energetic functions in defence and copulation. All observers who have studied bull seals over the breeding season are struck by their loss of weight and the increasing flabbiness of their skin as the weeks pass. During this time they draw on their blubber reserve and if this is below normal they may well be emaciated by the time they leave to go to sea and face the rigours of a north Atlantic winter. The blubber is not only a food reserve, it is their chief means of insulation. Further, the less blubber the less easy it is for them to remain at the surface so that extra energy has to be wasted in maintaining position in stormy waters. It is thought therefore that the breeding season imposes a very great strain in the resources of the territorial bulls and that many die in the following winter. It is probably significant that the cows proceed to moult shortly after breeding; bulls postpone this operation for several more months until they have had a prolonged bout of feeding in an attempt to restore their condition.

Further evidence in support of this explanation has recently come from Canada. Here, as already mentioned, there is a near 1 : 1 ratio of bulls to cows in the breeding areas, the pairs being widely separated along the coast-line or on the ice. There is thus no necessity on the part of the bulls to obtain and maintain territory in the manner found in Great Britain. Their period of starvation is little if any longer than that of the cow. Bulls of ages well up in the 20's and even some in the lower 30's have been recorded by Mansfield at the Canadian Arctic Unit.

Most of the information detailed in this chapter on the ages of maturity, longevity and mortality rates is necessary before the structure of a population can be determined. There is one other fact of great importance and that is the pregnancy rate or the percentage of mature females which are carrying young. The numbers that are doing so is of course the same as the numbers of pups born and they can be counted. But the non-pregnant ones cannot be counted. If the collection of mature cows were entirely at random, then the proportion of non-pregnant ones could be easily found out. The non-pregnant cows consist of nulliparous cows and those breeding cows who lose their pups in the first week after birth, leave the rookery, go to sea and are not mated with territorial bulls. Unfortunately the collections made are not entirely random. If it were then the pregnancy rate would be 75%. If it were not, and it probably has a too high proportion of non-pregnant cows, it would be higher. The only other figures that there are for comparison are those of the northern fur-seal where it is 80%. As this is close to the grey seal minimum, it is likely that it is a fair estimate for the grey seal too. But there may be occasions and places where the percentage is higher.

The result, then, of being able to determine the age of a grey seal and the collection of a limited amount of material has been to give us a much clearer picture of the birth to death career of both males and females. Immature males, from their leaving their natal rookeries until at least their fourth birthday, show no signs of impending sexual activity. Most of them do not show signs until a year later and it is not until they are six years old that it can be said that all bulls are potent. From that age until 9 or 10 years they are, in the breeding season, potent but unable to obtain territory in a rookery unless they are exceptional in some way or another. Their life as territorial bulls may be very short, actuarially speaking an expectation of rather less than four years. In any case well over 95% are dead before reaching 20 years of age and only a very small minority creep into the lower 20's.

Immature females approach puberty at their fourth or fifth birthday, and thereafter are capable of bearing one pup each year. Only a few live beyond 30 years of age, although up till then the death rate each year appears to be low. During the first few years of maturity a significant proportion remain nulliparous although probably very few exceed their tenth year without becoming pregnant. The virgin cows are joined each year by older post-pregnant cows who loose their pups after only a week or so and the means by which these two groups of cows become pregnant is not yet altogether clear.

CHAPTER 4

THE GREY SEAL – REPRODUCTION

IN this chapter we shall consider in detail the changes which take place in the reproductive organs in both male and female during their life time (sexual maturation) as well as those which occur during the course of one year, (reproductive cycle). It is necessary to study both together because each yearly cycle replicates to some extent, particularly in the male, the final stages of sexual maturation. Moreover the reproductive cycle must be viewed over a period of two years for during the first of these there will take place the maturation of the sperm and ova which, after fertilisation, give rise to the embryo. This in its turn will take nearly a year as a foetus before being born as a pup.

THE MALE

The male organs or testes of the grey seal are similar in many respects to those of most mammals. They are originally formed as elongate bodies on the dorsal wall of the abdominal cavity, close to the kidneys (Pl. 10). From this position they 'descend' at a very early age, namely between 90 and 100 days of active gestation. * 'Descent' really means moving backwards to a more posterior position where the cavity becomes so narrow that the testes can pass sideways and downwards through a gap in the abdominal musculature and wall which has been specially formed and is known as the *inguinal canal*. So far, so good; the same applies in all mammals which do not retain abdominal testes. In most other mammals with descending testes however, the testes come to lie close under the skin near the mid-line of the body and two flaps of tougher skin grow down at the sides and join each other to form a bag or '*scrotum*'. This is usually so much 'outside' the body wall that the testes are described as 'external' as opposed to the 'internal' or abdominal position. Now in the seals, first of all there is no scrotum and secondly the testes only just pass through the inner or muscular wall and remain covered by the blubber and the normal hide of the outer part of the abdominal wall. Thus although the testes have 'descended' they are not truly external (Fig. 16). This must be considered an adaptation to the marine habit for truly external testes might well be subjected to such low temperatures from the surrounding water that the germ cells would fail to develop.

Accompanying the testis in its descent is the epididymis, a long and much convoluted tube which acts as a storage organ for the sperm. The inner end

* The precise meaning of the term 'active gestation' will be explained later (See page 83).

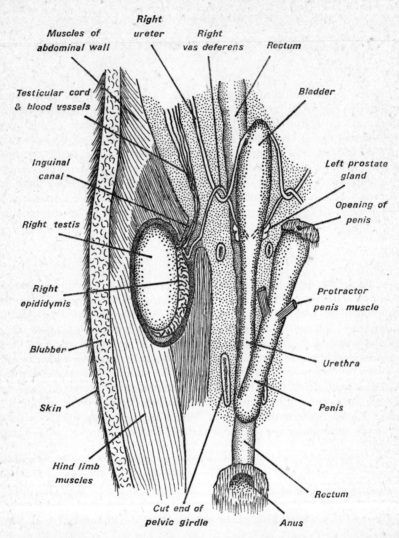

FIG. 16. The male grey seal genitalia. A view from below. The skin and blubber
have been removed to display the testis and epididymis lying in the thin-walled
pocket. The inguinal canal has been opened up to show the connection with the
main abdominal cavity, in which the rectum and bladder are lying. To show the
prostate gland and the urethra leading to the penis, the ventral part of the pelvic
girdle has been removed. This also shows the rectum passing back to the anus. $\times \frac{1}{3}$

of the epididymis runs as the *vas deferens* up the inguinal canal into the body cavity and thence, joining its pair from the other side enters the urethra at the base of the penis. Into the *vas deferens* enter the seminal vesicles, (another reservoir of ripe sperm) and the prostate gland which provides fluid in which the sperm can be transferred to the female.

During foetal life the testis and epididymis grow at a rate comparable with the other organs until the last few months, when they become disproportionately large. At birth the testis weighs about 18 grammes which is near the weight of the testis in a 3–4 year old bull. This is because during the last period of pregnancy it has come under the influence of the gonadotrophic hormones of the cow, which have been mounting to produce a period of heat soon after the birth of the pup (*post-partum oestrus*). During the first few weeks of life after birth the testis regresses and becomes quite small again; about 6–8 grammes. Thereafter normal growth takes place year by year until an average weight (of testis and epididymis together) of around 40 grammes is attained, but there are considerable variations in the weight in the age groups of 4–6 years. If these weights are related to the dates on which they were collected, we can see that the variation is seasonal and is becoming greater year by year (Table 2 and Fig. 17). Moreover in bulls which are quite certainly mature (e.g. territory holders aged 10–15 years) the weight can vary from as little as 80 grammes in April to as much as 250 grammes in October. Referring to the Table again you can see the point in age when the annual growth with some seasonal fluctuation, is succeeded by very great seasonal fluctuation and very little, if any, annual growth. This is the point of sexual maturity and is at the age of 6 years on average.

To find out to what these seasonal changes in weight are due, we must examine the contents of the testis and of the epididymis by cutting and staining sections of them and examining these under the microscope.

When we do this we find that the microscopic appearance changes very markedly through the year almost month by month. The photographs of sections of testes and, as a basis for comparison, the immature state are seen in Plate 9. The immature testis is made up of a great number of tubules which do not appear to have any clear tube or lumen down the centre. Between the tubules there is other tissue called the 'interstitium'. All the sections of mature testes (Pl. 9) show tubules which are much larger in diameter, with a large lumen. Those taken from bulls killed in the months January–July have walls in which there are only 1–2 layers of cells. From September to November however, there are many more layers, the tubules reach their maximum diameter and we can see spermatozoa in the lumen. If we examine these last sections very carefully we can see that the cells nearest the lumen are smaller than those below (and so are their deeply stained nuclei). In fact we can detect two sizes, one half the size and the other, still nearer the lumen, one quarter the size of the large basal cells. These small cells are the result of the so-called maturation divisions of the sperm-

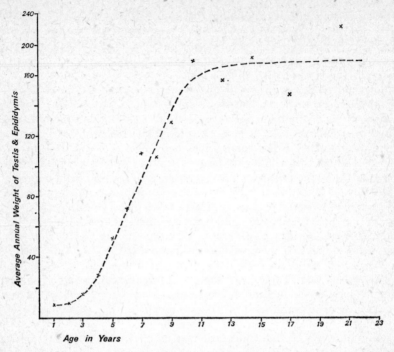

FIG. 17. Growth and maturation of the testis of the grey seal. Plotting the average annual weight of the testis against the age of the bulls, puberty is seen to become marked during the 4th year. Although sperm are formed from the 6th year onwards, it is not until about 10 years of age that the testis and epididymis reach their combined mature weight. The fluctuations between 150 and 250 grams in the average annual weights of mature testes are the result of different proportions of seasonal variations in the available yearly samples. (*See Figure 18*)

mother-cells which end in the production of 4 sperms from each sperm-mother-cell. The final stages of sperm formation can be seen on Plate 9, where the superfluous protoplasm is being sloughed off and the nucleus is being condensed and elongated into the sperm head, while the tail filament grows out. This stage is known as a 'spermatid'.

Turning to the photographs of epididymides on Plate 10 the story is somewhat simpler. From the immature condition there is a steady growth in size of the tube and of its wall, until at maturity we can see that the lumen has been lined with cilia, minute protoplasmic hairs which beat strongly in one direction and which will be used to push the spermatozoa down the tube. Again we can see a seasonal variation in the size of the tubules so that those accompanying testes in the earlier months of the year are much smaller than

Table 2. Weights of Testis and Epididymis

Years	1	2	3	4	5	6	7	8	9	10–11	12–13	14–15	16–18	19–22
Mean Annual Weight (g)	8.2	10.2	15.9	28.1	52.3	72.1	108.5	106.0	128.6	168.9	156.0	170.4	146.8	190.5
Mean Weight (g) for 'Lesser' half-year	8.3	12.6	13.4	26.8	50.9	63.9	92.6	88.5	102.8	122.7	107.1	115.0	97.8	122.8
Mean Weight (g) for 'Greater' half-year	7.1	10.7	22.0	54.5	89.2	145.1	165.9	158.3	155.8	172.0	194.9	175.4	182.0	228.5
Status	Immature			Pubertal			Non-territorial Mature			Territorial Mature				
Differences	−1.2	−1.9	+8.6	27.7	38.3	81.2	73.3	69.8	53.0	49.3	87.8	60.4	84.2	105.7
Mean Differences	1.8			49.1			65.4			77.5				

those of the autumn when ripe spermatozoa are being formed. It has been shown in other mammals, easier to experiment upon than seals, that the diameter of the tubules of the epididymis is a good measure of the amount of male sex hormone (testisterone) present in the blood. This hormone is produced by the 'interstitium' of the testis and, by appropriate staining techniques, we can show the increased activity there during these later months.

It is by studies such as this that we have been able to establish the period of the year when the males are really potent. At other times of the year their libido is reduced considerably and they tend to behave more non-sexually; they have no urge to establish territories on land or to exert their social position in a hierarchy such as we find in the 'breeding season'. Nor do they approach cows with a view to mating. In other words they seem to regard both other bulls as well as cows as being of the same sex or rather of no-sex.

We are now in a position to give an account of the male reproductive cycle starting at the point when the mature territorial bull leaves the rookery in late November or December after mating. He is usually rather exhausted having lost a lot of blubber. The testes although large are not very heavy and average about 170 grammes. They appear 'empty' and flaccid. The tubules are still large with large lumens but the walls are reduced to a single layer of primordial germ cells. Only a residuum of sperm remains in the epididymis. During January and February the testes become smaller, the tubules closing up and the walls more solid looking but there is no regeneration of the germinal epithelium. The epididymis too has become smaller and the tubules decreased in size. In March regeneration begins; the primordial germ cells divide and so increase in number. This process continues through the next 2 or 3 months although the overall weight of the testis continues to drop until the end of April (90 grammes). This is probably due to a reduction in the amount of interstitium. In June a few early stages of the maturation divisions can be seen and this is continued and increased slightly in July, but so slow is the process that mature sperm or even spermatids are absent. Not even one 'generation' of maturing sperm takes place over 4 to 6 weeks or even perhaps more. In August more activity is observable; the first 'generation' or batch of sperm comes 'off the production line' but is rarely seen in the epididymis. In September a speeding up of the process takes place, as the concentration of the sex hormones in the blood increases. It is in late August and September that the bulls begin to make their way towards the breeding grounds from the feeding areas (as Morton Boyd has shown (1963)). Anyone visiting the rookeries in July and August will be disappointed at the very few bulls (or cows for that matter) which can be found. They are all dispersed feeding and only towards the end of August and into September will they begin to congregate. Even so their libido is not yet high enough to make them aggressive holders of territory on the rookeries (Fig. 18).

October sees the height of testicular activity, several 'generations' of sperm-mother-cells are undergoing maturation simultaneously so that enormous masses of sperm are produced and the enlarged epididymis is packed with them throughout its length (Pl. 9). In the behaviour of the bull too great activity is seen; they take up territories and vigorously defend them

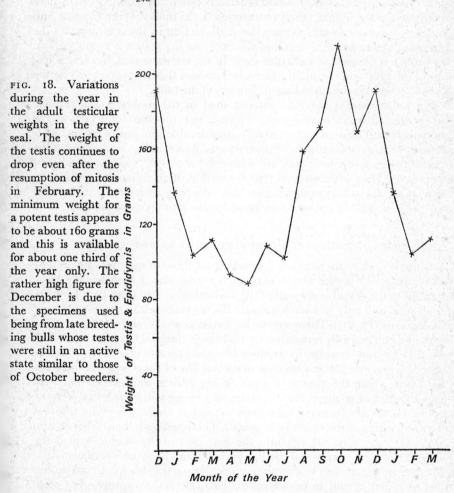

FIG. 18. Variations during the year in the adult testicular weights in the grey seal. The weight of the testis continues to drop even after the resumption of mitosis in February. The minimum weight for a potent testis appears to be about 160 grams and this is available for about one third of the year only. The rather high figure for December is due to the specimens used being from late breeding bulls whose testes were still in an active state similar to those of October breeders.

Weight of Testis & Epididymis in Grams

Month of the Year

against late-comers and as the cows come into heat after pupping they actively pursue and mate with them. By November however many will have ceased to produce more sperm and will use only that in the epididymis. Towards the end of the season a late-pupping cow may even approach a bull who has been long on the territory without eliciting an attempt on his part to mate. (This was first seen by Fraser Darling.) However, there will be late-comers among the bulls too so that the season is spread over a number of weeks. These tired, exhausted bulls then leave their territories and the cycle is complete.

One feature stands out clearly in this story and that is the astonishingly short time each year that each bull is actively potent. It is only because there is variation in the time of yearly maturation in the bulls that the pupping and mating seasons are so prolonged. (We shall see that in the common seal the 'pupping' season is very short and that the mating season is equally short. We do not yet know the testicular cycle in the common seal, but if it is like that of the grey seal the main difference between the two species will be the absence of wide variation in time of potency of the bulls.)

The bulls spend 4–6 weeks without food in the rookeries and indulge during that time in considerable activity, not the least of which is the production and expenditure of a very considerable amount of sperm. Now sperm consists almost entirely of concentrated nuclei and it is known that the nuclear-proteins of which they are comprised is a very 'expensive' material to produce. Thus when we find that the weight of an exhausted testis is, on the average, 80–100 grammes lighter than the fully active ones, we can see that reproduction may place a very considerable burden on the male.

THE FEMALE REPRODUCTIVE ORGANS AND CYCLE

The female organs are not very different from those of most mammals. The *ovaries* are ovoid bodies about 1–1½ inches long and ¾–1 inch wide lying attached to the dorsal body wall of the abdominal cavity (Fig. 19). They are rather solid and only in a section under the microscope can the minute 'egg' cells be seen (Pl. 11). These are to be found near the under surface of the ovary and can be easily recognised by their huge nuclei. During the life of the cow they do not increase in number like the sperm-mother-cells, but are limited. Once the cow has become mature a few of these 'egg'-mother-cells will mature, with the growth of an enclosing follicle, and one of these will reach the surface of the ovary, break it and the egg will be released into the abdominal cavity. In many mammals the egg is directed by cilia into the internal opening of the egg-tube or *oviduct*. This opening is funnel shaped and its beating cilia waft the egg into the first part of the oviduct called the *Fallopian tube*. In the grey seal the lips of the funnel have grown enormously to form a complete cover to the ovary, enclosing part of the abdominal cavity. Such an ovary is said to be 'encapsulated'. It certainly ensures that eggs, liberated from the ovary in the process known as ovulation, are not lost. The special ciliated funnel can be seen in Fig. 19, the capsule having been opened up. The Fallopian tube is very short and leads into the principal part of the oviduct in a mammal, the *uterus* or womb. In the seals this is more complicated than in the human because there are two 'horns' to it each leading from a

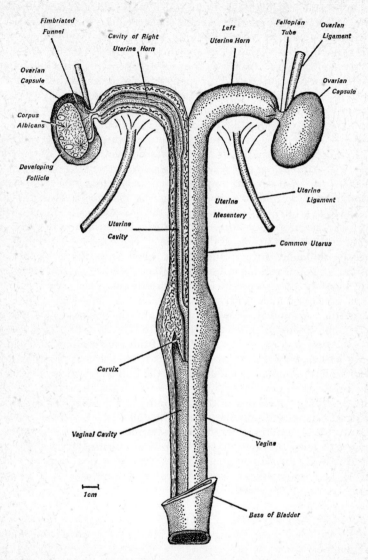

FIG. 19. The female grey seal genitalia (adult). A ventral view, the bladder having been removed. The left side (right side of the cow) is shown in section down the length of the organs to display the ovary lying inside its capsule and the cavities of the uterus and vagina. $\times \frac{1}{2}$

Fallopian tube. These join lower down into a 'common' uterus which ends at the *cervix* or 'neck'. The uterine portion of the oviduct is very muscular and potentially very vascular as we shall see later. Internally it is lined with a delicate cellular layer called the *mucosa* which undergoes remarkable changes during pregnancy. Below the cervix the oviduct opens out into a wide toughly lined *vagina* or copulatory part. This opens to the exterior just below the anus, where it is joined by the urethra through which the urinary bladder is emptied. The uterine horns in the non-pregnant adult are about 3–4 ins. long, the common uterus another 3–4 ins. and vagina about 6–7 ins.

The ovary of the newly-born pup is, like the testis, very large indeed, for the same reason. It weighs about 20–25 grammes but regresses soon to about 5 or less (Fig. 20). During the next few years slow growth takes place but not until near sexual maturity are any of the egg cells enlarged. From then on each year a few will undergo a process known as 'maturation' and this can be seen in the fully adult cow. The first sign is the growth around the primordial 'egg' cell of a layer of tissue known as a *follicle*. This increases in thickness as time goes on, and also in size so that the 'egg' cell comes to fill only a small part of the follicular cavity; the rest is filled with fluid (Pl. 11). The primordial 'egg' cell will have to undergo the maturation divisions (like the 'sperm') but only *one egg* is produced with three minute *polar bodies*.

Let us begin the female yearly cycle just after the birth of the pup. During the period of lactation the cow is antipathetic to the bull. This might be thought to be a simple protective reaction of the cow to guard the pup, because she will also repel any other cows from approaching her pup. But there are many occasions in some rookeries when she may go down to the water far from the pup and viciously repel the bull who approaches her, but not pay any attention to other cows. We may safely say, therefore, that this is a sexual reaction. A lessening of this antipathy can be observed towards the end of lactation so that finally she accepts the bull.

We do not know anything about the sex-hormonal condition of the cow at this stage but must presume that she is in heat or *oestrus* since she ovulates spontaneously. Even non-pregnant cows, that have not been mated, are known to have ovulated, as shown by an examination of their ovaries in January, February or March when a well-developed *corpus luteum* can be found.

However we do know some of the things that are going on in the ovary. Even while lactation is still taking place, in the ovary on the side on which the last pregnancy did *not* take place, one or two of the larger follicles containing maturing eggs grow very rapidly so that by the end of lactation there is at least one large enough (and the egg fully mature) to reach the surface of the ovary, burst and liberate the egg-cell. This is the usual climax of oestrus and is called *ovulation*. It takes place in the grey seal only once each year and then in alternate ovaries. From this sort of information we can see that the cards are very definitely stacked against the production of twins. Only one case of two ova (one from each ovary) is known to me in the grey seal and then only one was fertilised. Perhaps the second ovulation took place so long after mating that no live sperm were available to fertilise it. I have found only one case of twin embryos derived from a single ovum because there was no

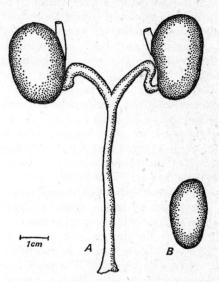

FIG. 20. The female grey seal genitalia at birth. A. the huge size of the ovary relative to the small undeveloped uterus and vagina is very marked. Within a few weeks the ovary regresses to the size characteristic of the 1st to 4th years of life (B). × $\frac{3}{4}$

1cm

A   *B*

evidence of a double ovulation. Even then both were dead, and one had been dead for so long that it showed signs of being resorbed. The explanation of apparent twins, two pups suckling from one cow, will be discussed later. Rae has reported one other case of twins.

Somewhere in the oviduct, probably in the Fallopian tube, the egg is fertilised by sperm and begins to develop as it moves slowly down the uterine horn. Now occurs a very remarkable phenomenon which is known in other seals (the common and elephant seals for example) and also in a few other mammals such as the badger and roedeer. It has been called 'Delayed Implantation' but a better term is 'Suspended Development' because that is just what it is. Having reached a very early stage (called the *blastocyst*) after about a week, further development ceases for the next one hundred days (roughly 3½ months). During that time the blastocyst (Pl. 12) lies quite free in the uterine horn, usually just in the 'bend' before the two horns unite externally.

The blastocyst consists of a hollow ovoid vesicle with a thick patch of cells at one end. Only part of this patch, known as the embryonic knob, will become the embryo. All the rest is used to develop membranes which serve in the processes of nourishing the embryo during its life in the uterus, and will be shed as the 'after-birth'.

Meanwhile the burst follicle grows enormously, thickening its wall until it is as much as 15–20 mm. across (Plate 11). This is known as the *corpus luteum* because it is yellowish-pink in colour. It can be easily detected from the outside of the ovary as a smooth round protuberance. Its function is to produce hormones which will enable the embryo to establish itself in the uterus and to obtain nourishment from the cow. It is, therefore, described as the corpus luteum of pregnancy. Oddly enough we find these corpora present in the ovary of grey seals whether there is a blastocyst present or not, that is whether the cows have been mated or not. The reason for this is not known. Neither is it known why there is this suspended development. One would think that with the well-developed corpus luteum development would proceed and the uterine wall become receptive for the attachment of the embryonic membranes.

However, this does not take place yet. We may note in passing that it is during this period that the cows undergo their annual moult and also put on much of the blubber which they have lost during lactation. Whether either of these facts is related to the suspense of development is not known and a lot of very difficult work will be necessary before an answer can be given.

Development begins again very gradually and at the same time changes begin to appear in the uterine mucosa or lining. It is not possible to give an exact date for this because just as pupping and mating are spread over 6–8 weeks or even more in exceptional cases, so the recommencement of development is spread. The peak is in mid-February, but it can occur a month earlier or later. Within a week or so the glands of the mucosa have enlarged and begin to secrete nutritive material which can be absorbed and used by the developing blastocyst. When this has reached a size of about 10 mm., wherever its outer layer of cells touch the lining of the uterus, this is broken down and soon the embryo is attached by its membranes to the uterine wall, a '*placenta*' is formed and nutriment can then pass rapidly from the blood stream of the mother through the tissues of the placenta to the blood stream of the embryo (Pl. 12). By the time the embryo is 5 cms. long, weighing about 7 grammes, it is quite recognisable as a seal (Pl. 13). Also shown in that figure are the 'membranes'. The principal part, of course, is the placenta, composed of the *chorion* from the embryonic side and the uterine wall from the mother's. It forms a band or zone encircling the whole complex, the two thin ends of the chorion not involved in placenta-formation can be seen to right and left of the embryo. The sac 'above' the embryo is the *yolk sac*. This helps to convey nourishment to the embryo in the very early stages, through its blood system. Although it does not contain any yolk it is so named because it corresponds to the same structure in birds and reptiles which does contain a massive reserve of yolk. Finally there is the *amnion*, a thin walled sac containing fluid which is largely water, surrounding the embryo and so cushioning it against any damage. At about this stage, when the embryo starts to look like a seal, we may begin to call it a 'foetus'.

Perhaps the real criterion is its rate of growth because up to this point growth has been slow, nourishment diffusing into the yolk sac slowly from the uterine glands and thence carried by the blood vessels to the embryo. However, when the placenta is established and in full working order the rate of nourishment speeds up. In consequence the growth rate increases to a steady figure which continues until birth. This is shown in Fig. 21. Nothing is known concerning the actual weights of the early embryos.

As the foetus develops so various external features appear. In chronological order some of the more obvious are listed in Table 3. The 'age' of the foetus is given in the number of days of active gestation, neglecting the 100 days or so of suspended development.

The over-all period of active gestation is about 250 days, which, with the 100 days of suspended development, makes a total of about 350 days, thus bringing the time of birth to within a fortnight of the anniversary of conception or mating. Coulson and Hickling have given an average of birth weights of 51 male and 23 female pups as 14,760 grammes (32.47 lbs.). It will be seen from Table 3 that the foetuses have achieved only half their birth weight after 185 days of active gestation, but all external features by that time are indistinguishable from the newly-born pup. The average length at birth (Coulson and Hickling) is 35 ins. measured from the top of the nose to the tip of the hind flippers.

FIG. 21. Foetal growth rate in the grey seal. Up to about 150 days from conception, 100 days are accounted for by suspended development and the other 50 by very slow embryonic differentiation and growth. The establishment of an allantoic placenta is the signal for the onset of the foetal growth rate which is strictly comparable with that of other mammals (except whales and primates) and which continues steadily until birth. A graph based on the length of the foetus gives an almost identical result.

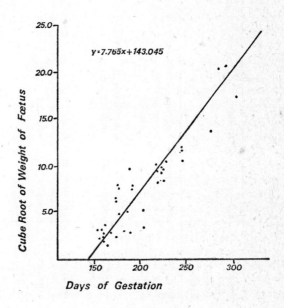

$y = 7.765x + 143.045$

Cube Root of Weight of Foetus

Days of Gestation

Table 3. Foetal Characters

Mean Age Weight Length	Skin	Eyelids	Vibrissae & Eye-Brow Tufts	Pigmentation	Last joint of digits – claws
60 days 7.2 g. 5.5 cm.	Delicate and transparent	Not completely covering the eyeballs	Follicles just visible as white dots	Absent	Just recognisable but no claws visible
70 days 35.0 g. 9.3 cm.	Delicate and transparent	Completely covering the eyeballs	Follicles raised as papillae	Absent except on edge of eyelids	Claw bed just visible, slightly whiter
83 days 133 g. 16.2 cm.	Now opaque but still delicate	Completely covering the eyeballs	Vibrissae hairs just protruding from follicles	Absent except on eyelids and part of face	Claws whitish and opaque
91 days 264 g. 20.2 cm.	Opaque		Vibrissae hairs just protruding from follicles (1–2 mm.)	Slight pigmentation on back as well as face	Claws whitish and opaque
101 days 500 g. 26.1 cm.	Opaque and thickening	*Hair on Body* Hair follicles visible on most of body	Vibrissae 4–5 mm.	More widely spread on back and belly. Fingers darker	Claws showing slight hook
115 days 937 g. 34.2 cm.	Tough	Hair visible on top of head, just visible on back	Vibrissae 7–10 mm.	Well developed showing sexual pattern differences	Claws becoming grey at base

Mean Age Weight Length	Fore- and Hind-Limbs	Hair on Body	Vibrissae & Eye-Brow Tufts	Pigmentation	Last joint of digits – claws
126 days 1468 g. 41.3 cm.	Very markedly darker than the body	Hair present all over body, longest on head, shortest on belly	Very long and prominent	Slightly obscured by the whitish hair	Claws of fore-limbs nearly all grey, of hind-limbs less so
136 days ? 56.7 cm.	Very markedly darker than the body	Hair covering whole body 2–3 mm. long even on belly		Pigmentation totally obscured	Claws large and nearly all grey
185 days 7400 g. 76.3 cm.	Indistinguishable from new-born pup, except for weight				

Meanwhile the cow has been at sea, feeding. The full story of this is not known but its outlines are interesting. After mating there does not seem to be much doubt that the cow goes to sea for long periods with infrequent haul-outs. This, it must be remembered, is during the winter with low temperatures, and she has lost a great deal of her blubber during the previous lactation. Consequently there is a strong incentive to feed and feed well, to replace this necessary blubber. Measurements of thickness of this fat layer clearly show that by February, on average, cows have recovered their condition. The evidence for this activity is largely negative and has been a cause of difficulty in obtaining specimens of free blastocysts and very early embryos. Table 4 shows that of 23 mature cows taken in January and February only 4 were pregnant, although 14 had been previously pregnant. The remaining 9 were young cows, either virgins or in their first pregnancy. This preponderance of young and non-pregnant cows can be compared with the collection of 26 mature cows in March to May inclusive of which 23 were pregnant. The absence of the pregnant cows at haul-outs has now been noted over a number of years and the difficulty of obtaining early embryonic stages has been noted also among the antarctic species of seal, notably the elephant seal.

During the spring the cows continue to feed, but the growing foetus is small and does not impose a great demand on her for food. By the summer however, with a large pup weighing 10 lbs. and upwards, the cows are less frequently found ashore and it is not until the breeding season approaches that they appear in any numbers near the breeding areas.

Let us take a last look at the foetus inside the mother. It is initially attached in one horn of the uterus near the point of fusion of the two horns. The

Table 4. Distribution of Pregnant and Non-Pregnant Cows

Months	Total	Immature	Mature	Pregnant	Non-Pregnant
January & February	30	7	23	4	19
March, April May	35	9	26	23	3
June & July	20	5	15	15	0
Totals	85	21	64	42	22
		85		64 mature	

Note 1. The proportion of immatures, c. ¼ is the same for the three groups.
     2. High proportion of non-pregnant in January–February, compared with the high proportion of pregnant in the other two groups.

placenta has formed as a band or zone extending all round the wall of the horn (Pl. 12c) and as the foetus grows, more and more of the horn is distended to contain it, until the whole of the 'pregnant' horn is involved. This is achieved by the time that the foetus is about half grown (Pl. 13). Thereafter, first the 'common uterus' is distended and finally even part of the other horn so that towards full term little more than the Fallopian tube and the upper third of the non-pregnant horn can be distinguished as separate from the enormously distended uterus.

CHAPTER 5

THE GREY SEAL – ANNUAL MOULT AND SPRING BEHAVIOUR

I T is extraordinary that until recently nothing was known about the moult. At the right time of year it is possible to visit a haul-out and find the rocks carpeted in loose hair. The beasts themselves present a curious parti-coloured appearance where the old coat has come away and disclosed the new pelt (Pl. 14). The only statement in the literature is an odd one made by Darling that the breeding (territorial) bulls stay ashore after the mating season is over until they have moulted. Nothing could be more wrong. In the first place the early territorial bulls leave the rookeries and make way for the later or replacement bulls; in the second these bulls have been ashore for six to eight weeks without feeding and are a shadow of the fat and sleek bulls which came ashore, as Darling himself remarks. Their need is for food to replace the lost blubber. Now we have the directly observed evidence of moulting bulls in March, April and even May.

An old coat is easily identifiable. During the year the hairs have tended to become bleached and most are split along their lengths, at least at the tips. This produces a paler coat and often rather uniform in colour and without sharply defined patterns. The new coat is more brightly coloured with sharp contrasts in the pattern of blotches and lighter marks. This applies to both cows and bulls and even more, as we shall see, to the yearling seals.

The first indication that was obtained of the period of moult was in a cow taken early in January 1956 in Pembrokeshire. She was, as luck would have it, pregnant with a free blastocyst. But she had started to moult, the new pelage being visible on the top of the head and around the base of the fore flippers.

The next observations also came from Pembrokeshire when Dr Backhouse and I visited the Island of Ramsey in April 1957. We had been unable to get there earlier in the year because of petrol restrictions following 'Suez', but our trips in April and May gave us most interesting information. We found a great haul-out of bulls in all stages of moult on a beach not normally used for breeding in the autumn (Pl. 14). The largest number we counted was 180, which, for the small population of south-west Wales, represented a considerable proportion of the available bulls. Five years later in Orkney, I saw a similar haul-out of bulls, also in April, this time far too numerous to count, but estimated at about 2,000. The following year (1963) haul-outs of predominantly moulting cows were seen in mid-February while a huge haul-out of bulls off Shetland in February a few years later showed no moulting. Many other observations in February, March and April give confirmation.

It must therefore be concluded that moulting cows will be found in January, February and March, while moulting bulls occur in March, April and May. What is not yet known is the time taken by *individuals* to moult. It may be only about a fortnight, although the new coat may not be fully erupted for another few weeks, but this is just guesswork based on the somewhat shorter time taken by the pups to shed their white coat and produce their first grey pelage. The thick mats of hair found on the rocks also suggest that the moult does not take very long and that the prolonged 'moulting season', whether of cows or bulls, is made up of individuals showing a considerable variation in the time of moult. Is this related to the variation in the time of pupping? That is, do late puppers moult late? We just do not yet know. Neither do we know whether the coincidence of the peak of blastocyst implantation and of the peak of moulting cows is other than temporal.

There is one moult which does not occur at these times of year, and that is the moult from the white pup coat to the first grey or moulter coat. This takes place on the rookery about the end of the third week of life and is therefore autumnal. This 'pup moult' also differs from the normal adult moult in that the first parts of the body of the pup to show moulting are the hind flippers, the fore flippers and the top of the head (Pls. 15 and 20). In the adult the moult seems to begin in the axils of the fore-limbs and the top of the head, then spreading backwards over the entire body. Other details of the 'pup moult' are described in Chapter 7.

There is no further moult in the first year, the next coinciding with the usual annual moult. Consequently the first grey coat has to last for well over the twelve months, probably for at least fifteen months. Like the adults at the end of a year the coat has become paler and in some instances almost white. This can be misleading because at a distance these yearlings may be mistaken for pups. I have myself made this mistake which was only corrected by examining the animal close to. It then is clear from its behaviour that it is not a pup. Size is not by itself a true guide, because yearlings are often well inside the range of size of a well nourished three week old pup and so, at a distance, may be wrongly identified. It is possible that some records of white pups which have an odd feature about them (in time or space) may be due to this type of error. In my case, mentioned above, it so happened that I knew the date and place of every pup's birth and the sudden appearance one day of what appeared to be an advanced pup, gave rise to immediate doubt.

Occasionally the pelage becomes extremely worn and tatty. I have seen yearlings almost bald over a great part of the body. The cause of this is not known, but might be due to the frequenting by the young seal of rocky haul-outs of particularly abrasive rocks.

The pups, of course, moult on their natal rookeries, but thereafter the haul-outs frequented by moulting bulls and cows are rarely, if ever, *exactly* the same as the breeding grounds. Not all of these haul-out points are known by any means, but some areas have been fairly well examined. In Orkney it is an even chance to find seals in a breeding island during the late winter and early spring. Only on two small islands is there any overlap and this only when the numbers hauled-out are high. On Ramsey Island, as already mentioned, a non-breeding beach is used by the bulls, and the cave portion of an extensive rookery by cows and some bulls. In the Farne Islands the moulting haul-outs take place on the breeding islands but equally on adjacent islands like the Blue Caps and Harcars (see Appendix D). Nothing is yet known of the moulting sites in the Hebridean and North Rona group, but the main Shetland haul-out appears to be the Ve Skerries, at least in February. Auskerry and the Pentland Skerries in Orkney, the Clerks off Ramsey need to be examined, while the relation of the West Hoyle Bank haul-out, off Wallasey, to the Irish Sea population needs to be more clearly defined. Unfortunately the weather conditions are not very good over the first four months of the year and it often requires five or six days of calm weather to allow the swell to subside sufficiently so that a boat can get out. Helicopter approach is probably the only safe and practical way, but is very expensive. Moulting adults can easily be identified by the patchy coats (Pl. 14).

A temporal connection between moult and the recommencement of development of the blastocyst was mentioned previously. There may not be any direct causal connection but there may be a connection in that the metabolism of the cow cannot cope with more than one process at a time. In other species of seal, such as the elephant seal, moulting is well spaced away from breeding activity of any sort. The moult is not just the shedding of an old pelage; it also involves the production of an entire new one and since hair is composed of keratin which is pure protein it can impose a severe demand on the animal. Birds always moult out of the breeding season and even in the domestic hen, which has been bred to produce eggs continuously, when the time for moult comes round, egg production drops dramatically. The metabolism is unable to stand the drain on its surplus protein in two directions simultaneously.

Is there anything corresponding in the male? The only point worth mentioning is that the lowest weight to which the regressing testis drops is found in May. Thereafter it increases gradually to its mature and potent size. This growth, it will be noticed, is also after the moult. In the grey seal we can see the new coat being produced in the skin below the old one if we take vertical sections. A complete new set of follicles are produced, each follicle giving rise to a new hair which emerges between the hairs of the old coat. The process is probably not a lengthy one as there is no sign of the new follicles at the end of breeding. But, while the actual shedding of the old coat and exposure of the new may only take a week or so, the preparation for this together with the growth of the new hair to its final length after moult, may well extend over several weeks.

Two further points need to be made about activity of the grey seal in the late winter and early spring. Both will concern only the Pembrokeshire group.

When Dr Backhouse and I were about to cross the Sound to Ramsey Island in April 1957 one of us said 'I wonder what we shall find this time.' The other answered, 'Pups'. I cannot recall which of us made this facetious remark but it indicates our preparedness for anything while investigating this hitherto unexplored time of year. Pups seemed as unlikely as mermaids. When, about an hour later, we stood at the top of the cliff above Porth Laoug at the southern end of Ramsey Island and looked down on the beach, we could not believe that the white thing lying 150 feet below us *was* a pup. But one end moved and a view through binoculars proved that indeed it was a pup. When we had descended we found that it was in very poor condition, suffering from a bad wound, suppurating eyes and repeatedly passing into rigors.* In the cave which led off the beach we found another pup in the first phase of moult – head and flippers in new coat. There was also the dead body of a premature birth, too far decomposed to estimate its foetal age. Later on we found another pup on Aber Foel Fawr along with a bull moulting haul-out and a few cows, including, of course, the mother of the pup. On returning to the mainland, the cox of the St David's Lifeboat told us that he had seen another white pup on one of the west-facing beaches about a week earlier.

Enquiries locally showed that these spring pups were seen most years and indeed we saw them ourselves (see Table 5). Many other rookeries have been visited in Orkney, Shetland and the Farne Islands in the spring months since then and no trace of pups or records of them have been found. It must, therefore, be concluded that this is a phenomenon restricted to this group of grey seals. It may still be shown that spring pups also occur in southern Ireland since there are indications that the populations of that coast and of west Wales are one.

Table 5. Spring Births 1957

Tag number	Place	Date	Age	Estimated date of birth
1148	N. Pembrokeshire	3.3.57	10 days	21.2.57
1258	Skomer	28.4.57	14 days	14.4.57
1281	Ramsey	22.4.57	8 days	14.4.57
1282	Ramsey	22.4.57	4 days	18.4.57
1288	Skomer	25.4.57	2 days	23.4.57
1290	Skomer	25.4.57	New-born	25.4.57
1291	Skomer	26.4.57	7 days	19.4.57

(From R. M. Lockley, 'Seal Marking'. Nature in Wales 1958 pp. 537–543.)

* We despatched it humanely.

Before we discuss the significance of this we must record the second peculiar feature which concerns the bulls. As already mentioned we examined other beaches at the southern end of Ramsey and on one, Aber Foel Fawr, found a great haul-out of seals. At that time, it must be remembered, we had not seen more than a few bulls during the breeding season and then mature big fellows. Neither had we found an easy way of determining the sex of younger grey seals when only head and shoulders were above water, or the back of a basking animal was only visible. We *thought* we could tell the difference between the sexes by the patterns of spots and blotches on the coat, but our experience had been limited to the breeding individuals. So it took quite a time for us to decide that practically all the seals were bulls. Several times we felt we must be wrong because of the behaviour of a seal and this is the interesting point. There was occurring a considerable amount of erotic behaviour, one seal attempting to mount another, nuzzling and flippering; the sort of actions one had associated solely with individuals of opposite sexes before mating. Yet these *were* bulls and the behaviour homosexual.

A large bull was seen to attempt copulation with a cow, the mother of a spring pup, the extruded penis being easily visible. Whether it was accomplished could not be determined for certain for they both sank below the surface. That they remained below for some time suggested that there had been coition because the same sort of procedure was later seen by us in the channels around the rookery on Eilean nan Ron in the Hebrides. Lockley has also recorded similar behaviour in Pembrokeshire in the spring. Just as remarkable was the absence of anything like territorial aggression or defence among the bulls.

Having stated the facts, now let us discuss their possible significance. Here we have pupping cows almost six months out of phase with the normal for British waters. It is close however to the pupping season of the Baltic grey seals. Was the grey seal originally di-oestrous, the Baltic group using only the spring and the British the autumn, while this special group in the extreme south-west retained both? There are difficulties in any explanation. If the normal gestation period, including 'delay', occurs following a spring oestrus then the bulls must be potent at that time of year. We have seen that in the northern group this would be quite out of the question but here in Pembrokeshire we do find some erotic behaviour in the bulls but this appears to fall far short of the full *libido* of territorial bulls. Unfortunately we have no testicular or ovarian material from this area and this alone, collected in late March or early spring, would show whether a copulation, if effected, could result in a conception. Another possibility exists if the 'delay' in development was omitted. But to produce pups in March the cows must have been mated in July a full three months before we have evidence of full sperm production and the same objection holds as before. A simple omission of 'delay' in October-mated cows would produce pups in June and not March. It is obvious that more evidence and material must be obtained before the right answer can be determined. But one thing is certain, and that is that whichever solution is correct, this group of grey seals is quite different from the Hebridean, those farther north and from the Farne Islands. Why they are different is still another problem.

All this may seem rather academic, but if the population of grey seals is to be controlled we must know whether its different geographical groups are really distinct or whether there is a free interchange of individuals and the whole population dealt with as a single unit. This evidence of the peculiarities of the south-western group suggests that these at least are a different, largely discrete population. Elsewhere more evidence of a different kind will be mentioned which suggests that there may well be several such separate population units round the British coasts.

CHAPTER 6

THE GREY SEAL – FEEDING AND FOOD; PRE-BREEDING ASSEMBLAGES

COMPARATIVELY little is known about the food of the grey seal either quantitatively or qualitatively, or about the means and place of capture. Direct evidence is difficult to obtain because digestion, as usual among carnivores, is very rapid and unless the seal is killed and examined within an hour or so of feeding, recognisable traces of food may be absent. A great deal of the information about the food is based on what the local fishermen say. Cornish fishermen say that the grey seals chase the pilchard shoals away. Hebridean ones say that they feed on saithe and codling. On the east coast of Scotland it is salmon. Nearly always the seals are said to be in competition with the fishermen. Only in Orkney it is said that where there are seals there will be lobsters, because the seals feed a great deal on octopus which in turn prey on lobsters. Probably there is something in all of these statements and seals feed on available fish, just as the fishermen go for the abundant available fish too.

Rae has given an account of the contents of the stomachs of grey and common seals shot at the nets off the east coast of Scotland.* As would be expected the remains are those of the fish for which the nets have been set. A less biased sample is described by Sergeant for the common seal on the Wash. This showed a wide spread of species, again with the commoner kinds predominating. E. A. Smith took the trouble to shoot grey seals in Orkney immediately on haul-out just after dawn. Here there was a preponderance of squid and octopus. I have seen a cow grey seal off Ramsey Island in Pembrokeshire bring an octopus to the surface and then eat it in two mouthfuls, first the body and then the tentacles. Three grey seals were captured as adults in Orkney and brought to the London Zoo. The two cows had weaned their pups and the bull was fully mature and territorial. The cows must have been in post-partum oestrus because for a week or two the bull remained extremely interested in them and repeatedly mated. None of them would eat any of the dead fish provided and they were obviously losing condition. It was decided to try them with cuttlefish which can be obtained easily and cheaply on the London market. This was immediately successful and all three went on to live several years and the cows to produce more pups.

All this goes to show that we do not really know what proportion of their diet is taken from the same species as required by man. Yet they

* This paper (1968) contains a good summary of all the evidence of food up to 1960.

probably eat many other species including eels which are great predators on the young of many species of foodfish. Until this proportion is known we cannot make out a balance sheet to show whether overall, in its predation, any particular species of seal is a pest or is beneficial.

Neither do we know how they capture prey. Their eyesight is certainly poor on land and the flattened cornea is said to be an adaptation to underwater vision. But seals can hunt in the dark and in opaque water. The North Sea as a whole is fairly turbid and visibility is greatly restricted when compared with the waters of the west and north coasts of Britain. Yet even in clear waters storms can stir up mud off the bottom. The cow, already mentioned, which ate the octopus was hunting in a thick fog. As she ate, floating vertically, the hinder parts of the body were invisible and the octopus arms, after the body had been bitten off, dropped out of sight within a foot or so of the surface and yet the seal dived and retrieved the second part of the meal. So if sight is used it must be a secondary sense only and unessential to feeding.

There are two other senses which could be used; the chemo-reception (smell, taste) and the tactile. Now it is worth noting that although the nostrils of seals are closed when they dive the rhinarium is still exposed externally. (This is the 'wet nose' of a dog and which is characteristically absent in all higher primates.) The seal cannot 'smell', as we understand it, under water but the rhinarium can pick up chemical stimuli and will therefore be able to produce sensations of 'smell-taste'. It is well supplied with nerves so it is clearly not a useless survival of the seal's land ancestry.

Another set of receptors with an enormous nerve supply are the vibrissae situated in the muzzle. These long hairs are very sensitive to touch in all mammals and must play a most important role in seals where they are very well developed and so plentifully innervated. Taking these two sets of receptors together, we guess that chemo-reception probably indicates the presence of prey in the vicinity and when the seal has turned into the direction indicated, the very close proximity of the prey is probably appreciated by stimuli received by the vibrissae from differential water movements produced by the prey. Direct touch of course would indicate a closeness which would enable the final bite to be made.

There is no doubt from my own observations that seals can use these two senses in ways quite beyond the comprehension of man. Eilean nan Ron is a small breeding island for grey seals in the Inner Hebrides. It is surrounded by a wide shelf of seaweed-covered rock exposed at low water. At that time access to the small sandy beaches on which the pups lie can be obtained along deep water channels from the sea. In 1957, when Dr Backhouse and I were there, a cow who was completely blind gave birth to a pup. We used to watch this cow coming up a channel, usually well to one side so that she was in contact with the weeds. How did she find the right entrance at the seaward end? How, if she took a wrong turning through following one 'bank' of the channel, did she recognise this almost at once and turn round and correct the error? 'Smell?' Touch?

Only two estimates have been made of the quantity of food eaten, one for each species, both based on information from zoos. Stevens gives the figure of 15 lbs. a day for the grey seal and Havinga gives 11 lbs. for the common seal. These figures are really not much use because they are more 'guess-timates' than exact observations. Further there are times in the year when seals do not feed at all or at most sparingly. Moreover we do not know how frequently they feed normally. Must they feed each day or will alternate days suffice?

In some grey seal rookeries it is clear that the cows must starve for after they have pupped they remain with the pup continuously. This is usual if the pupping has taken place far from the sea. In others (sometimes in other parts of the same rookeries) the cows go to sea quite frequently. On Ramsey it is the exception for the cow to be seen on land. But wherever the movements of the cows at sea can be observed it is clear that they do not go off in feeding cruises. They are usually swimming to and fro quite close to the shore, sometimes 'standing' vertically quite stationary for long periods within sight of the pup. It is *possible* for these cows to feed a little, but I do not believe that they do.

The bulls are certainly without food for nearly 2 months while they are winning and holding territory. The bulls are firmly attached to their territory. If they leave it another bull will slip in and occupy it. There is nothing to do except to sit it out and starve. The supply of blubber with which they have come ashore stands them in good stead. Nonetheless as time goes on the effects can be seen in sagging skin and obvious loss of weight. Before the breeding season the blubber may be $2\frac{1}{2}$–$2\frac{3}{4}$ inch thick in the mid-ventral position. At the end it may be much less than 2 inches and in some little more than 1 inch.

Similarly during the periods of moult the presence of large numbers of seals hauled-out means that fewer are at sea feeding. Probably there is no complete starvation during moult but there is clearly reduced activity and therefore less opportunity to feed. Alternating with these periods of reduced feeding are two phases of very active feeding indeed. The first, coming after the breeding season, is to restore the lost blubber. The females' loss of blubber has been due as much to transfer of fat to the pup during suckling as from starving. Measurements of the thickness of the blubber show that the loss is largely restored by the late winter, thicknesses of 2 inches and more being quite frequent in February.

The bulls do not go into moult until a little later and so have more time to recover. The indications are, however, that many die from lack of sufficient blubber to insulate them from the cold of winter and that this is the period of maximum mortality in the year. Thus in both sexes the winter feeding period is vital.

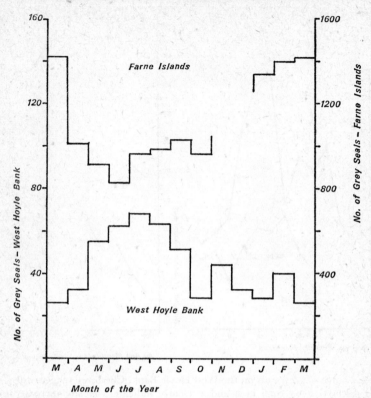

FIG. 22. Counts of grey seals hauled out on the Farne Islands and on West Hoyle Bank, Cheshire. Comparison between these is interesting. They are counts of *non-breeding* seals, but the Farne Island ones are on islands close to their rookeries while the West Hoyle Bank seals are over 150 miles from 'home'. The latter have their peak numbers during the main fishing season of the summer and the Farne Islands have their lowest counts during the same period.

The second feeding phase is throughout the late spring and summer. This is suggested by the smallness of numbers hauled-out in and around the breeding areas. Large haul-outs can be found however elsewhere. From the counts by Craggs and Ellison of grey seals hauled-out on West Hoyle Bank at the end of the Wirral Peninsula, between the estuaries of the Dee and Mersey, there are no breeding rookeries within 150 miles or more, yet the numbers there can exceed 200 animals in the summer (Pl. 22). The fluctuations of numbers during the year is the exact reverse of the numbers seen on the breeding grounds (Figs. 22 and 23). These observations have been made on a population based on the Welsh and Irish coasts within a closed

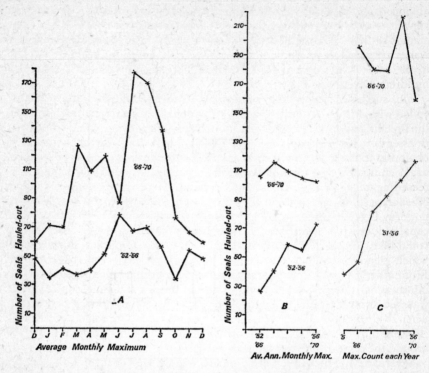

FIG. 23. Counts of grey seals on the West Hoyle Bank, Cheshire, 1952 to 1970. The graphs for 1951/2 to 1956 in B and C clearly indicate a steady increase in the numbers of seals using this haul-out. Ten years later the numbers appear to have stabilized. Another change is indicated in A. In the '52–'56 graph the maximum numbers appear during the summer months when grey seals are normally away from their breeding centres (see Fig. 22). But by 1966 to 1970 they appear to be using the Bank for moulting haul-outs in February and April as well, instead of returning to Pembrokeshire. (*Data from Craggs and Ellison 1960 and pers. comm.*)

sea. What happens in the Hebridean group and in the Northern Isles is not known, any more than for the Farne Island group whose North Sea area is much more extensive than the Irish Sea and which does not provide convenient hauling-out points far from the breeding centres. Some grey seals are always to be seen near the latter (e.g. on the Longstone End in the Farne Islands) but whether they represent a part of the population which does not wander far or is a constantly changing sample of the entire population is not known.

We are inclined to think of this summer feeding period as a pelagic phase of the grey seal, but of course we have little direct evidence other than absence from haul-outs on and around the breeding grounds. Against this view it is sometimes argued that as fishermen rarely see seals at sea they cannot be there. The sea however is large and seal heads bobbing among the waves are small. It would be interesting to know how often seals are sighted in the Mersey Bight when we know that there are upwards of a couple of hundred in the area.

This survey of feeding habits has taken us through much of the year and ended with an apparent dispersal over a wide area in search for food far from the breeding grounds. At what point is this tendency reversed and when does re-assembly begin? What are the signs to look for? Direct evidence is obviously difficult to obtain, perhaps impossible in some areas, but a start has been made by Dr Morton Boyd who organised a system of watching and recording along the west coast of Scotland. Here the presence of many off-shore islands, and consequently the presence also of narrow tracts of sea, not only suggested that any movement of the seals would be to some extent canalised, but it also provided a double shore-line from which observations could be made. As a result of this effort he was able to publish in 1962 data which clearly indicated a movement towards the main breeding centres. From other areas not so favourably situated geographically the same sort of information is not available, at any rate not in such a definite form. I have watched from the cliffs of South Ronaldsay in Orkney during September when the breeding colonies were already beginning and seen many seal heads. *All* were moving northward in towards the main breeding grounds which lie around the central waters of the archipelago.

Several days of such observation spent along the west coast of Wales, on the Northumberland and Durham coasts and elsewhere would I am sure produce evidence of *directional* movements. This can be shown by a *majority* of observed movements in one direction or another. Simultaneous notes on the state and flow of the tides or coastal currents are of course necessary to avoid mis-interpretation but this is a field open to anyone to work on.

The indirect evidence is provided, of course, by the observed increase in numbers on the breeding grounds. The period of such an increase varies with the group, but mid-August to mid-September is a fair estimate covering the more spectacular build-ups. Thereafter numbers continue to increase well into October but by the middle of that month some of the early arrivals among the cows may well have begun to move away again.

It has been mentioned in Chapter 3 that there was a question as to where the 'other' bulls were; the other mature bulls not holding territory. It has also been recorded that eventually (in 1961) I obtained material which provided the answer. But meanwhile chance took a hand and gave me an opportunity in 1954 to make field observations which later proved to be most helpful in interpreting the data about the age structure of the populations of seals. This needs some explanation.

Dr Morton Boyd, whose later work has already been mentioned, was at that time interested in the fauna of the shell-sand beaches of the Hebrides. One island he visited in 1953, and stayed on for some time, was Shillay off the west end of the Sound of Harris. Here, in September, he found grey seals hauled-out on the east facing shell-sand beach. This was not quite the sort of fauna he had come to study but like a good zoologist he made observations on them. These he passed on to Dr Harrison Matthews, Scientific Director at the London Zoo, who had been concerned with the grey seal work carried out in Pembrokeshire. He, in turn, passed it on to me, knowing that I would be interested. Now the observations that Boyd made were, quite simply, that, as far as he could make out, there were as many bulls on the beach of Shillay as cows. Pupping had only just started but even so this proportion of bulls was quite unlike anything so far reported from any breeding ground.

I went to Shillay twice, in 1954 from 22nd September to 30th September and again in 1955 from 21st September to 14th October. These two visits enabled me to make counts of the adult seals almost day by day as well as of the pups. The data so obtained confirmed Boyd's observations. On 28th September, 1954, there were more than 30 bulls, although there were only 7 cows with pups. There were however over 40 cows without pups nearly half of which had arrived since the count on the previous day when there were 27 bulls and 30 cows (6 with pups). In the following year a similar high number of bulls was counted, varying between 34 and 50 on the 27th–29th September. Thereafter the numbers of bulls decreased while the number of cows rapidly increased. Another most interesting and informative observation was concerned with the size and status of the bulls. It must be remembered that I had no means of exactly judging their ages. However, many of them were distinctly smaller, less bulky and without the very pronounced 'roman' nose of the typical rookery bull. In fact it was sometimes difficult to be certain whether they were cows or bulls from their size and general appearance alone. It was here that I began to use the colour *pattern* which later was shown to be quite reliable for separating cows and bulls. The really big bulky bulls behaved in a somewhat special manner (Fig. 24). They were grouped in two lots, one at each end of the beach (Pl. 3), spent their time basking and in all instances of contact with the 'younger' bulls assumed a dominance which was immediately accepted by these smaller seals. The 'younger' bulls were to be found mixed up with the unpupped cows in a 'herd' in the centre of the beach. Between them there were frequent contests, often when one landed from the sea (Pl. 16). One piece of behaviour which would often start a fight was the 'challenge'. This is made by lowering the head and opening the mouth, while emitting a prolonged hiss. I never heard a snarl and sometimes there appeared to be only an expiration without any distinct hiss. If the challenger was one of the 'old' bulls, other bulls would move out of his way.

Such confrontations ended by one or other retreating, either to another part of the beach or eventually into the sea, thus gradually reducing their numbers. The final number of bulls with established territories by mid-

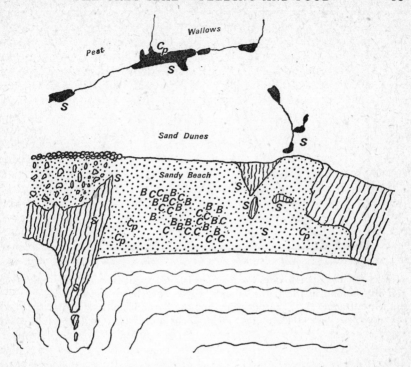

FIG. 24. Early stages in territory formation on Shillay. The large segregated bulls are indicated by S. Three of them have already established territories in the wallows area. The other seven are separated into two groups one at each end of the beach. The three cows with pups (Cp) are also at these end positions. The centre of the beach is occupied by a herd of cows and bulls in about equal numbers. Many of these bulls are obviously young ones, some of whom do not obtain territories. The cows are all pregnant and nearing full-term.

October was 20 of whom 10 were 'old' bulls. There was no doubt in my mind that I had witnessed an annual 'graduation' ceremony at which the more aggressive and dominant bulls among the younger non-territorial ones had succeeded in obtaining territories for the first time. Such a sorting out process had never been observed before. Did it occur elsewhere? The shell-sand beach on Shillay* was, of course, a perfect place for confrontations, charges and retreats and it could well be that elsewhere under different geographical conditions the ceremony would be different.

In the following two years, 1956–57, I (with Dr Backhouse) visited Eilean nan Ron off Oronsay to see what happened under the very different

* It is unique as an approach to a breeding rookery. All others are either rock or pebbles.

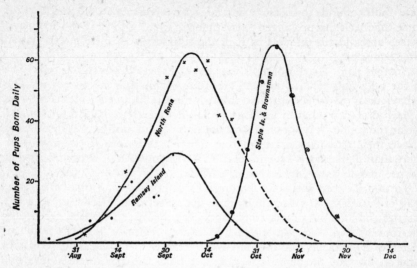

FIG. 25. Daily pupping rates for Ramsey Island, 1948; North Rona, 1959; Staple and Brownsman in the Farne Islands, 1970. The curves are all similar in shape but the later ones show sharper peaks and the Farne Island pupping season is compressed. (*Data from: Davies, 1949; Boyd, Lockie and Hewer 1972; Bonner and Hickling 1971*)

conditions there. Here the 'pre-breeding assembly', as we had come to call it, took place on the skerries which appear at low water between Oronsay and Eilean nan Ron. As the tide went down and the skerries appeared, so seals began to haul-out. A large proportion of these were bulls. The confrontations appeared to take place as a bull attempted to land and find a basking space. It may well be too that contacts made in the water assisted in sorting out the more dominant ones. Here there was a rise in numbers followed by a fall as first the 'defeated' bulls left and then the older bulls and the successful younger ones moved off to establish territories around the island of Eilean nan Ron and its neighbour Ghaoidmeal.

Since then the appearance of pre-breeding assemblies has been recognised in other areas and although details, particularly of individual behaviour, are not known because of observational difficulties, the general picture appears to be similar throughout.

This assembly breaks up and disappears with the establishment of territories by the bulls. It also synchronises more or less with the real onset of pupping. In most rookeries some pups appear well before there are territorial bulls, but there is usually a time when the number of pups born daily takes a sudden upward turn (Fig. 25) and it is then that the territories will be found to be established over most of the rookery area. However, in large rookeries 'late' bulls continue to trickle in and establish territories on the periphery for some time. It is this prolonged overlapping of events which, in the first place, makes observations difficult and, in the second place, their interpretation often equivocal.

Another point worth noting is that the objectives to which the behaviour of the bulls and cows is directed are quite different in the two sexes. The behaviour of the bulls is directed towards the establishment of territory with a view to mating; that of the cows to finding a space on which to pup and suckle the young. It is not until weaning that post-partum oestrus in the cows directs their activities towards mating. There is thus no *biological necessity* for more than the broadest synchronisation in the activities of bulls and cows in the pre-breeding and early breeding periods.

To sum up then the main features of this pre-breeding time when grey seals of both sexes are assembling near the rookeries: the cows use adjacent skerries and haul-out points simply as collecting areas. A few will proceed to the rookery itself and pup whether bulls are present or not. The numbers increase often sharply and then fall away as more cows come to full term and land on the true breeding rookeries. The bulls similarly assemble nearby, perhaps on the same ground as the cows, and pause before going to the rookeries. The 'older' bulls, survivors of previous breeding seasons, exhibit a dominance which is recognised and accepted by the 'younger' ones. They make no attempt to approach the cows or to molest them in any way. Gradually they move off to take up station on territory. The 'younger' ones sort themselves out in ways which are not always apparent or recognisable by us, but the upshot is that many are turned away while those remaining go to the rookeries to establish territories. How they do this is another story dealt with in Chapter 8.

CHAPTER 7

THE GREY SEAL – THE BREEDING ROOKERY: COW AND PUP

THE grey seal's year is usually divided into 'the breeding season' and the non-breeding period. This is unfortunate because the breeding season contains two distinct elements. The first is the period of 'pupping' and the second is the period of 'mating'. In the grey seal (but not necessarily in other species of seal) these follow each other closely and, because each has a considerable time range for any given rookery, overlap. For any individual cow pupping and mating are separated by about a fortnight as previously mentioned.

The literature contains many references to differences in the dates of the 'breeding seasons' between different groups of grey seals. Such differences can only be measured if we have a clear and precise definition of the 'season'. As the two parts are linked in time it should be enough to define one and the pupping period is the easier to evaluate since the pups are easily seen, can be counted and their age fairly accurately determined. Mating occurs only temporarily and can be missed even with almost constant observation. For a number of years therefore 'pup censuses' have been made at various rookeries and the pattern of pupping at them has been established. This work has shown that, in terms of the number of pups born daily, the pupping season starts slowly, gradually increasing in pace to a fairly high rate, slows off at a peak of daily numbers and then decreases again in almost a mirror image of the onset (Figs. 25 and 26). If the rate of decrease is *exactly* the same as the rate of increase the date of the peak is the same as the date on which 50% of the pups will have been born. This latter date is known as the *mean date of pupping* and is the best single date by which the pupping period can be defined. In some rookeries there is a suggestion that the decrease in pupping rate is slightly greater than the increase. This means that the halfway mark (mean date of pupping) is slightly earlier than the date of peak pupping, perhaps by a day or two. There are other dates which can be used further to define the pupping period, but they are not so useful as the mean date of pupping when comparison between rookeries or groups of rookeries are being made. These dates concern the *range* of dates over which pupping takes place. It will be seen by the graph of the North Rona rookeries that the onset and tail off of births is at a very low level for some time and, generally speaking, the larger the number of pups born the more constant will be the date of the first birth. This means that in a small rookery it may be necessary to make observation of this first birth date over a number of years to arrive at a mean

FIG. 26. Daily pupping rates for neighbouring rookeries. The combined figures for Brownsman and Staple Island give a typical pupping rate curve. Taken separately there is a clear indication that pupping on Brownsman starts later, reaches its peak later and finishes later. In 1956 very few pups were born on Brownsman compared with Staple Island. Only recently have the numbers been about equal. These graphs show that Staple Island still has a priority over Brownsman as a site for pupping.

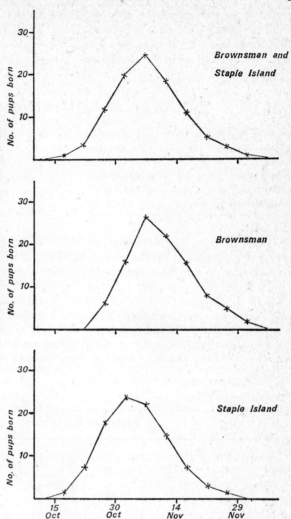

date of onset. Where this has been possible as in the Farne Islands and where the numbers are high, it can be as useful as the mean date of pupping as a criterion, but elsewhere it is not so.

Two other dates are worth noting. These are those between which 90–95% of the pups are born. The exact percentage is somewhat arbitrary and is actually decided mathematically, but in ordinary language it means that within these dates the vast majority of pups are born. Outside them the numbers are insignificant. If the rate of increase of pupping up to and away from the peak is steep as at Shillay and North Rona, these dates are relatively fairly close to the mean date of pupping. If the rates of increase and decrease are very gradual as in Pembrokeshire (Ramsey Island) they will be wide apart.

Table 6. Mean Dates of Pupping

Ramsey Island	1–5 October	(No very precise peak)
Oronsay group	1–5 October	
Shillay	7 October	(Sharp peak)
North Rona	9–10 October	(Sharp peak)
Orkney	c. 12 October	
Farne Islands (1964–70)	7 November	(Sharp peak)

Too often in the past statements on the 'breeding seasons' have been based on records of births at the extreme ends. These, as we have seen, are the least reliable data to use. Consequently the differences in time have been much exaggerated. Table 6 gives a list of the mean dates of pupping of some rookeries or groups of rookeries. From this it will be seen that for all the west and north coast rookeries there is an overall range of only about a fortnight but that the Farne Island group is a month later than the mean of these. Nevertheless there is overlap in the pupping periods of all. This means, of course, that inter-breeding between grey seals in British rookeries is just possible.

Table 7. Mean Pupping Dates in November in the Breeding Islands of the Farnes

	Av. '56–'61	'64	'65	'66	'67	'68	'69	'70	Av. '64–'70
Staple Island	9.7	7	2	3	3	3	6	4	4.0
North Wamses	9.3	6	8	8	7	6	9	7	7.4
Brownsman	21.0	12	9	10	9	8	13	9	10.0
South Wamses	16.0	24	20	19	11	10	15	11	14.4

If the dates of pupping in rookeries belonging to the same group and even in close proximity are determined it is found that there are considerable variations. This has been done in the Farne Islands over a number of years, and the results are shown in Table 7. Not only is there a range from 2nd November to 24th November overall, but each island clearly shows average differences such as those for 1964–70 ranging from 4th November to 14th

November. An interesting feature, apparently associated with the very considerable growth in numbers, is that over the fifteen years, 1956–70, there has been a steady progress towards earlier pupping in all islands. Another noticeable fact is that the earlier pupping dates are on the 'favoured' islands. Brownsman, the last to be used as a rookery, comes up from fourth place at 21st November to third at 10th November.

It is time now to turn to the rookeries themselves. What determines the site of them? Why are they crowded in places and in others scarcely used? These and other questions will be discussed in this chapter. In the previous one we have seen that the cows tend to collect in the neighbourhood of the rookeries before the breeding season proper begins. There can be little doubt that the majority of the early arrivals are cows at full term who will be among the earliest to pup. These then proceed to come ashore and pup on the rookeries. This they do whether or not bulls are already there. If bulls are found as the first inhabitants of a site, they are the large and older bulls who 'have been there before'. Much more frequent, taking the picture as a whole by including *all* pupping sites, large and small, is the beaching of the early cows. It can therefore be supposed that it is the cows who choose the sites of the rookeries and are so responsible for changes and expansions of the breeding rookeries. This aspect of the cow's behaviour is important to the ecologist if he wishes to establish a system of management and conservation. Are there any definable features of rookeries which can be seen to be favourable?

Basically one must regard the grey seal as conservative. Rookeries continue to be used during population growth long after the numbers appear to have reached a level above which sufficient ground space for the efficient rearing of the pups can be ensured without undue interference from neighbouring cows. This conservatism only becomes apparent however in the later stages of the evolution of a rookery when over-crowding becomes significant. We will return to it later.

Firstly the site should be accessible from the sea. The degree of difficulty tolerated by the seals varies from area to area depending largely on the gross geographical features of the coast-line. Davies has pointed out that the grey seals of Pembrokeshire and Cornwall are forced to use the small and often shallow beaches below the almost continuous cliff-line if they are to breed in this area at all (Fig. 27). The southern part of Great Britain being so densely and continuously populated, the fact that these beaches are relatively inaccessible *to man* is an important factor. In the absence of man the wider beaches, often at the mouths of streams, would be used and may well have been so in the past, just as they are today in the north and west where interference by man is minimal. Nevertheless, at the present time, in this south-western part of Great Britain, the *first* sites to be occupied by the cows each year are caves. In fact the term 'cave-breeding' has been applied to the grey seals of south and west Ireland, Cornwall and west Wales, including the small islands of Lundy and Lambay. Only later, when the caves are 'full', do they come ashore on the open beaches. The attractive feature of the caves may not be the cover they possess, but the deep water approach to the beach itself. It is very noticeable on the open beaches that access to them is

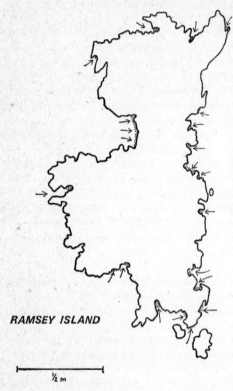

FIG. 27. Breeding sites on Ramsey Island. The breeding sites are nearly all caves at the head of small inlets or small pebble beaches. The only exception is Aber Mawr which is a broad beach on the west coast and which is used for pupping only after the other sites have been occupied.

RAMSEY ISLAND

½ m

confined to a few deep channels. If too many cows attempt to use them there is a great deal of interference. This is important in this type of geographical set-up, where the beaches are narrow and do not really provide much room for the cows, who tend to patrol offshore, coming in only to suckle.

I have noted occasions when a cow, whose pup was situated close to the head of a deep water channel, was so interrupted in her suckling of the pup by other cows that after three quarters of an hour or more she had hardly given more than a minute or two of suckling time, and had prevented other cows from reaching their pups.

Protection from the weather (in the form of high seas) is also a clear advantage. This must of course be considered in relative terms only since storms may arise from more than one quarter. Moreover, accessibility may be an overriding factor as it certainly is on the west coast of Ramsey Island for example. Examples of the effect of storms on site choice may be quoted from North Rona and from the Oronsay area. On North Rona in 1959 the onset of a severe autumn gale resulted in a very considerable drop of births in the south-western rookery on Sceapull and a rise in births on the most protected rookery of Braeside which faced north-east and whose approach suffered least from swell coming round the end of the island. In 1956 Dr Backhouse and myself were disappointed at the number of births on Eilean nan Ron during the fortnight we were there. Throughout this period the seas were too rough to allow us to visit Ghaoidmeal which lay to the north-east in the lee of Oronsay. However, the day after we left Eilean nan Ron, we were able to visit it from Oronsay and found far more pups than anticipated. Together with those from Eilean nan Ron they made up the same total as found on the same date in 1955 when the weather had been much calmer (Fig. 28).

A word of explanation is perhaps necessary here to distinguish between wind wave action, tides and swell. The latter is an oceanic phenomenon and that affecting the British Isles is the Atlantic swell. This a pulse of large frequency, the distance from crest to crest being a quarter of a mile or more. Its amplitude can also be great and may run up to 30 or 40 feet or more from crest to trough. The mass of water involved in a swell wave is therefore enormous and its effect on any obstacle quite devastating. The west coast of North Rona is a cliff about 60–70 feet high but swell can break in solid masses over the top. Even in so-called calm weather, that is without wind-formed waves, the splash zone extends to the top of the cliff as demonstrated by the presence of marine snails which are normally found (i.e. in sheltered positions) only just above the water mark, the 'typical' splash zone.

Wind-formed waves, the so-called 'white horses', are small and comparatively powerless. By the time they are five feet high the crest breaks and is swept away by the wind as spume. Between these two sorts of waves lies tidal action which, if the channel is restricted, may set up a local swell. Sometimes it results in peculiarly smooth water which has the appearance of 'boiling' or swirling. Almost the whole of the North Sea tide must enter and leave by the North Channel, much of it in the southern sector comprising the Pentland Firth, Wide Firth in Orkney and between Orkney and Shetland. As distinct from wind and wave and oceanic swell which are largely *vertical* movements, tidal swell results from true *lateral* movement of water attempting to pass through a narrow passage thus building up a pulse shown as a vertical swell. Such swell is usually described in terms of the speed of the lateral movement which may reach 8–10 knots. The three types of water movement are independent of one another. When two or more of them become involved, such as an oceanic swell backed by a wind storm operating in the opposite direction to a tidal swell, particularly dirty water is experienced. For some reason we do not know, most grey seal breeding areas are situated where such combinations are likely to occur. The importance of accessibility by reason of a beach or geo in the lee or protected by a promontory must therefore be

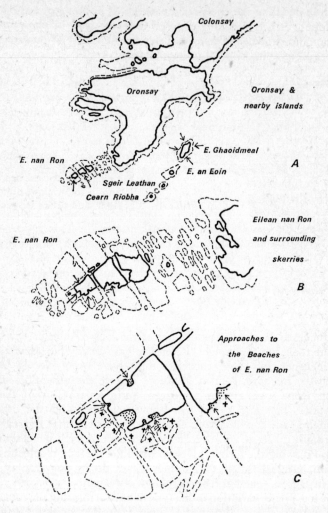

FIG. 28. Breeding sites on Eilean nan Ron and Eilean Ghaoidmeal, Oronsay. A.
shows the position of the two breeding islands E. nan Ron and E. Ghaoidmeal. A
very few pups are born on E. an Eoin. Sgear Leathan and Cean Roibha are used
as haul-outs only. B. shows the importance of the lowered beaches covered in kelp
which surround E. nan Ron. The skerries between Oronsay and E. nan Ron are
used for the pre-breeding assembly of bulls and cows. c. shows the position of
territorial bulls marked X. The small breeding beaches are connected to the sea by
the deep-water channels, Although the beaches lead by easy slopes to the grassland,
no pupping takes place inland. This clearly separates the Inner and Outer Hebridean
groups of seals in behaviour.

rated high in deciding the choice of a rookery. If pupping occurs on a beach or rock slope which is suddenly exposed to severe seas, all the pups will be swept away and drowned. Davies has put the mortality of pups on Ramsey from this cause as at least 10% in a normal year.

FIG. 29. Breeding sites on Shillay. Pupping begins on the beach and spreads inland to the wallows later. The area of grassed sand dunes between is not used.

It is difficult to assess the importance of the lack of interference by other seals on the rookeries themselves. Reference has already been made to over-crowded beaches, but some rookeries must have been selected originally because of the freedom from molestation, despite the difficulties of access. On North Rona two groups appeared quite separate from the heavy concentrations, one about 120 feet above sea-level and the other over 200 feet high at the top of a steep escarpment, so steep that the seals had to mount straight up it; to have tacked would have merely sent them rolling down hill. Probably the weight given to the different factors affecting choice varies from one individual to another. Cows do in fact display a wide variation in aggressiveness and opposition to disturbance.

There is too a wide variation in the type of terrain forming the rookeries. In the south-western group and in the Inner Hebrides, only the beaches are used even though, in the latter, access to grass-covered ground farther inland is easy. Yet on Shillay the sandy beach is used first and when this becomes fairly full cows proceed over grass-covered dunes to boggy ground farther inland (Fig. 29). On Gaskeir access is by narrow geos to a grassy plateau with bog pools like the inland part of Shillay. On North Rona no beaches as such exist and all the pups are born either on rock slopes or grass-covered ground inland (Fig. 30). In the Farne Islands the same is true, although the islands are much lower and suffer little true swell (Figs. 31 and 32). In Orkney and Shetland there is a range of rookery sites varying from a typical North Rona or Farne condition, such as those in the Greenholms, to beach rookeries almost like the Pembrokeshire condition, such as those on South Ronaldsay and on the coast-line of Fitful Head in Shetland.

When inland grassy sites are used there are always wallows or pools of

Lisgear Mhor

Sgor na Lice Mòire

Fianuis

Escarpment

Toa Rona

Sceapul

Lòba Sgeir

NORTH RONA

Gealldruig Mhòr

FIG. 30. Breeding sites on North Rona. All the rookeries are inland but despite overcrowding, particularly in some of the Fianuis sites, not all of the available grassland is used. Pupping seems to concentrate round pools and streams. Even the groups on the escarpment area have peat wallows.

water present, at least at the beginning of the breeding season. Later these may be flattened out into muddy patches. The presence of water (either fresh or sea) is therefore an essential element for the selection of a rookery site (Plate 6b).

While the general pattern of requirements is clear, with variations largely due to geographical features, certain puzzles remain. Why, in archipelagos such as the Farne Islands and the Islands of Orkney, are some islands used and not others? On many of the unused islands haul-outs are formed in the non-breeding times of the year, so that the questions of access and of human interference does not arise. Is the conservatism of the cows a sufficient explanation?

Associated with the different types of rookery site are different patterns of

OUTER FARNE ISLANDS

FIG. 31. The Outer Farne Islands. The grey seal now only uses the Outer Farne Islands for breeding. Staple Island, Brownsman, and the two Wamses each have rookeries. The other islands are used for non-breeding haul-outs (moulting and fishing), Knivestone, Big Harcar, Longstone End and Crumstone being the most favoured, yielding on average over 60% of the haul-outs. 11% are found on the Inner Farnes and only about 15% on the breeding islands. (*See Appendix D*)

cow behaviour (Fig. 33). At first these seem to be dictated by the nature of the site itself, but this is not altogether true. Darling regards the condition as found on Gaskeir and North Rona as more or less typical or ancestral. Whether this is so or not it forms a good starting point for a description. Here, as in other rookeries where pupping takes place on grassland behind and above the beach, the cows tend to stay alongside their pups, rarely going into the sea. The presence of pools enables them to immerse themselves periodically, but this does not seem to be a necessity. At the other end of the scale is the condition found in the south-western area where it is usual for the cows to patrol in the sea and come ashore only for suckling. The situation in the Inner Hebrides is intermediate. Here, owing to land movements, the islands are surrounded by 'lowered' beaches, penetrated by deep water channels. The cows appear to divide their time fairly equally between the beaches, on which the pups are, and the sea beyond the 'lowered' beach using the channels as the usual routes for movement. In general it may be said that where beach pupping occurs, either exclusively or as part of a wider

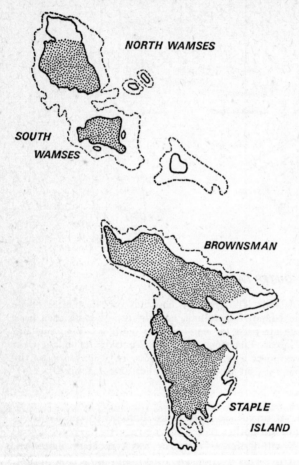

FIG. 32. The breeding sites in the Farne Islands. Only four of the Outer Farne Islands are now used for pupping. With the increase in numbers almost the whole area above high-water mark on all four is used for breeding.

rookery, the cows with pups on the beach will enter the sea more frequently and for longer spells than where the pups are inland. (There are associated differences in bull behaviour.)

Let us return to the question of the conservatism of this grey seal. A correct appraisal of its importance is desirable because it affects the possibility of spread of the species particularly if there is an increase in the population in any given area of breeding. The Farne Islands are interesting in this respect, because there are historical records. At present, breeding takes place on

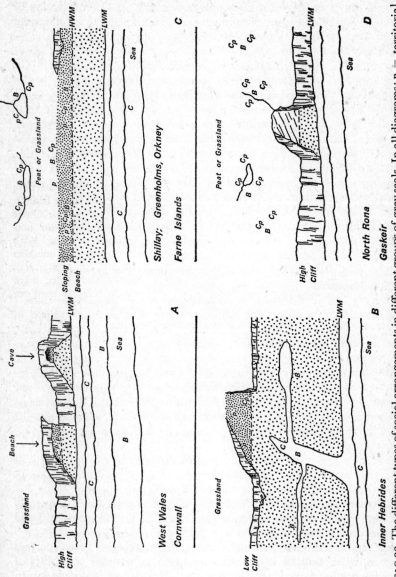

FIG 33. The different types of social arrangements in different groups of grey seals. In all diagrams: B = territorial bull; c = cow; p = pup; LWM = low-water mark; springs; Widely spaced dots = intertidal zone; Broken line = high-water mark, springs; Close dots = sandy or pebbly beach.

Staple, Brownsman and on the North and South Walmses (Fig. 32). The
intensive use of Brownsman and of the Walmses is of very recent date.
Certainly in the early 1950's only a few pups were to be found in Brownsman
on the side facing Staple across Brownsman's Gut. It is also known that in the
past seals bred on Inner Farne and the Wide Opens. Has the increased
accessibility of the latter to man been the reason for their desertion? North
Rona too presents a problem. It now has the greatest single concentration of
breeding grey seals in the world producing about 2,500 pups a year. It is at
the moment not inhabited by man, nor has it been for about 125 years,
except for a few visitors who have remained only for a few weeks. Yet up to
the beginning of the 19th century it was lived on by up to 30 people,
perhaps more. Administratively they formed part of the Parish of Barvas on
Lewis and records exist of their exports and imports. Yet there is no mention
of oil or skins, a natural source of revenue. Even in the first account in the
16th century seals are not mentioned. *Yet* the island is called Rona.
(*Ron*=seal *a*=island) and the hermit St Ronan lived there. Was it once a
great seal colony before human habitation? If so it must have been a long
time ago for the 16th-century author Martin Martin refers to the inhabitants
as being of a very ancient race bearing names quite unlike any Scottish or
Norse ones. Mr Bonner has suggested to me that the Old Norse 'Hraun'
meaning a 'wild place' (cf. Ronas Hill in Shetland) is a likely derivation.
I am inclined to agree.

Clearly grey seals can form new rookeries for within the last few years
breeding has been found on St. Kilda, the Isle of May in the Firth of
Forth and the Island of Coppay off the Sound of Harris has apparently
taken on an overflow from Shillay, while Haskeir to the south has now
hardly any pups at all. All the Hebridean Islands are uninhabited. The
Isle of May has a bird observatory on it so that previous pupping would have
been noticed had it taken place. Scroby Island off Gt. Yarmouth too has
seen recent pupping and although it is difficult to prove that it did not do so
before it was noticed in 1959 the vicissitudes of the 'island', which is a sandbank, are fairly well known and it disappears from time to time and then
reappears.

We have seen that the cows often precede the bulls in the early days of
rookery formation. Within a week or so however the bulls will have begun to
establish territories. The cows move in 1–2 days before pupping. They are
usually accosted by the resident bull. Even on Ramsey Island where the
bulls are out to sea, the cow is frequently chased by him as she makes her
way to the shore. The cow always repels the bull turning on her side,
'flippering' and sometimes 'hooting' at him. She may even make a lunge
towards him. The bull in reply always withdraws without making any
defence. It is probable that the bull attacks *all* intruders, fights invading
bulls but retreats from incoming cows as soon as they are recognised as such.

The evidence for cows coming ashore a day or two before parturition is two-fold. In many cases individual cows can be identified by the markings on the neck and chest so that observers can make quite certain of the time they are present before they pup. In a more general way, particularly in small groups of a dozen to twenty cows, as the numbers grow it can be recorded that the number of cows present is always a few more than the numbers of pups. A full term cow can easily be recognised if she is lying on her back, and the distortion of her abdomen is apparent. When she is lying on her belly, especially on uneven ground it is not always possible to be certain, and observation must continue for some time to make certain that she is not attached to a pup.

The actual birth of a pup is not often seen (Pl. 16). There are several reasons for this. First, in crowded rookeries the observer must be able to have a downward view to see any happenings other than on the nearside edges. Unless the rookery is underneath a cliff this is often impossible. Secondly there is no doubt that the majority of births are extremely rapid. I have missed seeing several by having my attention diverted by, say, agonistic behaviour between bulls or some other incident which required noting. On returning observation to the cow it has been found to have given birth. I have a filmed record of a birth which took less than a second from the first appearance of the hind flippers to the pup landing on the ground. It is also worth noting that births seen by what I might term 'casual' observers (nothing derogatory being implied) have nearly all been of durations over 1 minute and up to 4 minutes. Attention of the observer has been recorded as being drawn by prolonged contortions of the cow, and one such birth being of a dead pup it could legitimately be assumed that the more prolonged periods of parturition are of 'difficult' births.

Thirdly, and this is a little more speculative, many births may take place at night or near dawn. The evidence for this is all indirect, but collectively not without possible significance. Despite the many hours I have spent in daylight observing rookeries, I have been present at very few occasions of birth (and seen in detail fewer). On the 1959 expedition to North Rona there were four competent observers and the numbers of pups born *daily* rose from 20 to over 60, yet again very few births were noted. On Shillay I made daily observations and counts on some sections of the rookery in the peat wallows, leaving off as dusk was coming on and returning not long after dawn (in some instances before dawn). Yet the numbers of pups increased although I rarely saw a birth take place. The number of after-births seen is also small and usually they are found only early in the day*. Seal rookeries are a happy hunting ground for greater-blackbacked gulls and fulmars who make short work of the placentae. More direct and numerical observation is required, of course, before this point can be finally settled. A birth has recently been observed on the Farne Islands by Bonner and Hickling (Pl. 16). It took

* Curry-Lindahl (1970) records that *all* grey seal pups births in Skansen Zoo have been at night.

eleven minutes, but they believed that their presence disturbed the cow. The photograph shows the protrusion of the pup's hind flippers in a breach birth.

If the birth is short and sudden the umbilical cord is broken by the violent ejection of the pup. There is no information as to how it is broken if parturition is slow. In the fur-seal the placenta follows the pup very shortly after the birth and may remain attached. It probably dries up with the cord and is eventually knocked off. This has never been seen in the grey seal, although the after-birth follows within a quarter to half an hour of birth.

The behaviour of the cow is quite stereotyped. Immediately after parturition she circles the pup clearing the ground of any other pups and cows as far as she can. She appears to regard this as 'territory'. Its size varies; some cows are aggressive and defend a wide area, others are tolerant. In most cases it appears that she is more aggressive in the early days of suckling, and many young cows (judging by their size) are more assiduous in their defence of the pup than older ones. This 'territory' concept is not attached to the land but to the pup. Often pups move around in the rookery, perhaps going into less congested areas and the cow will continue to defend an area around the pup wherever it may be. I have seen a cow hoot and flipper at a bull until he moved away only because her pup had moved too near (in her view) to the bull.

The cow nurses the pup within the first hour and thereafter 3 or 4 times a day usually for about a quarter of an hour each (Pl. 19). In land based rookeries it may be more frequent and perhaps of shorter duration. In the shore rookeries of Ramsey Island the cow leaves the pup ashore and only comes back to nurse. This is usually only twice in the day time, once around high water, (usually before) using the incoming tide to assist in coming ashore, and once again just before dark. During the night on Ramsey the cows are out at sea, often quite a distance away. This may be an adaptation to the severe water conditions. Most of the beaches and cows are on a lee shore so that the effect of storms can be highly dangerous if the seals are too close inshore in the dark. I have visited these beaches before dawn and failed to get any response from adult seals in the water. When they are frightened they dive bringing the hind flippers on to the surface of the sea in a clap and splash. No such sounds were observed. Soon after dawn the heads of a few cows would be seen standing perhaps 100–150 yards offshore. They would come in and then nurse the pups. Whether this is a general feature on Ramsey I do not know, but if it is then this would constitute a third nursing period.

The proportion of time spent by the cow ashore near her pup varies considerably and depends on several factors. First and foremost is the distance the pup is from the sea; the farther away it is the more likely the cow is to remain with the pup. Thus on North Rona, Gaskeir and similar rookeries the proportion of cows present in the pupping area is high. On some of the Orcadian Islands such as the Greenholms and in the Farne Islands where the pupping area is continuous from the beach to higher grassland, the ratio of pups to cows increases as one passes down towards the sea. Even so on the Farne Islands, Coulson and Hickling record that there is a 'minority' of cows in all parts of the rookery. On North Rona where exit and entry on the shore-line is very difficult there are many more cows but with the same gradient of the pup to cow ratio.

It is usually assumed that the cows do not feed during the nursing period. This still requires positive confirmation, but like all negatives it is difficult to prove. Where the cow hardly ever leaves the pup, if at all, it is clear that she can survive without feeding and the variation in the frequency of visits to the sea already mentioned suggest that it is not a necessity. On Ramsey Island, where most of the cows spend most of the time in the water, there is ample opportunity for feeding, but despite many hours of observation from the high cliffs above into crystal clear water with bright sunlight, I have never observed any attempt at feeding. The weight of the 'non-evidence' is, therefore, against feeding. To this may be added the loss of weight and a thinning of the blubber layer which has been positively established.

It is difficult to see how the pups could grow as they do without at least three sucklings a day. The increase in pup weight and size has been measured in the Farne Islands by Coulson and Hickling. They have shown that the average weights at birth for a male pup is 32.8 ± 4.2 lb. and for a female 31.0 ± 6.1 lb. The difference between the sexes is not significant and each may vary by several pounds each way. An average pup puts on about 4.0 lbs. per day, but really well nourished ones may put on much more; 5.1 lb. per day has been recorded. Coulson omitted in his calculations those pups which were definitely losing weight owing to neglect by the mother. Nevertheless it is difficult to be very precise about weight increase except to point out that it can be prodigious. On average a pup weighing 31 lb. at birth reaches a weight between 90 and 100 lbs. by about 17 days of age, and many of over 1 cwt. have been recorded at moult. Nearly all this increase is represented by blubber under the skin, very little in real growth. This is shown by the fact that the increase in length over the period of puppyhood is quite small; only an inch or so on to the 33–36 inches of the newly born.

How is this achieved? In 1950 milk samples were taken and analysed by Prof. Amoroso and his colleagues. This showed that there were approximately 70% solids (50% fat) in this extremely rich milk. To get some idea of how rich it is it may be recalled that the fat percentage permissible for cow's milk sold in Gt. Britain is only 3.5%. The same workers also showed that the cow lost about twice the weight of blubber as the increase of weight in the pup. Suckling, therefore, presents about a 50% efficiency in fat transfer from cow to pup.

The newly born pup has a slack skin usually disposed in rolls round the body (Fig. 34) (Pl. 17). The amount of fat and consequent smoothing out of the body is an indicator of age provided that nourishment is normal. For the first three days the umbilical cord is present and this marks out the early stage; thereafter ageing is marked in weeks. The figures show typical individuals of the first four weeks and were used by the observers on the 1959 North Rona investigation so that all would be using the same criteria. Of

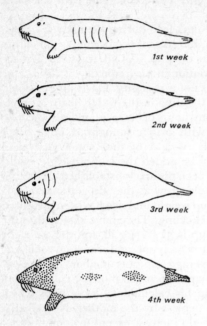

FIG. 34. The grey seal pup in the first four weeks. It is possible to estimate the probable age of pups (and thence their date of birth) from their general appearance. Subjectively allowance may have to be made for malnutrition but on the whole the method has been found to work well.

course misjudgements are made if the rate of nourishment is markedly less or more than the average. But if the intention is to obtain approximate numbers of the different age groups, these variations cancel each other out. Consistent data have been obtained using this method.

The pup fur is long, creamy coloured and silky in texture. Some individuals tend to have greyish hair on the muzzle and the fur on the top of the head and along the middle of the back may have greyish tips. The proportions of pups showing this feature varies in different groups, that in Pembrokeshire being rather high compared with the others. There are several references to this appearance as a 'pre-natal' moult. In fact it has nothing to do with the moult. It is due to grey *tips* of the hairs and can be seen first in the foetus at about 120 days of active gestation, little more than halfway through the foetal period.

Pups are capable of swimming at once although this is only done under compulsion. I once saw a pup which had been born only a few minutes swept into water on a rising tide. It continued to swim around attempting to crawl out for over three quarters of an hour until it eventually succeeded and was able to have its first suckling period. Others, born on land, may not come into contact with water for weeks. In Pembrokeshire the pup tends to enter the water within the first 24 hours and take a swim in company with the mother after each suckling period. It then crawls out and goes to sleep on the beach. For the first 3 or 4 days its movement on land is obtained by dragging motions of the fore flippers, the digits being recurved, and digging into the substrate be it sand or pebbles or rock. The fore flippers are *moved alternately* as one would expect of a dog or other mammalian young and it is only later that the use of *both* flippers simultaneously is displayed so that the typical seal motion is developed during puppyhood. This later simultaneous motion of the fore-limbs is accompanied by a humping action of the pelvis and hind flippers, again similar to the adult motion.

These Pembrokeshire pups *appear to learn* to swim. For the first ten days or so their swimming movements are clumsy and while the hind-limbs and the hind part of the body form the principal motive organ (as they do in the adult) the fore-limbs are also used in a rather haphazard way like a dog paddling clumsily. By the third week of life, however, the fore-limbs are being used less and the hind flippers are swung more purposefully. Nevertheless their degree of co-ordination is markedly less than that of a moulter in the sixth or seventh week. In the Hebrides and elsewhere where sea conditions are almost prohibitive for the pups or where the pups are born on land away from the beach, some may be able to indulge in swimming in pools of either sea or fresh water, but these are few in number (Pl. 19). Consequently it may be said that most of these pups become moulters, fully weaned, and ready to go to sea without previous swimming experience. Indeed on North Rona the moulters usually prolong their stay ashore by moving up on to the higher ground above the main rookeries and remain there for a week or so before going into the sea. We should conclude from this, therefore, that the *learning is only apparent* and that successful swimming is dependent upon a fully developed muscle system and adequate neuro-muscular control. These will develop in the course of time whether there is actual practice and experience or not.

Vocalisation by the pup is considerable; there are two kinds. A 'snarl', rather like clearing the throat before expectoration, is used defensively to repel other pups and human intruders. The other, indicative of hunger, used to call for the mother, is a high pitched 'bawl', it can be imitated by calling 'mum' or 'help' without pronouncing the labials distinctly about an octave and a half above middle C. (Easy for a tenor, but just a little of a strain for a baritone!) This call may, if it fails to bring the mother, after some time become almost a whine. The excitement of snarling and repelling humans stimulates the tear glands. Even the slightest secretion results in copious tears pouring down the face of the pup because seals have no orbito-nasal duct. (In man this duct draws off much of the lachrymal-secretion and produces the well known sniffle of the tearful child.) Its absence from the seal means that all the secretion must come on to the surface of the eyelids. Even without excitement the eye of the pup can often be seen to be surrounded by a wet ring of hair. This is most easily seen in dry weather with sunlight when the secretion has to increase to keep the surface of the cornea moist despite a high evaporation rate.

The presence of 'moist eyes' and the 'pitiful bawl' excite the emotions of human observers. The resemblance to the behaviour of a human child is however purely superficial and any attempt to handle the pup will result in savage repulsion and serious damage. Only for the first 24–30 hours of life can a pup be handled without evoking this reaction. The bite of a pup can be serious because teeth begin to erupt at birth. The milk dentition is produced during the foetal stage and is resorbed. Consequently it is the adult dentition which erupts during puppyhood (Pl. 17). This is truly a remarkable affair. In the newly born the crown is already formed with its covering of enamel with only a few millimetres of 'root' which is almost paper-thin. Within three weeks this root has grown to a length of 12–15 millimetres, the 'upper' part, nearest the crown, thickening considerably. This 'pup' dentine contains a very dense layer which increases the strength of the root, a necessary adaptation for the 'lower' part is still very thin. In young seals taken in their first year, the root can be seen to have circular ridges at irregular intervals (Pl. 8). These are probably formed when the young seal bites on to a hard piece of food, slightly distorting the root and the formative bed of dentine-producing cells. The full length of the root is not achieved until about the end of the first year of life.

Nursing by the cow is variable in length. It is generally agreed that the normal time is about 14–17 days, but instances have been recorded of pups sucking later. It is doubtful whether the mother solicits suckling at these later ages. As a rule a cow will nurse only her own pup which she identifies by smell (Pl. 18). Should she scent a pup not her own she will hiss and snarl at it or even snap at it, pick it up and shake it (Pl. 18). Because of this the presence of two pups sucking at one cow has often been recorded as evidence for the birth of twins. Embryological evidence however suggests that twinning is extremely rare if it takes place at all. All twins *in utero* have shown either one or both embryos or foetuses dead (Rae 1969). I have found only one instance of double ovulation in 50 pregnancies and then only one egg was fertilised to produce an embryo. I have, however, recorded 'double' nursing by a cow. Here there were two cows each with a pup, on a small beach. One of the cows was totally blind. (The hand could be passed across her eyes within a few inches, cutting off direct sunlight, without producing the slightest reaction.) This cow nursed *both* pups while the other nursed only her own. The normal aggressive reaction was never exhibited by the blind cow. The most probable explanation of 'twin' nursing is that a pup, probably an orphan or deserted by its mother, manages to suck alongside the true offspring while the cow is stretched out on her side to expose the teats. When once the 'strange' pup has thus made a physical contact with the cow, it 'smells' right and is accepted. Smith (1968) has recorded a number of 'adoptive' nursings of various kinds, but this is not the general rule and must have been brought about by human interference in the rookery while taking censuses and pursuing other researches. The proportion of adoptive nursings reported by Smith has not been confirmed by Susan Fogden who took the utmost precautions not to cause interference or even to be seen. Her detailed account of cow–pup relations is excellent (1968).

Whether nursing ceases at the end of the second week, or not, it certainly decreases in the third and this is simultaneous with the onset of the post-partum oestrus of the cow. Her attention is less and less attracted to the pup and she becomes more receptive to the approaches of the bull until she eventually mates. By this time the pup is usually completely deserted by the mother.

Moulting of the puppy coat of creamy white hair normally begins at the end of the third week of life (Pl. 20). Again normally speaking, it is completed in the fourth week, taking about 4–5 days. Earlier moulting times have also been recorded. Dr Backhouse and I saw one beginning to moult at 12 days. There are however, many records of much longer times and these are due apparently to malnutrition. The Farne Islands' rookeries have been the scene of a great deal of careful and accurate observation and measurement over a number of years. Here, with the individual tagging of pups, the careers of each could be followed. Much of this work has been done by a team, led by Mrs G. Hickling, of members of the Northumberland, Durham and Newcastle-upon-Tyne Natural History Society and more recently Dr J. Coulson of the University of Durham has assisted. He has also shown that during moult the pups lose weight since they are no longer being nursed and have not yet taken to the sea to feed.

My own first observations on the moulting pup were made on Ramsey Island. I was struck by the fact that there appeared to be two methods of moulting (Pl. 15). Both showed that the first parts to be moulted were the fore and hind flippers and the muzzle. From these centres in one type, the pup hair became loose and came off progressively until only a tatty patch remained on the back. In the other, the pup hair apparently became thinner all over so that the pattern of the adult coat showed through the remaining white coat. The explanation was really quite simple. There were two types of *behaviour*; in one the pups remained almost stationary during moult, rubbing off the hair as it became loose in tufts which formed a bed of fur around the pup. In the other the pup continued to enter the sea during moult and the hair from any part of the body which was loose washed off, so that moulting was a continuous thinning process. In the first type much of the remaining hair is in fact already loose and can be freed at the lightest touch. In the second the remaining hairs are still embedded in their follicles and require a definite pull to free them. Naturally in the north where the pups rarely enter the water the first type is nearly universal. Only when pools or wallows are available will the second be seen.

The moulter coat is at first quite short when exposed, 2–3 mm., but rapidly grows out to its full length, 5–6 mm. It has all the characteristics of the normal adult coat including the sex difference in the pattern (Pl. 20). As mentioned earlier, these patterns are visible as dermal pigmentation in the foetus at about 115 days' active gestation.

After moulting the behaviour of the young seal (moulter) varies according to the locality. In Pembrokeshire they leave their natal beach, swim away and haul-out on another beach. This was brought home to me very dramatically in 1951, almost my first 'breeding season' of observation. I wanted some photographs of moulters and I had to leave by a certain date so that I could be ready for the beginning of the University term. I saw the occasional moulting pup on completely inaccessible beaches but, on the other that I could get to, all the pups were too young. Would any moult before I had to go? (As mentioned earlier in this chapter the caves and inaccessible coves were the preferred rookery sites so these held the older pups.) I had my eye on one or two who might make it just in time. Suddenly to my surprise and joy a beautiful bull moulter appeared on one of my beaches. And my own chosen pets with only a single tuft left on, equally suddenly disappeared!

Where the pups are born and nursed on land, they appear reluctant to enter the sea. Probably they do so eventually only when driven by hunger. Coulson and Hickling give 32 days as an average of age before leaving the Farnes' rookeries. They mention that the moulters move on to unused sites on the islands in the centre and on higher ground. North Rona is perhaps the most extreme situation where the moulters move away from the sea on to the less congested higher ground. The old sheep fank, which we used as our store base and radio station, became surrounded by moulters which had to be chivvied out of the way when we wanted to enter. This is so marked a phenomenon that Darling was led into an error (very rare) in thinking that they remained ashore all winter. These moulters are really very beautiful creatures if well nourished. They weigh anything from 90 to 110 lbs. and are covered in the short coat of bright new hair, the black of the bulls having an almost bluish tint. On North Rona we were visited by a lobster boat from Camaret in Finnisterre, Brittany. The crew had never seen seals before and were entranced. I caught a moulter and held it by the hind flippers so that the skipper could stroke it. This he did rather timorously, his face split in a wide grin as he turned to me and said, '*Comme*' *c'est douce!*' And soft like velvet, the coat is.

Davies was the first to record the sex-ratio among pups. This he did on Ramsey Island using some 49 pups of which 24 were males and 25 females. This looks like a 1 : 1 ratio and later counts seem to confirm it using much greater numbers. Out of a total of 803, 399 were male and 404 female. There were however slight differences in the ratios from different areas: 1 : 0.89 for

Pembrokeshire, 1 : 1.06 for the Farne Islands and 1 : 1.21 for Hebridean rookeries. Were these differences significant and if so what was the cause? This is a nice example of how careful one should be. Bias can be introduced quite unintentionally, because here the cause was based simply on the dates when it was convenient to visit the rookeries. Coulson, by a careful study of the sex-ratio of pups born throughout the season on the Farne Islands, has shown that there is a preponderance of males at the beginning of the season and a preponderance of females towards the end. He found that from 14–27 October the sex ratio was 1 : 0.718; from 28 October–10 November, it was 1 : 0.901; from 11–24 November, 1 : 0.996 (almost 1 : 1) and after 24 November, 1 : 1.357. Taken as a whole 1,433 pups had 731 males and 702 females giving an average sex-ratio of 1 : 0.96.

Of very considerable interest and importance is the question of pup mortality. Here again Davies was the first to give any estimates based on individual records. He gives 14.5% as a minimum figure for mortality on the beaches. Darling gives a 'guesstimate' of 10% for North Rona and Treshnish, but this is far too low for North Rona. The enormous rookery of North Rona is very diverse in character and the density of pupping varies widely. As

Table 8. Pup Mortality on the Farne Islands 1956–70

	Staple	Brownsman	N. Wamses	S. Wamses	Total
56	11.3	10.7	9.5	11.3	10.5
57	19.9	10.8	15.2	10.7	16.3
58	19.7	2.5	11.4	7.2	13.6
59	19.4	17.0	10.9	9.7	14.5
60	21.1	11.8	12.9	2.3	16.3
61	23.0	13.1	14.9	11.3	17.9
62	15.7	15.8	12.8	16.4	15.1
63	20.9	16.1	15.4	14.3	18.0
64	23.6	17.5	14.5	6.0	19.0
65	28.6	20.3	13.0	7.3	21.0
66	23.9	20.9	17.1	10.2	20.2
67	24.9	17.2	9.0	4.4	16.9
68	23.0	14.0	16.6	9.0	17.0
69	22.0	16.9	11.8	13.7	17.3
70	27.3	19.6	17.1	13.9	21.1

	Mean Mortality 1956–62	Mean No. of calves/100 m of shore-line
Staple	18.6	77
Brownsman	11.9	14
N. Wamses	12.5	42
S. Wamses	9.8	10

shown by Boyd *et al.* the mortality could vary between 12.4–13.0%, on the more sparsely populated ground of Sceapull and Fianuis South, to 19.2–19.5%, on the heavily used areas of Fianuis Central and North. Even this does not do justice to the influence of density for in the Main Gullies of Fianuis North mortality rose to 29%. Boyd and Campbell have given the pup mortalities figures for North Rona for all the years 1959–68. Two 'death censuses' were made each year except in 1961 and 1966 when there were only one each. The average for the eighteen readings over 10 years was 19% ranging from 14–15% in 1963 to 25% in 1961.

The accumulated observations on the Farne Islands have been published by Coulson and Hickling (Table 8). These figures must be judged against a background of varying densities on the different islands and a general and steady increase in total numbers of pups as shown in Table 9.

Staple has been the most densely populated island throughout the period, with an almost consistently high mortality; only in 1962 did it fall below 20% and over the last few years it has averaged 25%. This is very high when considered as applying to nearly 700 pups, over one-third of the Farne Island production. Brownsman and South Wamses both show a build-up of population, the former approaching the 20% mortality at a pup total of nearly 500. South Wamses is under-populated and density is obviously not yet playing any major part in producing mortality. The same may be said for North Wamses which does not appear to show quite the same steady build-up of numbers. It presents difficulties of access which may limit its population before it reaches a level which could seriously affect mortality.

Table 9. Numbers of Pups Born in Farne Islands 1956–70

	Staple	Brownsman	N. Wamses	S. Wamses	Total
1970	672	654	385	245	1956
1969	637	703	365	212	1917
1968	614	694	296	189	1793
1967	670	534	343	229	1776
1966	694	493	351	177	1715
1965	546	453	276	123	1398
1964	636	423	310	67	1436
1963	560	397	241	56	1254
1962	529	297	235	55	1116
1961	495	168	403	71	1137
1960	517	228	224	43	1019
1959	350	53	433	62	898
1958	320	40	440	69	869
1957	362	93	315	84	854
1956	311	84	294	62	751

It can be seen from the figures quoted that it is very difficult to state an average mortality or even a range which would be significant. The best that can be done is to say that a pup mortality of 10–15% may be considered quite normal, but in the presence of high density it may rise to 25% (or over). Generally speaking such high mortality is confined to sections of a breeding rookery and, where this does occur, taken in association with the lower mortality section, the overall mortality may lie between 15% and 20%. In terms of the individual pup born this means that it has a 5 or 6 to 1 chance of survival to moulter stage.

CHAPTER 8

THE GREY SEAL – THE BREEDING ROOKERY: BULLS, TERRITORY AND MATING

WE have seen in the previous chapter that the behaviour of the bulls and cows is, in the early stages of the formation of a breeding rookery, largely independent. Even though some cows come ashore before any bulls, sometimes bulls may come ashore before any cows, and later bulls often take up positions where there are no cows at all, even though they have the choice of establishing a position among already pupped cows or remaining on the periphery where they may later be joined by cows and pups. It seems clear that the sole preoccupation of a bull on arrival at a rookery is the establishment of a position around which a 'territory' can be maintained.

Some territories (and positions) are established immediately and without any opposition by other bulls. This occurs in the early days and such bulls are always large and massive. They also appear 'to know their way about' to use a human analogy. On Shillay two bulls took up positions inland over a sand-dune, which completely barred them from sight of the sea, long before other bulls had sorted themselves into territories on the beach. One had a cow and her pup in his territory, the other none. Again on North Rona a bull established himself at a height of over 200 ft. on the Saddle and another at about 120 ft. on the escarpment. Neither had cows present at the time and the former position was completely out of sight of the coast-line.

From observations on Shillay it appeared that about half the final total of territorial bulls were of this category (Fig. 35). The rest appeared younger and more tentative in their movements towards the establishment of territory. Even some of the 'seniors' might take 3 or 4 days before they finally stayed on the one location permanently. During this time they visited the site and progressively spent longer and longer on station. The movements of the 'juniors' are roaming, often coming into contact with a sequence of established bulls, each of which in turn will drive the intruder away. This often leads to a return to the sea and he will not return until the next day. At last he will accept a more peripheral position from which he is not attacked by other established bulls (Pl. 6). He in turn will have to defend his territory against even later intruders.

This general behaviour has been described in terms of a land rookery, partly because it is easier to visualise and partly because it is in such places as the Hebrides and North Rona that the necessary observations have been made. In the Oronsay group of rookeries, the bull territories are established

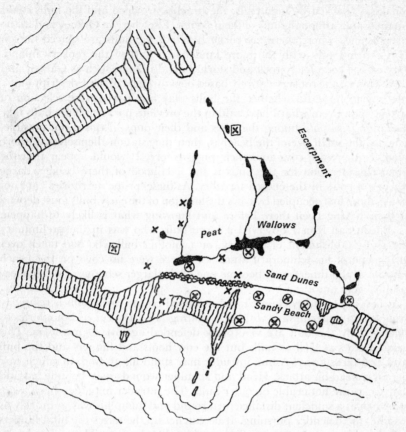

FIG. 35. Bull territories on Shillay. The central positions taken up by the bulls are indicated by X. Those surrounded by a circle were those established early, the three on the wallows being the first, followed by those on the sandy beach. The two surrounded by a square were the last, one bull having one cow, the other none by October 15.

in the same way, but on the seaweed-covered 'lowered' beach which surrounds the islands. For part of the day it is used as land, for the rest it is sea and the bull swims on patrol over his territory. In Pembrokeshire and the south-western group generally, territory is held at sea, a bull considering a length of shore as 'his'. This might comprise only half a wide open beach such as Aber Mawr on Ramsey Island, but equally it might consist of three or four narrow inlets or ogofs each with one or two cows and pups. It is interesting to note that in Orkney where there are a few beach rookeries, as in South

Ronaldsay, backed by high cliffs, the beaches are deep and the bulls could remain ashore although some of them do not. Elsewhere in Orkney and in the Farne Islands where there are rocky beaches, the bulls are spaced out on them continuously with the more land based part of the rookery inland. Only on the completely rock and storm bound islands, such as Gaskeir and North Rona is the rookery entirely based on a turf peat of some description.

It is very doubtful whether the bulls play any part in the selection of rookery sites. From what I have said in the previous paragraph the bulls take up station *if possible* among the cows and their pups; if this is not possible, owing to the small size of the beaches, then they station themselves offshore wherever there are cows and their pups ashore. It would appear that the prime consideration for the bulls is the likelihood of there being a large number of cows in the chosen territory. As these 'prime' territories* are not always those first occupied by cows the location of the early bulls must depend on their having been there before and knowing what is likely to happen. On Eilean nan Ron I observed a large bull, who was in the preliminary stages of establishment of territory, oust another bull who had taken over during one of his temporary absences. There were no cows on the beach opposite at the time, but it became one of the larger sections of the rookery within a week or so.

At first the territory claimed and defended by the early bulls is relatively large; much larger than it will be at mating (Pl. 21). Yet its boundaries as conceived by the bull are vigorously defended against *all* intruders. This includes cows as well as bulls but the cow hoots and flippers and the bull stops and turns away. A bull intruder may stand his ground, in which case there is a head-on attack. Head and shoulder wounds may be inflicted and many scars are noticeable on older bulls. The intruder may then back away and when at a sufficient distance turn round and hump his way as quickly as possible, the defender pursuing. If he catches up, he seizes the hind flippers or tail in his teeth and can inflict considerable damage. The pursued may either tear himself away in accelerated flight, or turn to face the attacker and repeat the performance of backing away and then fleeing. The defending bull rarely goes beyond the edge of his territory. If the intruder, at the approach of the defender, turns away and makes off, the defender will rarely pursue. In this way bulls space themselves out over the potential rookery. The later bulls work round the periphery and bide their time.

This can be made use of if one is attempting to reach a good position for observation and has to pass through established territory. Any prone object about the size of a seal (such as a man) will be noticed and attacked. If one turns away and then works round the edge, as it were, of the tolerance of the bull it is quite possible to avoid attack. There is no real danger because in the last resort one can stand up and the attacking bull will hurry off thoroughly frightened. But the day's observations will be ruined.

* From the bull's point of view.

There is of course considerable variation within this main pattern. Some of it concerns individual bulls, some of it due to difference in rookeries. One of these differences of great interest concerned the 'roll'. I first observed this on the Island of Shillay in the Outer Hebrides in 1954 and again in 1955. It was a very distinctive performance which I called the 'victory roll' when I noticed that it was performed almost without exception after a territorial bull had chased an intruder from his territory. Let me describe it in detail. First the bull comes to a halt, at the end of the pursuit, at the edge of his territory. He usually leans his head forward, opens his mouth and emits an almost silent hiss. (This is similar to the challenge made by a bull coming into a pre-breeding assemblage.) He then clearly dismisses the intruder and slightly turning his head to one side rolls his whole body over one complete sideways turn. Owing to the tapering shape of the body this brings him round more than half facing back into his territory. He then begins to lumber back to the central position to resume guard. Referring to my field notebooks I find almost every encounter between a defending bull and an intruding one terminated in this way. I also have recorded seeing it (and have filmed it) without any chase, when two bulls were at the limits of their respective territories almost side by side, but facing each other. Each gave the challenge and remained stationary. Then one very slowly rolled completely over back into his own ground.

By this time I had come to the conclusion that it was a signal implying, 'This is my territory, this far and no farther' rather than a sign of victory. I had also noticed that cows, in repelling bulls from proximity to their pups, usually rolled on to their backs, hooting and 'flippering'. To 'flipper' successfully a seal has to turn somewhat on to its side, otherwise the flipper strikes the ground on the downstroke. Consequently for a time I took the 'half-roll' of the cow as an occasion when she had rolled a bit too far off balance. However, I now saw that in resuming her normal posture the cow frequently did not roll back, but continued so as to make a complete turn of the body. The prolonged hooting and flippering had confused me so that I did not connect the two halves of the roll. This too I have filmed. Here again it obviously implied a statement of territorial possession.

Why had no one seen and mentioned it before? Especially such an acute observer as Fraser Darling on North Rona. I had not seen it myself in Pembrokeshire, but then the bulls were hardly ever ashore and the cows rarely. Later in 1956 and 1957 on Eilean nan Ron I did not see it although I watched for it carefully. But here again the bulls were stationed on sea-weed-covered rocks and the terrain was hardly suitable for rolling. The final answer came during the visit to North Rona in 1959. Here there were four observers and, for over three weeks in October, they had under observation a huge rookery with about 150 bulls. Many encounters between bulls were seen as the later arrivals tried to establish territory on the periphery of the aggregations. Yet the 'roll' was seen only three times. It would be interesting to know what its frequency is on Gaskeir and on Coppay, but, as so often in the study of the grey seal, the difficulties of observation are very great. This peculiar behaviour pattern must therefore be regarded as variable, probably not entirely confined to Shillay, but certainly very characteristic of that rookery.

The first phase of bull activity, therefore, concerns the establishment of territory. When the surrounding area is also occupied and demarcation is recognised there comes a period of comparative quiescence. Naturally enough this first comes to the prime bulls who have occupied the most favoured places in the centre but it will spread outwards as the boundaries of more and more bulls are established. This period extends to about a week or so, since none of the cows within the territory are yet ready for mating, unless they had already pupped before the bull took up station. Sooner or later however the 'earlier' cows come on heat and the bulls are stimulated to mate. Nothing is known about how this stimulus arises. It may be due in part to a chemical stimulus from secretions of the cow. It may also come from a rising libido in the bulls themselves, but I do not think so (see 'young' bull behaviour, p. 135).

The consequence of this altered behaviour of the bull is to lessen the defence activity. His attention is now turned towards the cows within his territory rather than towards intruding bulls from outside. The total area of his territory is thus often eroded by adjacent bulls or even by the intrusion of a new bull (and a new territory) between himself and his previous nearest neighbour. The patchwork of final territories on an extensive rookery may therefore be quite complex. Younger or later arriving bulls may occupy territories in the centre of the rookery as well as on the periphery, during the later stages of the breeding colony.

The sign that mating is about to begin is usually the approach by a bull to a cow whose pup is about 2 weeks old. The first attempt at copulation is not always successful as the cow may not be fully receptive. This results in many bull–cow battles quite unlike those approaches made earlier when the full-term cow is arriving in the territory. The bull attempts to seize the cow by the scruff of the neck in his jaws and to hold her while he mounts her. If she is not ready she will struggle to free herself and get away from him. If she is ready, she is much more passive, and will raise her tail to allow the bull to insert his penis to one side of it into the vagina, her hind flippers being, at the same time, widely spread. The bull is always assymetrically placed over to one side although his fore flippers embrace her shoulders anteriorly (Pl. 21). On Eilean-nan-Ron it was possible to watch the progress towards successful mating. Here the cows on the small beaches made frequent visits to the sea and to do so swam out along the deep water channels which cut through the bull territories. An unsuccessful attempt at mating was signalled by a great deal of splashing and turmoil in the water, the cow often escaping sideways on to the seaweed-covered rock. The heavier bull found it more difficult to

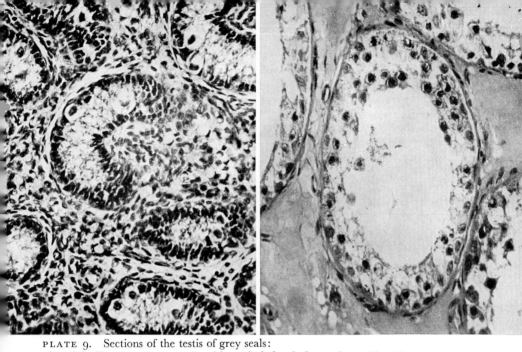

PLATE 9.   Sections of the testis of grey seals:
above left: The immature testis with occluded tubules and considerable inter-
stitial tissue (1–3 years old). × *c.* 30
above right: The mature but regressed testis with large open tubules but with
thin walls only one or two cells thick (January–March). × *c.* 30
below left: The mature and active testis with large open tubules having thick
walls producing the first batch of spermatids and spermatozoa (September–
October.) × *c.* 30
below right: An even more active testis at the height of breeding with spermatozoa
and many layers of future sperm (October–November). × *c.* 30

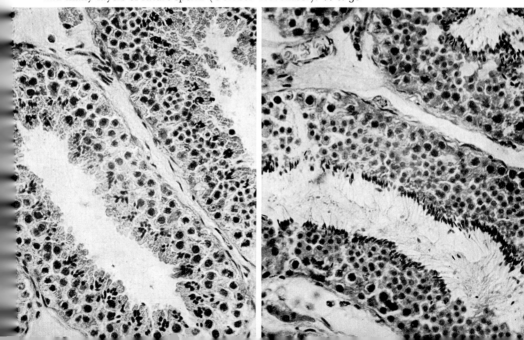

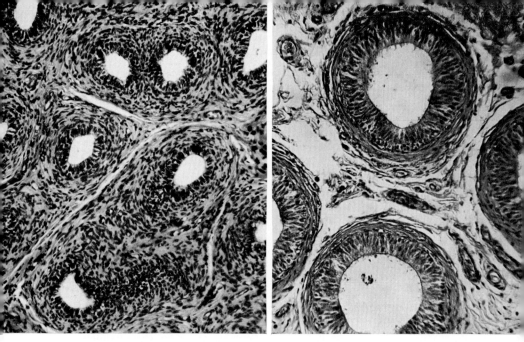

PLATE 10. Sections of the epididymis of grey seals.

above left: The immature epididymis with small tubules and thin walls (1–3 years old). × *c.* 15

above right: The mature but regressed epididymis with large tubules and deep inactive walls but with no sperm in the lumen. × *c.* 15

below left: The mature and active epididymis. The tubules are filled with sperm and the walls deep and active. × *c.* 15

below right: A dissection of an early foetus of 82 days' active gestation. The testis (arrowed) is still abdominal and close to the lobulated kidney. × 2.0

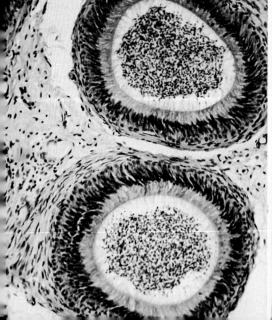

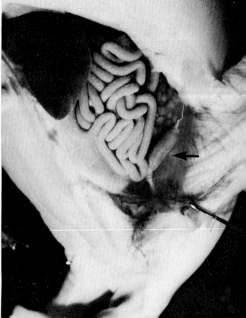

climb out of the channel and usually allowed her to escape. Later when the cow was fully ready to mate, copulation took place quite unobtrusively. On several occasions one would note that a cow had left her beach and begun to swim out to sea. Five minutes later one would suddenly see two heads, a bull's and a cow's, one above the other, surface in the channel to breathe and then sink slowly down again. Copulation had taken place under water quietly and without a struggle. I have also seen this quiet acceptance many times on land on North Rona.

It has been stated that the bull seizes the cow by the back of the neck and holds on viciously during copulation. This may be true exceptionally when the cow is not fully receptive and co-operative, but the most usual is for the bull to lie passively on top of the cow. Seizure may also occur during the initial positioning and insertion.

From what I have just written it is clear that mating can take place on land or in the water. I have the impression, however, that, if water is available, this is preferred but *shallow* water is even better for the bull to be able to contact the bottom in order to position himself properly. Thus I have seen copulation on Ramsey Island in the water along the shore-line as well as in deeper water; on Eilean nan Ron it always took place in the channels leading from the beaches to the sea; on Shillay the peat wallows were much used but not always since they were limited in their distribution through the rookery; and on North Rona the majority of matings took place on land since the shore-line was rocky and precipitous and rock and peat pools few and sparsely scattered, but if pools were available they were used. There is no apparent difficulty either in the sea or on the land.

Copulation lasts for some time, anything from 10–20 minutes. The bull makes repeated thrusts at intervals and this may indicate several discharges of semen. One bull may mate several times with the same cow. Whether a cow will accept more than one bull is not definitely recorded, but there does not seem to be any fundamental objection, since she may well pass through several bull territories on her way to the sea. Darling has observed that whereas in the earlier stages of a rookery it is always the bull who makes the first advances, in the later stages a bull may become worn out before leaving his territory. Here a cow may approach such a bull and if he is still un-responsive she will move over into another's territory to find an active bull.

This leads to a consideration of 'replacements' of worn-out bulls in the last stages of a breeding rookery. Darling has recorded that on North Rona the prime bulls leave their stations and are replaced by others; Davies also on Ramsey. I have seen this myself towards the end of October on North Rona and as the rookery continues well into November (when Darling noted replacement) it may be quite extensive. Its significance is in relation to the bull to cow ratio of a rookery. It would mean that the number of territories was less than the number of bulls involved and that the ratio was less than expected from territorial evidence only. Personally I do not accept this argument fully because there also occurs a 'replacement' of cows. On North Rona I was able to observe at close quarters part of the rookery in North Fianuis. This area is densely populated from an early date so that by mid-October a high proportion of pups had become moulters. As these moved off on to higher ground they were replaced by newly born pups; not in the same numbers possibly because to reach the area the cows had to pass through the very active zone of cows and pups surrounding it. As a result this area, one of the first to be used and densely populated, became a 'new' area less congested than the surrounding. Not until a detailed numerical study has been made of the latter half of the pupping season will the precise significance of the phenomenon of 'replacement' in both bulls and cows be known.

Meanwhile the data on the bull to cow ratio must remain imprecise. Perhaps it always will be because of the range of the ratio which has been observed in rookeries. On Shillay there was one territory which had 27 cows in it and another with none. On North Rona in 1959 counts of bulls and pups every four days enabled us to get some idea of the *average* ratio. Here it ranged from 101 bulls with 1,043 pups (pups give a better figure than cows, a fair and unknown proportion of whom may be in the sea) with the ratio of 1 : 10 on 7–8 October, to 156 bulls and 1,899 pups, ratio 1 : 12 on 24–25 October. Allowing for a continued rise in the ratio during the rest of the season it was suggested that the average lay between 1 : 10 and 1 : 13. The validity of this range was tested by supposing that it could be extended to 1 : 9 and 1 : 14. In the latter case, on a total pup production of 2,300 only 164 bulls would be required. This figure had almost been reached by 25th October with six or seven more weeks of mating to go. The lower figure would require 256 bulls which is an increase of 46% on the 25th October count. This seems an excessive allowance since most of the bulls had probably already been accounted for. Thus we concluded that a ratio of 1 : 10–13 probably included the true average requiring 230–177 bulls respectively.

Elsewhere various 'guesstimates' have been made. On Shillay I estimated the total pup production at 160 and the bull territories at 20. Allowing for some 'replacements' in the prime positions later on (say 4) this gives a ratio of 1 : 6.7. In Ramsey Island 1 : 7 seemed reasonable but not firmly based on counts since pups in caves could only be estimated. It may be that the smaller the group or rookery area, the lower the ratio.

Despite the indefiniteness of this ratio we are left with the fact that with a sex-ratio at birth approximating to 1 : 1 some explanation will be necessary to account for this discrepancy on the rookery.

Before we leave the bulls there is one more subject to be considered. As a feature of the true breeding rookery it is by way of being a non-event. This is the problem of how virgin cows are mated. Let it be said straight away that there is no direct indisputable evidence on this at all. All that follows is speculation, but it is based on several observations all of which point in one direction. First of all no one has seen virgin cows on a breeding rookery.

Every cow either has a pup or is obviously full-term. When a cow loses her pup she may stay for a day or so looking for it, but then moves away and from the present point of view joins the virgins as an unmated cow. It has also been shown that the territorial bulls mate only with cows on their territory and the majority become exhausted before they leave the rookery.

As mates for the virgin cows we are, therefore, left with non-territorial but sexually mature bulls. Now on the shell-sand beach of Shillay there were present a large number of such bulls *before* the rookery was fully established. Some of them undoubtedly later came to possess territory, but at the time they formed a good proportion of the herd on the beach they did not. These 'young' bulls were seen persistently to molest cows; they were always repulsed because the cows were either full-term or had just pupped. *Such molestation was never attempted by the large 'older' bulls who did not yet have territory either. These 'younger' bulls, aged between 6–10 years, are therefore the only ones which will approach or molest cows without being in possession of territory* and so have a behaviour pattern which could, if confronted with a virgin cow on heat, lead to mating.

The next questions arise, if not on the breeding rookery, where and when? Since there is no evidence that virgin cows pup at times other than normal it is highly probable that mating must take place during the normal season. The short period during which bulls are potent supports this. As to where, we must recall observations by many workers such as Davies, Darling and myself that near to a rookery, often on nearby islands or skerries there are 'reservoirs' of seals not actively engaged in pupping or territory holding. Nearly all these places are very difficult to get at and even more difficult to make observations on. Davies points to the string of islands known as the Clerks to the west of the Pembrokeshire mainland, Darling to Loba Sgeir, Lisgear Mhor, Sgor na Lice Moire etc. close to North Rona, I mention Eilean an Eoin, Sgeir Leathan and Cearn Riobha near to Eilean nan Ron and Ghaoidmeal off Oronsay. In Orkney there are similar assemblies on, for example, Boray Holm but on Rusk Holm the aggregation occurs on skerries to the south of the main island (where breeding takes place) which are connected by seaweed-covered rocks at low water. I have been able to stalk these groups and undoubtedly 'young' bull seals form a very significant element among them. Observation even here is difficult because the majority of the seals are in the seaward facing slope and not clearly seen from landward, while any attempt at an approach from the sea immediately puts them all in the water. However, Darling records having seen a copulation on Loba Sgeir part of which can be observed from the mainland of North Rona with good binoculars. This is the nearest to direct evidence but of course there is no knowing the exact status of either bull or cow even if the observation was many times repeated.

Faced with all these difficulties of obtaining direct evidence we may have to be content with an explanation which seems reasonable, not contrary to known facts and to which there does not seem to be any good alternative. This is to be regretted because it would be useful to know the probability of virgin cows being mated. Certainly a number are not on their first coming into heat or even later. Table 10 shows how the proportion of pregnant cows increases:

Table 10. Proportions of Virgin Cows in Age-groups 3–8

Years	Total Cows	Virgin Cows	Pregnant Cows
3	16	16	—
4	21	20	1
5	18	14	4
6	17	7	10
7	18	2	16
8	14	—	14

CHAPTER 9

THE GREY SEAL – MOULTERS, DISPERSAL, MARKING EXPERIMENTS AND LATER MOVEMENTS

WE left the just-moulted young seals in Chapter 7. On North Rona they had moved on to higher ground away from the rookeries, while in Pembrokeshire they had moved from their natal beaches to adjacent ones. The difference however did not end there because we had seen that the southern ones had had considerable experience in swimming while the land-based ones of the north had not. From the Farne Island rookeries we have a similar picture to that of North Rona. It would seem that, swimming experience or none, the young moulter pauses as it were for perhaps as long as a week or more before setting out on its sea life to fend for itself. Probably it is hunger that drives it for Coulson has clearly shown that there is a distinct loss of weight after moulting before the young seal goes to sea. By that time too a fuller development of their neuro-muscular co-ordination has taken place. There is a great difference in the control of the swimming movements between the white coat and the moulter ready to go to sea. So far there is no real evidence as to the reasons why a moulter should go to sea – hunger? – weight? – neuro-muscular development?

Until the 1950's nothing whatever was known about the further life of the young seal. Then in 1951 the Northumberland, Durham and Newcastle-upon-Tyne Natural History Society under the direction of Mrs G. Hickling began a programme of marking young seals and obtaining returns. This has been carried on ever since in one form or another. In 1952 I began marking pups on Ramsey Island and this continued for many years under the West Wales Trust. Elsewhere marking has been done in the Hebrides (myself *et al.* 1954–), North Rona (Nat. Cons. 1959–), Orkney and Shetland (E. A. Smith *et al.* 1959–) (Pl. 4).

It was soon apparent that the principal problem was to ensure permanence of the mark. In the Pribilov Islands the U.S.A. Fish and Wildlife Service had used 'hog tags' (like cattle ear tags) clipped to the fleshy skin fold lying in the axil of the fore flipper of the fur-seal; this had proved most successful over a number of years. Such a position of the marker is protected from water drag and from becoming caught on rocks and torn off. Since in the grey seal no such fold exists, the trailing edge of the fore flipper being about one inch thick and leading directly on to the body, the most convenient attachment for such a tag was through the web of the hind flipper. This position is however subject to severe water drag and there was no doubt that they soon pulled out. Nevertheless at least one astounding record was made, needless to say with the first tag ever used. This was fixed on a moulter on the Farne Islands who appeared, a fortnight later, near to Bergen on the Norwegian coast.

Encouraged by this success of Mrs Hickling and her helpers, I tried to develop a more permanent tag of the form shown in Fig. 36. This may have been better, certainly records exceeding six months were obtained, but none

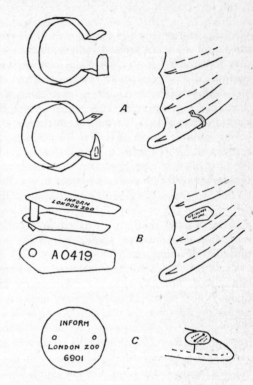

FIG. 36. Types of marker used on grey seal pups. A. the earliest types based on the cattle ear-tag but which encircled the 5th toe as shown on the right. The upper one was made from stainless steel the lower from monel metal. B. was a 'batchelor's button' type fixed in the web of the hind flipper. C. was a disc fixed by german silver wire on the tail. Both B and C types were made of coloured plastic, a different colour for each year or rookery, so that some information was available even if the individual identification was not possible.

over a year. There was difficulty too in ensuring that they could be applied quickly and firmly. I have marked over 100 in 3 hours without trouble, but at other times have had failures of the spike to penetrate the slot and turn over. The ring apparently gave too much opportunity for mechanical play to ensure success every time.

E. A. Smith tried other tags attached to the tail. The cattle tags and rings were of Monel metal. The tail tags were of plastic and different colours could be used for different years. But again there was a persistent failure to obtain records over more than a few months. Many different patterns of tags were tried, some of them illustrated in Fig. 36, but all prove too impermanent.

Eventually it was decided that branding was probably the only sure method. Again in the Pribilov fur-seal this had been done, but not followed up as no continuous research programme was then in force. Many years later, when tagging every year was started, one or two bulls were seen with these brands on them, showing that it was possible to brand successfully and for the mark to be recognisable over a number of years. Early attempts in the grey seal met with varied success. The great differences in time of application of the hot brand, depending on the degree of wetness of the pelt and, in moulting pups, on the amount of hair present, led to difficulties in standardising the procedure. On the whole, it proved a useful method and has been used on some rookeries for the past ten years or so. It can, however, only be used to mark a year-group from a particular rookery; individual identification is not possible (Pl. 22). The first results from this, other than those concerned with dispersal, have tended to confirm the age of maturity of cows and the age of territory holding by bulls as determined by anatomical methods (Table 11).

Table 11. Reappearance of Branded Seals of Farne Islands

58 pups branded, 13th and 14th December 1960, with a cross on the right shoulder.

	Reappeared	*Description*	*Date*	*Age*
1966	Megstone	Almost fully mature ♂	11. 6.66	6 years
	Brownsman	Breeding ♀	25.11.66	6
1967	Staple Island	Breeding ♀	8.11.67	7
	Brownsman	Breeding ♀	10.11.67	7
1968	Brownsman	Breeding ♀	15.11.68	8
	Brownsman	Breeding ♀	15.11.68	8
	Brownsman	Breeding ♀	15.11.68	8
1969	Brownsman	Breeding ♀	9.11.69 and 13.11.69	9
1970	Brownsman	Breeding ♀	10.11.70	10
	Brownsman	Breeding ♀	10.11.70 and 22.11.70	10
	N. Wamses	Breeding ♀	11.11.70 and 22.11.70	10
	S. Wamses	Breeding ♀	22.11.70 and 29.11.70	10
	N. Wamses	Territorial ♂	18.11.70 and 22.11.70	10
	Staple Island	Non-territorial ♂	29.11.70	10

Reappearance of Branded Seals of North Rona

Oct. 1963	Fianuis, N. Rona	Cow with pup	18.10.68	5
	Fank Brae, N. Rona	Cow with pup	19.10.68	5

What have been the principal dispersal results of the marking work? A summary of tagging work is shown in Table 12a and samples of the returns are shown in Tables 12b and 13. The first (12b) shows how many of the early returns, particularly of under-nourished pups, came from reports of dead pups close to the rookeries. The second (13) shows the considerable distances which must have been travelled by some young seals. Outstanding examples of distance are: Pembrokeshire to Bay of Biscay and Galway Bay; Farne Islands to Norway, Germany and Faeroes; Orkney to Iceland. Many of these long distance voyagers were found alive and well, and some of the distances appear to have been travelled in a remarkably short time.

Table 12a. Summary of Seal Tagging 1951–61

	Total tagged	*Total recovered*	*Percentage recovered*
Farne Islands	2,927	205	7
Orkney	1,660	122	7
Hebrides & North Rona	1,461	31	2
Pembrokeshire	1,141	68	6
All areas	7,189	426	6

b. Summary of Recoveries 1951–61

ex *Farne Islands*

Farne Islands	47
Scottish E. Coast	70
English E. Coast	62
Orkney & Shetland	3
Norwegian Coast	9
Danish Coast	2
Dutch & German Coasts	11
Faeroe	1

ex *Orkney*

Orkney	30
W. of Orkney & Hebrides	4
Scottish N.E. Coast	36
English N.E. Coast	1
Shetland	7
Faeroe	6
Norwegian Coast	35
Irish Coast	3

ex *Hebrides and North Rona*

Hebrides	18
Faeroe	3
Orkney & Shetland	6
Norwegian Coast	2
Irish Coast	2

ex *Pembrokeshire*

Welsh & Lancs Coast	34
English W. Coast	12
Irish Coast	14
French Coast	7
Spanish Coast	1

In view of these discoveries which, after a few years, tended to repeat themselves, showing that the initial observation was not unique, serious consideration was given to their interpretation. Firstly there were no records of young seals, reported hundreds of miles from their rookeries, being later seen back near their point of origin. The nearest to this was the instance of a young seal who, in a short time, moved across the North Sea and back again. Again there was the remarkable appearance of two young seals within a day

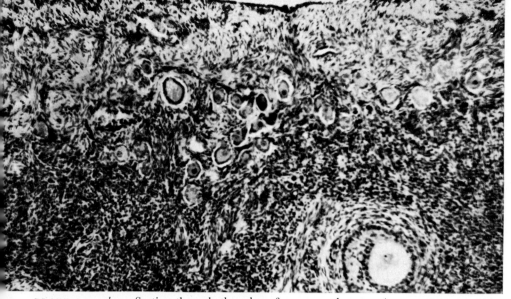

PLATE II. *above:* Section through the edge of a grey seal ovary. An oocyte beginning to mature can be seen in its enlarging follicle (right bottom). Above it are a number of germ cells awaiting development. × *c.* 30

Hand sections of the right and left ovaries of a grey seal:
below left: Right ovary of pregnant side with a large *corpus luteum* (with small cavities). An old *corpus albicans* is just below it and maturing follicles lie further down still. × 2.1
below right: Left ovary of the post-partum side with large star-like *corpus albicans* from the last pregnancy. Three smallish developing follicles are also sectioned. × 2.1

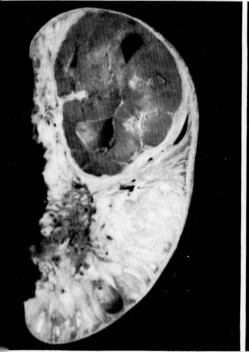
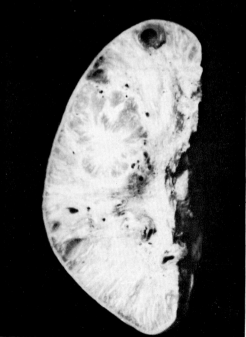

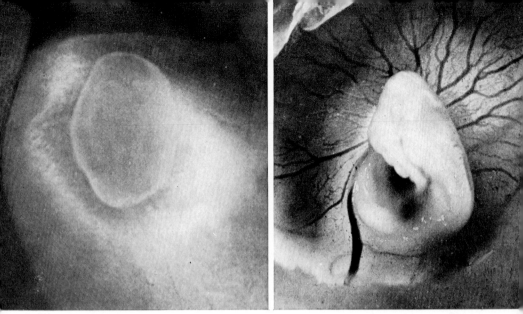

PLATE 12. *above left:* An unimplanted blastocyst of the grey seal (2 × 1.3 mm), lying in a depression in the wall of the uterine horn. (January 1956.) × 20
above right: An embryo of about 31 days after implantation. The yolk-sac blood-vessels are obvious and very active. A fore-limb can be seen as a lobe to the left of the head. (March.) × 10
below: A very young foetus of about 55 days' active gestation lying in its membranes in the uterine horn. Surrounding the foetus is the amnion, and below it the yolk-sac. The placenta is well established as a band, sectioned above and below the foetus (limits are arrowed). × 1.5

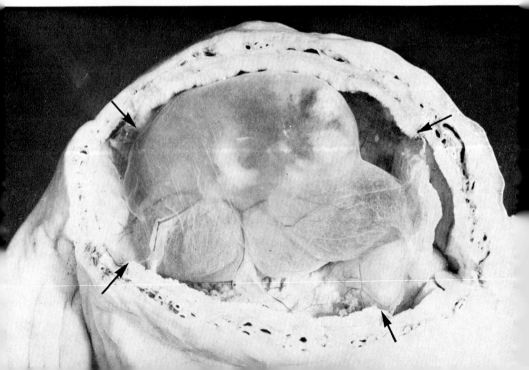

or so of each other turning up on the coast of Britanny, one near Roscoff, the other near Quiberon. Other instances of this sort of thing were noted and led to the idea that the prevailing winds might have something to do with it. This was confirmed when the meteorological records were looked into.

Now it so happened that at the time there was great concern over the drifting ashore of oil waste discharged at sea and information was being collected by the Admiralty to find out, if possible, safe distances beyond which discharge could be permitted under International Agreements. Some of the results were surprising and wholly pertinent to the young seals. For example, two batches of return postcards, enclosed in polythene envelopes, were dropped off Valencia Island south-west of Eire on different dates. Most of the returns from one batch were sent back from Norway, while the coast of the Bay of Biscay and even farther south gave most of the records from the other. It appears that for the top 18 inches of the sea, at least, the effect of the wind is more important than currents or seasonal bulk water movements. The speed of a young seal would rarely exceed 3 or 4 knots, i.e. of the same order as currents. Many if not all of the very long distance records of young seals, therefore, must be regarded as due to the action of winds, and there is no evidence to indicate that such seals ever find their way back again. On the other hand, if several such seals drift in the same direction it presents the possibility of the establishment of the species in areas which would not lie within the usual range of dispersal.

Another point of significance was the variation in the percentage of these marked which were recovered, dead or alive (Table 12a). The Farne Island marking was by far the highest at $\pm 8\%$ whereas others were much lower, below 3%. The factors involved undoubtedly included the proximity and extent of a shore-line. The almost enclosed North Sea presented shores nearly all round in which dead or exhausted youngsters could be washed up. Moreover most of its shore-line was inhabited and often visited. The west coast groups had only the coast to the east representing less than one half of the available circumference, assuming random dispersal, and much of it sparsely populated and infrequently visited, especially in winter. However, there was some evidence against random dispersal from the Farne Island recoveries which suggested that there was a coastwise movement north-ward disproportionately large. It was difficult however to get any truly significant figures because the total numbers were small.

The real gap in knowledge, which still exists, is in the dispersal seaward into deeper water. There were several records of young seals caught, well out from the coast, by trawlers which suggest that there is a general dispersal, besides a coastwise movement, but how much of this is due to wind drift is not clear.

There certainly is overlap of the dispersal areas (Fig. 37). For years the salmon net fishermen of the Aberdeen-Kincardine coast on the east of Scotland have shot predatory seals at the nets and on haul-outs. Since

Table 13 a. Notable Recoveries of Tagged Seals (Farne Islands)

	Tag No.	Date Marked	Place Recovered	Date Recovered	Age
Norway	1	16.12.51	Jaeren, nr. Stavanger, Norway	30.12.51	c. 3–4 weeks
	97	21.12.52	Off Utsire, Norway	3. 4.53	15 weeks
	3421	30.10.57	Eigerøy (nr. Egersund) Norway	31.12.57	9 weeks
	5195	29.11.58	Vigdel, Co. Rogaland (nr. Stavanger), Norway	10. 1.59	6 weeks
	5412	23.11.59	Kvalavag, Karmøy, Norway (Seen Isle of May, Scotland, 21.12.29)	30.12.59	c. 5½ weeks
	6494	1.11.61	Gösvear, Solund, Norway	3. 2.62	14 weeks
	6624	10.11.61	Off South-East (West?) coast of Norway (58° 13′ N 2° 15′ E)	21. 2.62	15 weeks
	6632	18.12.61	Solsvik på Sotra, Norway	2. 2.62	9 weeks
	6806	18.12.61	10 m. off Sandefjord, Veierland, Norway	—. 1.62	3–7 weeks
	A0752	23.12.64	Nr. Hiskjo, Bergen, Norway	20. 1.65	5–6 weeks
	A0890	10.12.66	5 m. West of Lindesnes, Norway	18. 1.67	5 weeks
	A1041	24.11.66	Lindesnes, Norway	9.12.66	6–7 weeks
	A1405	18.11.67	Maunefjorden, nr. Mardel, Norway	23. 1.68	16 weeks
Sweden	A0438	10.12.63	Humeboostrand, Sweden	3.1.64–24.1.64	5½–8½ weeks
Denmark	3686	16.11.57	Skagen, Denmark	25. 1.58	11 weeks
	6194	12.11.60	Nissum Bredning, Lim Fjord, Denmark	4. 2.61	12 weeks
	A0897	10.12.66	Off Kardestederne, Grensen, Jutland, Denmark	20. 1.67	10 weeks
	A1043	24.11.66	Vejrestrand, nr. Blaavand, Denmark (Seen Scarborough, Yorks, 11.3.67)	27. 2.67	13½ weeks
	A1073	24.11.66	Klitmoller, Jutland, Denmark	17. 2.67	14 weeks
W. Germany	61	6.12.52	Mouth of River Elbe, Nr. Cuxhaven, West Germany	9. 2.53	10 weeks
	5167	24.11.58	Juist, E. Frisian Island, West Germany	27. 1.59	9 weeks
	5412	23.11.59	Wangerooge, Nr. Wilhelmshaven, West Germany	2. 1.60	6½ weeks
	6151	17.12.60	Norderney, E. Frisian Island, West Germany	31. 1.61	10 weeks
	A0622	22.11.64	Sudstrand, Borkum, E. Frisian Island, West Germany	12.12.64	5–6 weeks
	A0690	22.11.64	Sylt, Nr. Frisian Island, West Germany	2 and 13.12.64	17–28 days

Table 13a continued

	Tag No.	Date Marked	Place Recovered	Date Recovered	Age
	A0877	25.11.66	Wangerooge, E. Frisian Island, West Germany (Seen Aldbrough, Yorks, 26.12.66)	4 and 5.1.67	6 weeks
Netherlands	A1214	8.11.67	Juist, E. Frisian Island, West Germany	7 and 9.1.68	9–10 weeks
	863	24.11.57	Uithuisen Dike, Uithuizermaeden, Netherlands	9. 1.58	7 weeks
	5178	27.11.58	Island of Amaland, Netherlands	3. 1.59	5½ weeks
	5451	5. 1.60	Callantsoog, Noord Holland, Netherlands (Seen Withernsea, Yorks, 17.1.60)	21. 1.60	c. 6 weeks
	5455	5. 1.60	Vlieland, W. Frisian Island, Netherlands	3–5.3.60	c. 12–13 weeks
	5754	16.11.60	Loosduinen, Netherlands	26.12.60	7 weeks
	6565	29.10.61	1. Oosterland, Wieringen, Netherlands	2.12.61	6 weeks
			2. W. Terschelling, Netherlands	29.12.61	10 weeks
	A806	27.11.62	Den Helder, Netherlands	12. 1.63	6 weeks
	A0981	16.12.66	30 m. N.W. of Ijmuiden, Netherlands	13. 1.67	5–6 weeks
	A1140	18.11.67	Texel, W. Frisian Island, Netherlands	17. 3.68	18 weeks
	A1980	10.11.70	Callantsoog, Noord Holland, Netherlands	22.12.70	6 weeks
	A2041	11.11.70	De Koog, Texel, W. Frisian Island, Netherlands	29.12.70	7½ weeks
Faeroes	3050	18.11.56	Boroyavik, by Klaksvig, Faeroe	26. 1.57	8 weeks

b. Notable Recoveries of Tagged Seals (Pembrokeshire)

	Tag No.	Date Marked	Place Recovered	Date Recovered	Age
France	201	28. 9.54	Ile de Batz, Finnisterre	10.12.54	>10 weeks
	331	28. 9.54	Porsdoun, Ouessant	12.12.54	>10 weeks
	?	26. 9.56	Loctudy	12.11.56	>6 weeks
	1060	5.10.57*	'West Brittany'	11.11.57	5 weeks
	1064	17.10.57*	'North Brittany'	30.12.57	10 weeks
	1352	27. 9.57*	'North Brittany'	9.11.57	6 weeks
	?	? 58	Pierre Noire, Finnisterre	?	?
Spain	1716	21. 9.60	Santoña, Nr. Santander	mid.12.60	>11 weeks
Eire	1183	2.10.56	Black Hd. Lighthouse, Co. Clare	30.11.56	>8 weeks

* Date of birth (? estimated).

marking began those with tags have been noted and these records show that
the first year seals on that coast are derived about equally from the Farne
Islands and from Orkney. In the Moray Firth there are more Orcadian seals
than Farne Islanders, while farther south the reverse is true. This raises the
question again of the discreteness of breeding groups which will have to be
dealt with later when all the pertinent data have been obtained. While
mentioning this source of information, it may be noted that there was a
peculiar sex difference shown. Thus on the Berwickshire coast the recoveries
were predominantly females (from the Farne Islands) while from the same
rookery it was principally bulls which were caught in the Aberdeen-
Kincardine area. No explanation of this is apparent. There is still a great deal
to be known about the movements even in the first year.

Before we leave these first year youngsters it should be mentioned that the
marking programme carried out on the Farnes was accompanied by the
collection of much other data (besides the sex-ratio already referred to).
Regular weighings of pups enabled individual histories to be built up, thus
connecting malnutrition with high post-moulter mortality and so on. When
access to the animals is so difficult and chancy it is well worth while to obtain
as much as possible in the way of information, and to construct a research
programme to cover as great a part of a life history as is feasible.

Dr Lockie in 1959 made a transect on North Rona in which 77% of the
pups were recorded as 'healthy and well grown'. Another 12.5% were
considered as unlikely to survive to moult. This leaves 10.5% as doubtful and
likely to die *shortly* after entering the sea. Dr Coulson has examined the
records of tagged pups in relation to their weight as moulters and has come
to the conclusion that any pup under 90 lbs. at weaning is unlikely to survive
for more than 6 months. Thus, from Farne Island records, this suggests that
about 20% can be placed in this category. It is also worth noting that the
weights of young seals recovered after natural deaths are all *below* the figure
of 90 lbs. So to the 15–20% 'pup mortality' there may well have to be added
a further 15–20% moulter mortality, up to the age of six months. The
mortality during the second six months to the end of the first year will add
still more to the death toll.

Turning now to what is known about the movements of older seals, we
come upon a field of almost total ignorance. What glimpses we have pose
questions rather than provide answers. Most of the observations have been
briefly mentioned in Chapters 4 and 5 in connection with reproduction or
the moult. Undoubtedly the movements of cows and bulls are dissimilar and
further, in mid-winter, those of the pregnant and non-pregnant cows are
different. Firstly it seems certain that *on the whole* the adult population (and
probably the sub-adult) do not remain close to the rookeries. The periodic
fluctuations on the West Hoyle Bank more than 100 miles from the breeding
grounds are quite clear and significant; at their minimum in the breeding
season, rising to their maximum in the late winter to early summer. Similar

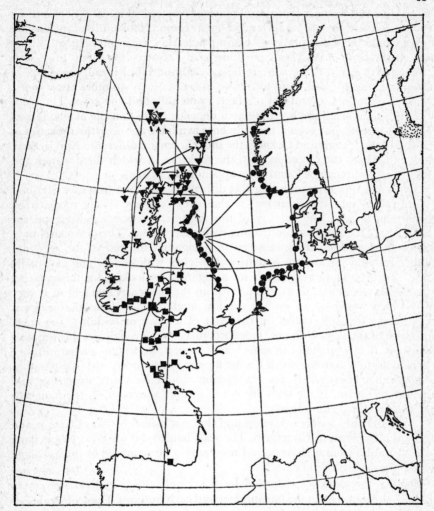

FIG. 37. Recoveries of young marked grey seals. Recoveries from three centres of marking are shown: Pembrokeshire – squares; Farne Islands – circles; North Rona – triangles. Not all records are shown as they would show continuous overlap on this scale in many parts of the coast. Those from Orkney are omitted altogether as they would have produced a very confused picture, mixing in among those from North Rona and from the Farne Islands. There is sufficient mixing of these on the Norwegian and east Scottish coasts and in Faeroe to show that the groups are not segregated in the first year of life.

figures for the Farne Islands are the exact converse (Fig. 22). A month by month count of the grey seals hauled-out at Donna Nook on the Lincolnshire coast would be of great interest in this connection. I can supplement this by an observation in Shetland when in mid-February very few grey seals (a couple of dozen or so) were to be seen around Fitful Head, the centre of breeding, and we had to go to the Ve Skerries nearly 50 miles away to the north-west to find a haul-out of about 1,000 bulls and 300 cows. The *actual* distance away from the breeding area depends greatly on the availability of haul-out points, but even if the only ones available are near the rookeries as in the Farne Islands and Orkney, the sites chosen are different. Nor is there any rule about the direction from the rookeries in which these winter and spring haul-outs can be found (See Appendix D, p. 219).

One objection to considering this dispersal as oceanic (distance of ±100 miles radius into the open sea) is that grey seals are rarely reported by fishermen at sea. The validity of this argument depends entirely on the accuracy of the fishermen in making such observations. Theirs is a strenuous life and apart from those engaged in navigation the rest of the crew are either busy on the various activities connected with the fishing or equally busy sleeping. Those responsible for navigation are looking for things larger than seals out at sea, or at instruments on the bridge. A seal's head is very small in a welter of sea and at the low angle of view from the bridge is completely invisible unless on the crest of a wave or within a *very* short distance of the ship. I do not, therefore, place much weight on this negative evidence. Unfortunately (in some ways) there is no pelagic sealing industry to help as there is in the north Pacific for the northern fur-seal. To mount a comparable effort solely for observation would be vastly expensive and doubtfully useful. If the seals are not in inshore waters or on the haul-outs they *must* be farther out to sea.

Thus the only *positive* evidence, and that not direct, is that of Craggs and Ellison referred to in Chapter 6. The seals hauled-out on West Hoyle Bank are 150 miles from a rookery and must surely be a sample of those feeding widely in the Irish Sea (Pl. 22).

Finally the evidence collected by Boyd indicates a general movement *towards* the rookeries in the late summer and early autumn. These observations have been made from the shore or from off-shore islands, but there is nothing to suggest that a similar drift of seals is not taking place shoreward from the more open sea.

Throughout this chapter the word 'dispersal' has been used to describe the outward movements from the rookeries. Often the term 'migration' is used, but this is to debase the word so that it becomes almost useless. True there is a 'return' phase from dispersal, but if migration is used to cover this, what can be used to distinguish a movement in which practically the whole population moves from one limited area to another and back, as happens, it would seem, with the harp seal. Let 'dispersal' and 'return' be used; they are adequate and do not imply more than is known to occur.

Reference has already been made to the establishment of new rookeries and the essentially conservative behaviour of the grey seal has been emphasised. Another difficulty can now be seen, because it is in the dispersal phase of their distribution that the *young* seals may encounter new favourable sites for rookeries. Yet their physiology is not keyed to react to stimuli connected with breeding, whether pupping or mating. Is it possible that new rookeries are founded, almost by accident, not by the young but sexually mature bulls (6–7 year olds) and virgin cows whose *libido* may not develop sufficiently early to permit a return to a distant natal rookery, but who meet when it is adequate to induce mating at some point far away. It should be possible to determine the age of the bulls and cows at newly established sites now that more workers are available to discover these places early in their history. The Isle of May has been going as a rookery for perhaps too long and the same may be said for the Cardigan coast and Scroby Sands, but St Kilda and other Western Isles are possibilities worth investigation. What are the ages of the seals now breeding there? Young (5–15 years) or old (15–30 years)?

CHAPTER 10

THE GREY SEAL – POPULATION DYNAMICS, MORTALITY AND PREGNANCY RATES

I N this chapter we are going to attempt to synthesise much of the information recorded in previous chapters, not in respect of the individuals of the species, but in terms of the populations as a whole. In doing so we shall come upon fields where our knowledge is sadly lacking and to arrive at any sort of general conclusion we shall have to make some assumptions.

Now for a species to maintain its numbers over the years, a sufficient number of each year's young must survive to sexual maturity in order to replace those of breeding age which have died in that year. But to understand how this may be achieved a number of factors, called parameters, must be known because the variation of any of them will cause fluctuations in the 'balance sheet' of the population. Because such variations arise from purely natural causes and because they may almost automatically give rise to compensating changes, the whole system of population control is regarded as 'dynamic' even though over the long-term the population itself may be regarded as 'stable'. The study of these parameters and their interactions is called 'population dynamics'.

First let us list the parameters which we require. They cannot be arranged in order of importance because all are necessary.

1. The number of young born to each cow on the breeding rookery.
2. The ratio of cows to bulls involved in breeding.
3. The sex-ratio of the young at birth.
4. The percentage of cows of mature age which are pregnant each year (pregnancy rate).
5. The age of sexual maturity of the cows.
6. The age of sexual maturity of the bulls.
7. Age of entry of the bull into a breeding rookery.
8. The potential longevity of the cows in breeding condition.
9. The potential longevity of the bulls in breeding condition.
10. The rates of mortality for each year of life.

To see these parameters at work let us look at a few a little more closely. It has already been said that only one pup is born to a cow on the rookery (1), but until we know the pregnancy rate (4) the number of mature cows in a population cannot be calculated from the number of pups born. Another interesting parameter is longevity (8 and 9). This is one which affects the

PLATE 13. *left:* A very young male foetus of about 62 days' active gestation, removed from its membranes. The skin is still transparent, the claws hardly differentiated and the follicles of the vibrissae and eye-tufts are the only indication of hair growth. × 1.5

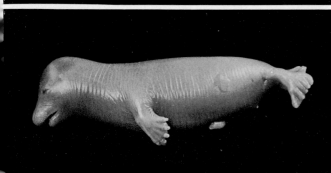

left: A young male foetus of about 72 days' active gestation, removed from its membranes. The head region is straightening out and the claws now visible as white tips to the digits. The skin is becoming less transparent. × 0.7

below: A male foetus of about 113 days' active gestation, removed from its membranes. Pigmentation is now apparent all over the body, but still there is no trace of hair except for the vibrissae. The claws are now very obvious. × 0.5

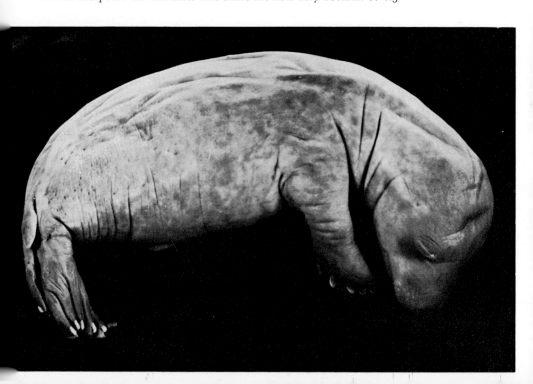

PLATE 14. *above:* Moulting haul-out at Aber Foel Fawr, Ramsey Island. Nearly all the grey seals are bulls. (April 1957.)
below: A closer view taken from the cliff-top above the haul-out. The great variation in pellage can be seen. Note the intense black of the newly-moulted bulls.

dynamics of a species quite fundamentally. Most insects, for example, replace all their breeding stock each year; some even several times in one year. Among mammals the short-lived shrews and small rodents (15 months–2 years) have to be dealt with very differently from the long-lived elephants, whales, larger carnivores and ungulates when attempting to regulate their populations.

All these parameters are taken into account and summarised in what is called a 'Life-Table', using average figures for each statistic and assuming that the population remains 'stable'. Even though the real population is 'dynamic' such a life-table provides a model from which we can find out what the effect will be of varying one or more of the parameters. This is what the practical ecologist (pest-controller or conservationist) has to be able to do if he is going to 'manage' a population and not let it get out of control.

Now let us see how far our knowledge of the grey seal will take us in this task by setting down in summary form such values as we have for each of the parameters.

1. One pup is born to each cow on the breeding rookery.
2. The ratio of bulls to cows involved in breeding varies from 1 : 7 to 1 : 12 say. This figure is problematical since within one rookery variations can occur between 1 : 2 and 1 : 15+.
3. The sex-ratio of the young at birth is 1 : 1.
4. There is no direct evidence for the pregnancy rate because an unbiased sample of mature cows cannot be collected. Percentages on biased samples give 93% and 66%.
5. Sexual maturity in cows appears normally at 5 years of age.
6. Sexual maturity in bulls appears normally at 6 years of age.
7. Bulls appear rarely to be found on rookeries before the age of 10 years.
8. The potential longevity of the cows appears to be 30 years +.
9. The potential longevity of the bulls appears to be 20 years +.
10. Only for the pup to moulter stage is there any direct evidence of a mortality between 15% and 20%. There is less direct evidence for a further 15–20% mortality in the next 5 months (up to 6 months of age). For the rest there is no direct evidence, but a heavier mortality must take place among bulls to account for their shorter life.

It is now possible to see where more information is required or where it may be possible by careful examination of the data available to be more precise, or to make reasonable assumptions.

The ratio of bulls to cows is not especially important to our basic calculations and can be left for consideration later (see p. 156). The pregnancy rate however is vital. Is it possible to get a closer estimate by examining the bias in the samples? The higher figure (93%) is derived from specimens collected from March to July inclusive; the lower figure (66%) is obtained if the specimens collected in January and February are included. Now it has already been pointed out that the cows hauled-out in January and February contain a very high proportion of young and non-pregnant cows, and in addition the total collected in those two months is above the average for the subsequent months. Thus there are two factors tending to bias the percentage of pregnant cows in a downward direction in the lower figure. No specimens in August or September have been included because these might well include early full-term cows coming into the breeding area which would bias the pregnancy rate in an upward direction. However, it is the general subjective impression that one does not see so *many* (in absolute terms) young cows in the months of May to July and consequently the higher figures may still have some upward bias. The halfway figure between the two is 80% but this may well be too low and perhaps it should be as high as 85%.

Here we might turn to what is known about the Pribilov fur-seal which has been so intensively studied by the United States Fish and Wildlife Service. Because there is a pelagic sealing fishery in the north Pacific during the non-breeding season an unbiased (so far as is known) sample of cows is available and from it a pregnancy rate of 80% has been arrived at. This is identical with our first, though slightly suspect, estimate and, since the biology of the two species is similar in many respects, it does not seem to be unreasonable to use this figure as the pregnancy rate until a better one can be obtained.

An 80% pregnancy rate means that for every 100 pups born on a rookery there is a population of 125 mature cows. However, the differences in longevity between cows and bulls will necessitate two separate life-tables, one for cows and one for bulls. So, taking the female life-table first and taking into account the sex-ratio of the pups (1 : 1) we must use as our basic data the statement that 250 mature cows are required to produce 100 female pups.

Now we know the longevity and the normal age of sexual maturity and it is in the age groups of the years between (6 to 30) that these 250 mature cows must be found. Further we can say that the total mortality of these cows in any one year must equal the number of female pups surviving, from the original 100, at the age of 5 years.

But before we consider mortalities in detail, let us see what is known on this subject in the Pribilov fur-seal. The extensive work on this species, already referred to, has been made possible by a peculiarity in its behaviour. Each year at the breeding season *all* members of the population, immature as well as mature, collect on and around the rookeries in the Pribilov Islands. It has also been possible to attach numbered tags to the pups (which weigh very much less than the grey seal pup, and are thus much easier to handle). These tags have been put on tens of thousands of pups and they can be examined year after year as the young seals turn up in the Islands. It has, therefore, been possible to determine the yearly mortalities directly with great accuracy in the cows throughout their life and in the bulls also, taking into account the commercial cull of young bulls for their skins. These mortalities can be used as a guide and a check on our own estimates for the grey seal.

Returning now to a 'standard' population with a group of 2,500 cows (this is 10 times the previous figure and will give 1,000 cow pups, but it is easier to use when dealing with mortalities and largely avoids referring to 0.5 cow!). This is spread over 25 years (6 to 30 years of age) and would therefore give an average of 100 cows per year-group if there were no deaths at all. But we must apply an annual mortality rate and if we do this *at a steady rate*, and we have no reason to do otherwise for the moment, we find that we should start with 200 in the 6th year-group. This is therefore the number surviving to the sixth year from an initial 1,000 pups. It is not difficult to see that the *total* mortality of the first 5 years must therefore amount to 80% or thereabouts. It will of course be unevenly distributed over these years and we have seen in Chapters 7 and 9 that a very high proportion of this occurs in the first six months. For the remaining period there is much less evidence, much of it indirect and we shall have again to make comparisons with the Pribilov fur-seal.

In Chapter 7 the overall mortality of pups was estimated at between 15% and 20%. In Chapter 9 a further 15–20% mortality was thought likely in the next five and a half months. In a paper by Coulson and Hickling there are some very useful data. They are not able to give figures for the various *causes* of mortality, but they give a graph which shows the growth rates of four 'classes' of pups observed in the rookeries. The first curve (Fig. 38) is that of a well nourished pup whose mother has easy accessibility, a minimum of interference and therefore it presents an optimum. Curve 2 is that of a less well nourished pup who proceeds to moult at about 60 lbs. and is *apparently* normal. The third curve is that of a poorly nourished pup who nevertheless hangs on, perhaps proceeding to moult at a late age and a weight hardly higher than at birth. The fourth is that of a very badly nourished, perhaps injured, pup who dies on the rookery, probably within the first ten days of life. Pup 1 (to name it after its growth curve) is likely to survive into its second year of life and stands a good chance of becoming a breeding animal in 4–6 years' time. Pup 2 will in all probability die within the first six months, certainly within the first year of life. Pup 3 will die within a week or two of moulting and leaving the rookery if it gets as far as doing so. Pup 4 represents what has been called the 'pup' mortality of 15–20%. What is wanted now are estimates of the *relative* numbers in these four categories. The sum of the percentages of categories 2, 3 and 4 would give a reasonable figure for the total of the first year's mortality. Starting with the fairly firm minimum figure of 15% for category 4, and, working on the assumption that the maximum mortality falls on the young mammal in the period immediately following weaning and release from parental care, giving tentative figures of 20% and 25% to categories 3 and 2 respectively, we would arrive at a figure of about 60% mortality (total) in the first year.

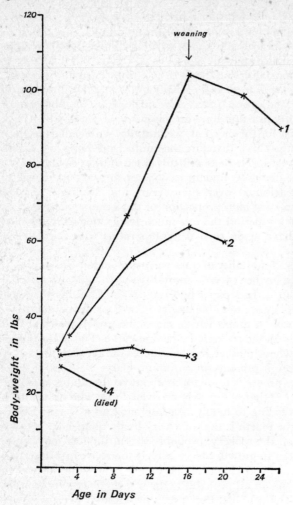

FIG. 38. Growth-rates in grey seal pups. These curves are for four pups which represent four types of growth dependent upon nutrition. (*Redrawn from Coulson and Hickling, 1964*)

Coulson and Hickling have given some more figures which bear on this mortality but they are not large enough and are not categorised in quite the right way to give really accurate answers. (This is no fault of the authors – it is just that the data cannot be got.) Table 14 sets out their data (in roman type in columns 1–3 and 6) and I have added three columns (4, 5, 7); column 4 is calculated from their data, the other two are estimated. Two points emerge from an examination of the figures. The first is that the percentage of pups born which put on more than 3.9 lbs. per day is 35.5% and that as this is the highest category of nutrition this percentage might

Table 14. Growth-rate and Survival of Farne Island Pups

Growth Rate	Nos.	Found Dead in <5 weeks	Known to have survived >5 weeks	Average Weight at 15 days	Approx. Curve No. in Fig. 38	% of pups born	Of 100 pups born there are: Dead within:		
							c. 6 weeks	c. 6 months	c. 12 months
	1	2	3	4	5	6			
Losing weight	19	10	0	<32 lb.	4	} 16.7	16.7		
0–1.9 lb./day	41	5	4	47 lb.	3		5–6?		
2–2.9	71	3	8	69.5 lb.	2	19.7		19.7	
3.0–3.9	101	1	9	84.5 lb.	1–2	28.1		4–5?	14–15?
Over 3.9	128	0	15	>99.5 lb.	1	35.5			5–6?
Totals	360	19	36			100			56.4±

Roman refer to figures taken directly or derived from Coulson and Hickling 1964 Table 11, page 504.
Italics refers to figures calculated or estimated by me.

well be taken as a *minimum* of those surviving the first year of life. The true figure almost certainly should include some of the next category, say a third of them and, since accident as distinct from malnutrition would remove some, a figure of 40% survivors would not be unreasonable.

The second point is that with several 'ifs' and 'buts' the total mortality of the first twelve months amounts to 56.4 ±, a fair approximation to the 60% arrived at by somewhat different arguments. It is also interesting to note that the percentage of pups gaining less than 1.9 lbs. per day plus those losing weight is 16.7 which corresponds to the 15–20% 'pup' mortality figure; while those gaining 2.0–2.9 lbs. per day total 19.7% which is not far off the 20% suggested for category 3 pups.

More recently Boyd and Campbell have published data which has been collected on North Rona over about ten years. Among this are a series of weights of moulters, taken at random. Table 15 sets out a summary derived from these measurements. It is the last line of this table which is significant because the percentage of those born which attain a weight of 90 lbs. or over comes out at 40%. Now on the Farne Islands the practice of weighing pups and moulters *and* tag-marking them enabled some trace of their fate to be obtained. Coulson (pers. comm.) thought it fairly clear that, although the numbers were small, no pup which had not reached 90 lbs. at moult had any chance of surviving into the second year.

The North Rona data contained another line of information similar to that already mentioned for the Farne Islands; the daily weight gains of pups. Here again I will summarise from the data in Table 15. The inclusion of several older pups whose weight gains were slowing down has reduced the numbers in the higher two groups so that comparison with the highest category of the Farne Island pups would probably necessitate adding the top two North Rona categories. This produces a figure of 35.2% of the Farne Island top group.

Both these sources of information tend to confirm that 40% is a fair guess at the *survival* rate for the first year. It is only by collecting data of different kinds that it is possible to narrow down the possibilities when direct observation is impracticable. The conclusion will always remain tentative but it becomes *not inconsistent* with more and more types of data.

Taking all the available data into consideration, it is not unreasonable to suggest the figure of 60% for the first year's *mortality*. This would allow a pass-on of 400 young cow seals into their second year. How is this number reduced to 200 by the end of the fifth year, i.e. in four further years? A steady *annual* mortality of just under 17% would achieve this, but again the earlier years must clearly have a higher figure. A comparison with the Pribilov fur-seal gives 28.3, 8.0, 6.0 and 5.0 as annual percentage mortalities for these four years (after a 60% mortality in the first), the last figure being the continuing annual mortality of the mature cow fur-seal. I have proposed 30, 12, 6.7 and 6.7 as tentative figures, again the last two figures being the

Table 15. Weights of North Rona Moulters

Moulters	No. of Specimens	Average Weight	Range of Weight
♂s	26	87.8 lb.	38–113 lb.
♀s	27	87.4 lb.	43–105 lb.

Distribution of moulters by weight

	less than 80 lb.	over 80 lb.	over 90 lb.	over 100 lb.	Total
♂s	5	21	12	7	26
♀s	5	22	15	3	27
♂s+♀s	10	43	27	10	53
As percentage	19	81	51	19	100
Assuming 20% pup mortality, as percentage of pups born	15	65	40	15	80

continuing annual mortality. In round figures the cow population to produce 2,000 pups (male *and* female together) is:

> Immature cows at end of 1st–5th year   1,360
> Mature cows (2,000 breeding)
>   years 6–31   2,500
>
>   3,860

It is time now to turn to the bulls. It will not be possible to use any of the Pribilov fur-seal data about bulls because there the commercial cull of young bulls completely distorts the life-table. We shall have to rely entirely upon our own data, and this is rather meagre, but some comparisons with the cow life-table are possible. For example, there is nothing to suggest that the mortality rates in the first few years of life to maturity are significantly different in the two sexes. We can, therefore, *assume* that there are 1,360 bulls who are immature in the first five year-groups.

One outstanding difference however concerns longevity. In the last few years the age of territorial bulls has been determined for some of those breeding off the coast of Nova Scotia. Here the bulls may reach ages comparable with those of the female and we also know of a Baltic bull which lived in Skansen Zoo for 41 years and was probably 42 years old when he died. Now the Canadian grey seals are practically monogamous and the Skansen bull did not breed, while the British bulls are polygamous and must

Table 16. Daily weight gains by pups from 8th October–15th October, 1962,
on Farne Islands. The pups were of various ages but *most* were
within a day or two of birth.

Total	Disappeared (Died?)	Negative	< 1 lb.	1.0–1.9 lb.	2.0–2.9 lb.	> 3.0 lb.
27	7	6	6	3	4	8
as %	20.4	17.6	17.6	8.8	11.8	23.5
					35.2	

fight to obtain and retain territory over some weeks. It is, therefore, not
unreasonable to suppose that polygamy and the territoriality of the bulls are
the cause of a differential mortality between cows and bulls in their years of
breeding leading to a shortened longevity of the bulls.

Although we know that sexual maturity in the bulls is about one year later
than in cows, this is not significant from the point of view of the breeding
population of bulls which consists (almost entirely) of bulls holding territory.
All the evidence we have, the development of the *os penis*, the weights of the
testes and the ages of bulls taken on breeding rookeries, lead to the conclusion
that territorial bulls under the age of 10 years are the exception. Consequently
this age of 10 years should be thought of as the start of the bull breeding
population. Twenty years of age (again with a few exceptions) is the upper
limit. Thus there are eleven year-groups in this population. Have we any
data to determine its absolute size? (In cows we had the number of pups as
a starting point.)

Now elsewhere (Chapter 8) I have tried to arrive at an average ratio of
bulls to cows on the breeding rookeries, and for North Rona I showed that a
figure of 1 : 10 was the most probable. If we now apply this to the cow
population of 2,500 we find that the bull breeding population is only about
250. I suggested that this ratio was probably too high for more scattered
types of rookeries and therefore the population of territorial bulls would on
average be more than 250. Perhaps 275 (c. 1 : 9) would be more realistic or
even 300 (c. 1 : 8). At any rate it is a very small number and spread over
11 years averages at 23 to 27 per year-group. (Notice how the apparently big
difference in the total (250 to 300) drops to 4 when considered on a yearly
basis.)

If we now do as we did with the cows and impose an even rate of mortality
to produce extermination by the 21st year, we find that we should start in
year 10 with about 110 bulls with an average mortality rate of about 40%.
This seems to be very high indeed but nothing less will accord with what
facts we do have. The figure of 110 bulls at year 10 is less by 40 when
compared with the number of cows surviving at that age. This can be

PLATE 15. Two pups in different types of moult, Ramsey Island.
above: This pup has not moved from the spot during moult and some of the shed hair can be seen among the pebbles. (September 1952.)
below: This pup has continued to enter the sea during moult and the loose hairs have washed off fairly evenly. Only the flippers and the top of the head are fully moulted. (September 1952.) (See also Plate 20, *top.*)

PLATE 16. *above:* Challenge by a newly landed bull grey seal on the shell-sand beach of Shillay. The open mouth and barely audible hiss is characteristic of a bull joining a pre-breeding assembly. The nearby cow retaliates by an aggressive hoot. (September 1954.)

below: Grey seal cow giving birth, Farne Islands. The hind flippers can be seen extruding in a breach birth, which is more frequent than a crown birth.

attributed to the extra mortality occasioned by bulls younger than 10 years holding territory so we must impose a higher than normal mortality rate (6.5–7.0%) for the years 7–8–9 say, 10%, 15%, 25% respectively during which the bulls are sexually mature, but in which few obtain territory. If this is done we find a total of 690 bulls in the year-groups 6–7–8–9 (compared with about 720 cows over the same range).

We can now summarise the bull population thus:

Immatures at end of 1st–5th years		1,360
Matures (but largely non-territorial) years 6–9		690
Territorial bulls years 10–21	say	270
		2,320

There is nothing so far in our life-table which conflicts with known numerical data, although much is guesswork and undoubtedly with more knowledge refinements can be made. But there is one feature which could be verified by direct observation, and it concerns the assumption of the very high mortality rate of territory holding bulls. If this rate is in fact true it means that of those bulls in a rookery one year, only a little over half (60%) will return the following year. No check on this has been made in one of the larger rookeries, but in 1954–55 I made observations on Shillay and noted a peculiarity of behaviour, namely, that some of the bulls coming in to obtain territory were 'large' (and possibly 'old') and that they were 'segregated' from the 'younger' bulls who fought among themselves *before attempting to establish territory*. I noted that the behaviour of these 'old and segregated' bulls suggested that 'they had been there before'. Several took up stations after a few days ashore where there were no cows at all, but which within a week proved to be the most densely populated with cows and pups. Fortunately, each day that I made a census of the seals in the rookery (and this was almost every day), I noted the number of 'old and segregated' bulls as distinct from the 'younger' bulls. When, several years later, I arrived at the conclusion that there ought to be this heavy annual mortality, I turned up my field notes on Shillay and found that there had been 10 'old and segregated' bulls and that when the rookery was fully established there were 20 territories. If I was right in thinking that these 10 'had been there before' then this represented about the right proportion of survivors. On such small figures and on the basis of one year's observations, it is not possible to be more definite or precise. (If, the preceding year, there had only been 18 territories the survival rate would have been 56%, compared with 50% had there been 20.)

Of course an increased mortality upon holding territory could reasonably be expected. These bulls must remain on station for the best part of two months without food and their emaciated condition at the end has been remarked on by more than one observer. Unless they pick up quickly to replenish their blubber insulation they have to face the hazards of winter with a strong likelihood of chilling with consequent pulmonary trouble and almost certain death. Alternatively, if they have not put on enough blubber during the summer they may enter territory without adequate reserve and with the same fatal effects in the winter. The greater longevity of the Canadian bulls with their almost monogamous breeding points to the same cause of high mortality.

If then we are prepared to accept the assumptions made, which result in figures not inconsistent with known data, we can summarise cow and bull populations thus:

	Cows	Bulls	Totals
Immatures	1,360*	1,360	2,720
Mature (but not breeding)	—	690	690
Mature (breeders)	2,500	270	2,770
	3,860	2,320	6,180

* About 210 of these are mature but primiparous so cannot be counted in the 'breeding' population.

and such a population will produce 2,000 pups a year. Thus, if we made a census of pups in any rookery or group of rookeries we can calculate the total population by multiplying the number of pups by 3.1. As such censuses are nearly always on the low side a figure of 3.5 probably gives a better estimate.

The great advantage that such life-tables give us is that absolute population numbers can be calculated from the one parameter which it is not too difficult to obtain, namely, the number of pups. It also allows us to take account of the immatures who otherwise are hardly ever seen on the rookeries and only on rare occasions, such as during the moult, outside the breeding season. For bulls this is particularly important since only about 11–12% of the total bull numbers are seen on the rookeries. I have been fortunate enough to see two or three of the very large haul-outs of moulting bulls and, even after considerable experience of the breeding rookeries, the numbers come as a shock. The same is true of a fishing haul-out such as that seen on the West Hoyle Bank (Pl. 22). Davies calculated the total number of pups on Ramsey Island as about 190, and in subsequent years my own observations agreed with his. He does not give a total figure for territorial bulls, but for three strips of coastline he records a total of 53 cows (and pups) with 8 bulls. This would give about 35 bulls proportionately for the total of 190 pups. Yet on 19th May 1957, we (Dr Backhouse was with me) counted 189 seals of which 'less than a dozen' were yearlings and the rest moulting bulls. In Orkney, which yields about 2,300 pups, on 2nd April 1962 I saw haul-outs on Ruskholm which were estimated in total at about 2,000, of which only a very few were cows, most in various stages of moult. On the same day a dozen or so large bulls were also seen on Boray Holm and of course there may well have been more elsewhere. In 1953, on 19th April, Dr Backhouse saw a huge haul-out of seals, most of whom were bulls, on the Longstone End in the Farne Islands. The total was estimated at around 800. At that time the pup production of the Farnes was reckoned to be 'between 550 and 650'. From photographs taken at the time it is clear that this was largely a bull haul-out. In all these instances the numbers of bulls involved are clearly of the same order as the number of pups, as suggested by the summary table on page 157 (2,320: 2,000). This is perhaps another case where our 'guesstimates' are not inconsistent with the observations.

What we have been discussing enables us to visualise the population as something alive, capable of change by variation of the many factors which combine to produce the flow of individuals into and out of the population. The model (life-table) states the position for a constant or stable population, even though there may be considerable variations in the totals in consecutive years. If numbers increase this may lead to a shortage of food, to interference with suckling and so on which increases mortality and so brings the total back to the normal. The greater the longevity of the animal the slower is the working of such effects (known as 'density dependent factors'). In the short-lived rodents maxima and minima may follow each other with only a very few years between. In seals such fluctuations may well be spread over a quarter of a century or more and it is often very difficult to identify the causes of the fluctuations. Grey seal groups in some British waters are fairly stable, judging by North Rona and Orkney, but there is evidence that the south-western group, of which Pembrokeshire is a part, is on the increase. The same may be true of the Outer Hebridean although there is not really sufficient data to be sure. The Farne Island group, clearly, are showing a very marked increase as shown by the pup counts in Table 9. The earlier figures may well be on the low side, but there is enough certainty over the last 10 years to make it quite clear that there has been an average increase of 7.8% per annum. This amounts to a population explosion, but so far no cause has been shown to be responsible for it. One of the difficulties arises because, in a long-lived animal reaching maturity at 5 years of age, the cause of the present increase in pups will have become operative years ago. The number of pups born is merely an indicator; it could be produced initially by an increased pregnancy rate although this seems unlikely in view of the persistent and steady increase. Alternatively it could be produced by reduced mortality in the years preceding sexual maturity so that the yearly intake of primiparous cows is increased or by a reduced mortality in the years of breeding so that there were more cows surviving for an extra year or so. It is even possible that all these contribute in some degree to the increase.

This is a good point at which to consider the natural causes of mortality. These have been listed for the pups by several workers (Table 17), and it is interesting that, whereas they agree in general on the causes, they differ considerably on the degree of importance of these. Basing their ideas on

observations made in places so different as Ramsey Island and the Farne
Islands, it would perhaps be surprising if they did agree more. Davies says
that the major cause of pup mortality was still-births amounting to one third
of the total deaths. Other causes in diminishing importance were storms
(washed away and drowned), oiling, accident and malnutrition. On the
Farne Islands Coulson and Hickling list the main causes in order of
importance as:

1. Starvation
2. Still-birth
3. Injuries caused by other seals
4. Infection
5. Misadventure

Boyd *et al.* also lists causes of pup mortality on North Rona. In a transect
across part of Fianuis North, 48 pups were examined. Five were ill-nourished
and one had serious septic wounds. This part of the island would not be
affected by storms, but other parts would and their effect would be serious
locally. No estimate could be made as to how many were so lost. The size and
complexity of the rookery also made the still-birth figure unobtainable, but
the high 'mortality' in the first week pups suggests that still-births may have
contributed substantially to it. At one place ('Saddle', 200 ft. above sea-level)
where the live pups all survived under ideal conditions of nutrition and lack
of interference and injury, there were several still-born pups; possibly a
result of the laborious climb of the mothers up the steep escarpment.

The principal causes of death among pups are therefore probably:

Still-births
Malnutrition
Storms
Injuries (followed by septic infection)

The order in which these would be placed according to importance must
vary with conditions of density, access and vulnerability to storms.

Table 17. Causes of Pup Mortality

Boyd et al. (1962)		Coulson & Hickling (1964)		Davies (1949)	
1. Ill-nourished	5	1. Starvation	6.5%	1. Still-births	6
2. Septic wounds (serious)	1	2. Still-births	4.5%	2. Storms	4
3. Storms	?	3. Injuries	2.0%	3. Oiling	2
		4. Infection	2.0%	4. Accident	2
		5. Misadventure	1.0%	5. Malnutrition	2
				6. Unknown	2
12.5% 6/48		16%		14.5% 18/124	

Among moulters there is no direct evidence except that all those dead moulters whose weights are known were well below that of an 'average' moulter (90 lbs.). Thus malnutrition is suggested as the primary cause although the immediate cause may include drowning or infection due to insufficient blubber. Predation may well play a part although killer whales, the only *known* predator, are not very numerous. In the later years disease and accident must play an increasing role, although we know practically nothing about the types of diseases involved. Glaucoma of the eye (one or both) may lead to blindness but as the sight of seals is not nearly so important as chemo-reception and perhaps touch through the vibrissae, its loss may not lead to fatal malnutrition. Indeed, as mentioned elsewhere, a totally blind cow has been seen to survive well enough to pup, to suckle and indeed to follow what appeared to be a normal existence.

None of the known parasites of the grey seal seem likely to lead to death. Externally there is a body louse *Echinophthirius sericans* recorded, although I have never come across it.* A mite, *Halarachne halichoeri*, is found in the trachea and nasal passages, often in considerable numbers, but I have only found one severe infection. This might, by stimulation of excess mucus, lead to respiratory troubles but it must be a very minor cause of death. The internal gut parasites are numerous and appear to be widespread. *Porrocaecum decipiens*, usually called the cod-worm because its sub-adult encysted stage is best known in the cod and related whitefish muscle, has increased considerably in recent years. It is not infrequent to find a ball of these nematode worms in the stomach as its only contents. So far as is known it does not directly harm the host; nor do the other less common round and flat-worms which have been recorded. In Table 18 are recorded the various parasites so far known to occur in *H. grypus*. It has been compiled from Miss A. Duncan's paper of 1956 but the very considerable amount of investigation into the parasite load of the grey seal which has been carried out in recent years has not added to the list. It has made it possible however to indicate with reasonable accuracy those species which are commonest both in incidence (proportion of infected seals) and in numbers occurring in individuals.

It has already been shown in this chapter how it is possible, from an accurate count of the number of pups born, to calculate the total population associated with a particular rookery. Where the rookeries are known and comparatively accessible as in the British Isles, it is, therefore, possible to arrive at a total for a considerable area. Elsewhere such as in the Baltic and on the eastern Canadian seaboard where there are not rookeries in the strict sense, and the individual cows and pups are scattered perhaps over miles of ice floe or along miles of coast-line, this cannot produce anything like so accurate a figure, even if enough were known to produce a life-table

* Mr Bonner tells me that he has found *E. horridus* on *H. grypus*, in addition.

Table 18. Parasites of Grey Seal

Group	Parasite	Infesting	Recorded by:	
Nematoda (Round Worms)				
†	Ascaris osculata = = *Contracaecum osculatum* (Rudolphi)	Stomach	Bellingham Allman	1844 1847
			Nehring Baylis Mohr Duncan *et al.*	1884 1920, 1937 1952 1956
†	*Porrocaecum decipiens* (Krabbe)	Stomach	Freund Stekhoven	1933 1935
			Baylis Legendre Mohr Duncan *et al.*	1920, 1937 1947 1952 1956
*	*Anisakis similis* (Baird)	Stomach	Baylis Dollfuss Duncan	1937 1948 1956
	Dioctophyme renale Geotze = = *D. gigas* Rudolphi	Kidney	Mohr	1952
Trematoda (Flat Worms)				
*	*Amphistoma truncatum* Baird = *Pseudoamphistomum* *truncatum* (Rudolphi)	Intestine Liver	Baird Freund Price Sprehn Mohr	1953‡ 1933 1932 1933 1952
* *	*Opisthorchis tenuicollis* (Rudolphi) *Metorchis albidus* (Braun)	Liver ⎤ Liver ⎦	Freund Price Sprehn Mohr	1933 1932 1933 1952
	Echinostoma acanthoides (Rudolphi)	Intestine	Mohr	1952

Group	Parasite	Infesting	Recorded by:	
Cestoda (Tape Worms)	Cryptocotyle lingua (Creplin)	Intestine (ant. and mid.)	Duncan	1956
	Schistocephalus solidus (Mull)	Intestine	Mohr	1952
	Lingula sp.	Intestine	Mohr	1952
Acanthocephala *	Corynosoma strumosum (Rudolphi)	Stomach and ant. to post. intestine	Porta	1909
			Freund	1933
			Wülker and Stekhoven	1933
			Baylis	1939
			Mohr	1952
			Duncan	1956
	Corynosoma semerme	Intestine	Wulker and Stekhoven	1933
			Mohr	1952
Arthropoda *	Halarachne halichoeri Allman	Nasal cavities and trachea	Allman	1847
			Nebring	1884
			Duncan et al.	1956
*	Echinophthirius sericans Meinert	Pelt	Ferris	1934, 1951
			Freund	1927
			Duncan	1952
	Fannia sp. (larvae only) (Two-winged fly)	Wounds on pelt	Duncan	1952

* Probably common   † Probably very common
‡ Recorded on this occasion from common seal (*Phoca vitulina*)

consistent with the different biological arrangements involved. Added to this in the Baltic it appears that the main breeding areas are on the eastern coast, approach to which is prohibited by political factors. On the Canadian coast physical difficulties are considerable, although in recent years attempts to visit the area have been becoming more successful.

E. A. Smith in The Report of the Interdepartmental Committee on Seals and Fisheries (1963) attempted to estimate populations of grey seals. Since then the Farne Islands population is known to have increased considerably and Mansfield (1965) has given an increased estimate of the western Atlantic or Canadian group. Table 19 has been revised with this new knowledge, but most of the provisos as to accuracy mentioned by Smith still apply. Of these figures, those for Ireland, Iceland, Faeroes, Norway and the Baltic are little more than guesses based on very meagre knowledge. Taken overall they are probably not far wrong, although the Baltic figure seems a high one. Most of the constituent figures for Scotland, England and Wales stem from counts of pups and to that extent have a numerical basis, but the accuracy of these varies from rookery to rookery, depending on accessibility. The Canadian figures are probably of a similar degree of accuracy as regards counts, but the multiplication factor has a slightly less firm basis. A round figure of 50,000 for a world population is probably of the right order, although arguments could be made for anything between 40,000 and 60,000. On present knowledge about four-fifths of these are round the British Isles, although this proportion must remain dubious since the odd one-fifth elsewhere contains the Baltic population about which so little is known.

For some reason which is not at all clear the grey seal is often referred to as 'the rarest seal in the world'. This phrase first occurs on page 217 of the 'Natural History in the Highlands and Islands' 1947 First Ed. by F. Fraser Darling and I suspect he has regretted it ever since. To start with, it presupposes that the numbers of the other species of seal are known to the same degree of accuracy (or inaccuracy) and this is of course quite untrue. But there are certainly two other seal species which readily qualify for this description: the Mediterranean monk seal (1,000–5,000) and the Hawaian monk seal (1,000–1,500), while the northern elephant seal has a population of only 8,000–10,000, and Ross seal and the Ribbon seal with populations of 20,000–50,000 would come into the same category as the grey seal. However, more recent estimates than Scheffer's suggest that Ross seals may number about 100,000 and the Ribbon seal numbers are more than 50,000. Several sub-species of seal such as the freshwater common seals of Seal Lakes in Northern Labrador (*P.v. mellonae*) and the freshwater ringed seals of Lakes Ladoga and Saimaa in Finland also fall in the 'less than 10,000' group.* These figures are given by Scheffer (1958) who quotes 25,000–50,000 for the grey seal. We may safely say, therefore, that the grey seal is among the rarer species of true seals, if we take 50,000 as the top limit of these, leaving 180,000–5,000,000 as the range of the upper category. If the three groups, western Atlantic, eastern Atlantic and Baltic are considered as sub-species then it is the western Atlantic and Baltic which may be thought of as very rare and the eastern Atlantic, centred on Great Britain, as the most flourishing with records of increasing numbers over recent years at least in Pembrokeshire and the Farne Islands. It is just as well to get the picture in perspective and as factually-based as possible.

Reference has been made to 'density-dependent' factors controlling the

---

* *P. v. kurilensis* is regarded by Scheffer as part of the *P. v. largha* sub-species but other workers have regarded it as a separate species with probably only a few hundred still living. (But see comments on pupping dates on p. 177, Chapter 12.)

Table 19. Grey Seal Populations

North-East Atlantic			
Orkney (counts)	10,500		
Shetland (partly counts)	3,000		
North Rona (counts)	9,000		
Hebrides (partly counts)	7,000*		
Total for Scotland		29,500	59.2%
Farne Islands (counts)	6,300		
Pembrokeshire (partly counts)	1,400		
Cornwall & Scilly Islands (estimate)	500		
Ireland (rough estimate)	1,000		
Total for England, Wales and Ireland		9,200	18.5%
Iceland & Faeroes (rough estimate)	3,000		
Norway (rough estimate)	100	3,100	6.2%
Total North-East Atlantic		41,800	83.9%
Baltic			
Baltic (very rough estimate)		5,000	10.0%
N.W. Atlantic			
Canadian Mari. Prov. (partly counts)		3,000*	6.0%
Total all areas		49,800	99.9%

absolute size of the population. At one time (in the late 1950's) it was thought that these might operate in the Farne Islands and stabilise the population at an acceptable level but unfortunately this has not taken place. Part of the explanation may be that newer rookeries have been established. Nevertheless the density on the older sites has increased and some interesting effects of over-crowding have appeared. One of these, a shift in the mean date of pupping, has been dealt with in Chapter 7, but the other, an increase in the aggressiveness of cows, may be considered now. A certain proportion of cows are always to be found who will refuse to leave their pups when observers

* Both these figures are now subject to revision (1972). Aerial counts by W. Vaughan in 1970 for the Hebrides amount to 2,893 (estimated annual pup production 3,300) giving an estimated total population of 11,550. This is undoubtedly partly due to a real increase.

Mansfield has further revised the Canadian figures dramatically to 17,000 on grounds of improved methods of estimation and more complete counts.

These two examples emphasise the dubious validity of 'rough estimates'.

invade the rookery, but this is usually small and this aggressiveness was taken to be due to individual variation in the intensity of maternal care. Even when, on visiting North Rona in 1959, we found a much higher proportion of 'intransigent' cows we did not attribute this to overcrowding. The evidence from the Farne Islands is however conclusive as the proportion of these cows has increased steadily with the overcrowding. It cannot be attributed to continued human interference because this is the one thing from which the North Rona population had been free in 1959 for twenty years. In fact, we did think it possible that the aggressiveness was due to a *lack* of contact with man. Just what effect this prevalence of aggression will have on a population is not clear but is certainly the most obvious effect of increasing density of cows and pups in the rookery.

A last word on the subject of population may now be said regarding the separateness of the different 'groups' of grey seals around Britain, or perhaps even of the various rookeries. First of all what positive evidence have we one way or the other? On the side of free interchange of populations there is clear evidence of its possibility in the very considerable overlap of dispersal areas from the various rookeries and groups. Although this can be demonstrated only for yearling grey seals, if we are correct in believing that the older and mature seals have an oceanic phase it must equally apply there. Against this must be set certain features peculiar to rookeries and groups which it is difficult to imagine persisting if free interchange occurred on a large scale. Two such features are behavioural; the first is the peculiar 'roll' of territory possession seen so frequently on Shillay and rarely elsewhere and secondly the social set-up of bulls and cows which differs so widely in different groups. Could a bull which normally took up his territory at sea change into a land-based animal as would have to take place if there were free interchange between Inner and Outer Hebridean groups? Between these two groups there is also a difference in pupping technique, the cows and pups always remaining on the small beaches in the Inner Hebrides while in the Outer full use is made of the grass-covered interior. The differences in mean pupping dates might also be considered a barrier to free interchange. However there are considerable periods of overlap between adjacent groups. Even between the Farne Island group and the Orcadian and Shetland this is true. Pups *are* born in Orkney in December though infrequently. Are they instances of Farne Island cows joining the declining rookeries of Orkney? Finally there is the very strong impression that at least the older bulls have 'been there before'. This might also be said to apply to cows such as those who make the laborious ascent to the Saddle on North Rona. How else can they know that conditions exist there for pupping and mating? To some extent this is the most important evidence of all for it implies that these cows were probably born there. Some observers have stated that they were convinced that they had seen cows pup on almost the same spot in consecutive years. This should be possible to prove since the markings on the cows is quite individual so that they are naturally marked. This would be a nice piece of work for anyone prepared to make right and left sketches of the markings, and the patience to record over a number of years the exact position of these known individuals if they reappeared.

On the whole I am of the opinion that the populations of the separate groups are, generally speaking, distinct although very occasionally there may be interchange. I also think that, in the absence of interference and disturbance, the same may apply to the rookeries, although interchange may be more frequent, particularly if the sites are adjacent, e.g. Staple Island and Brownsman in the Farne Islands.

CHAPTER 11

THE COMMON SEAL – INTRODUCTORY

WE now come to the second resident species, the common seal (*Phoca vitulina*). Despite its English name it is probably not commoner than the grey, except on the east coasts. Its American name of harbor seal is really more appropriate for it is an inshore seal through most of the year, if not always. On the west coast of Scotland, Darling calls it 'a seal of the sea-lochs' rather than of the open sea. Its fondness for sandbanks in the Wash must not prevent us recognising that it will haul-out just as well on rocky slabs in Orkney, Shetland and elsewhere.

It has been used as the typical member of the family and sub-family even though for many years the genus *Phoca* included most species of the sub-family now separated as distinct genera. It is distributed throughout all the coastal waters of the north temperate oceans and seas and has penetrated into inland waters which are now fresh (Fig. 39). Although it is instantly recognisable wherever it is found in its wide range, there are minor differences which have led to the description of numerous sub-species. Scheffer, however, considers that only five of these can be justified, one each for the eastern and western coasts of the Atlantic and Pacific Oceans, and one for the clearly land-locked population of Seal Lakes in the Ungava peninsula of northern Labrador. Even so the stocks of the eastern and western Pacific meet in the Bering Sea and separation of individual specimens is not always easy or definite. However the habit of the species not to travel far from shore suggests that local races could arise more easily than in other species with more widely ranging individual animals. The five sub-species are:

P. vitulina vitulina of European waters, that is of the eastern Atlantic coast-line including the North and Baltic Seas. Although it penetrates as far north as the Murmansk coast it does not occur in the northern Baltic (Gulf of Bothnia) and its occurrence in the Bay of Biscay to the south is rare. Icelandic specimens are considered to belong to this sub-species.

P. v. concolor is the western Atlantic form with about the same range of latitude as on the eastern side, along the coasts of Greenland, Newfoundland and Nova Scotia, the New England States and penetrating into Hudson Bay.

P. v. richardi is the eastern and *P. v. largha* the western Pacific forms meeting in the Bering Sea. They both appear to penetrate farther south (to latitude 30° N.) than do the Atlantic forms. In the distributions mentioned it is commoner in the centre of the range where its typical and favoured habitats are found.

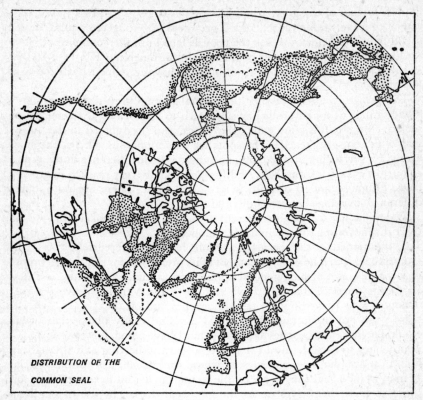

DISTRIBUTION OF THE
COMMON SEAL

FIG. 39. World distribution of the common seal. Although circumpolar in general terms their coastal habitat has allowed separation to occur sufficiently for some five sub-species to be recognised.

P. v. mellonae is confined to the Upper and Lower Seal Lakes of Ungava. *

A case could be made out for only three sub-species, Pacific, Atlantic and Ungavan. What is quite clear is that it is a circum-polar species, united in the last inter-glacial in one large population within the Arctic Circle, which has now suffered some degree of separation owing to the enlarged ice-cap (Fig. 8).

The common seal is a small seal with little difference in the maximum sizes of bull and cow. The adult male length is 5–6½ ft., the female 4½–5 ft. with a maximum weight around 250 lbs. Compared with the grey seal the common has a short head resulting in a more spherical vault to the skull. Both in profile and full-face the dorsal outline is rounded with no tendency to the

* Although this sub-species was accepted by Scheffer (probably on grounds of geographical isolation) Mansfield doubts its validity.

flatness typical of the grey. The nasal region is also shortened producing a rather concave profile more like the grey seal pup than the adult. Another useful field-character concerns the nostrils which, in the common, are set at a wider angle and the ventral points are almost touching (Fig. 11). All these features are visible when the head only is showing, which is all too usual (Pl. 23b).

The pelage is much browner than usual among grey seals. But there is a wide range of tone from yellowish-brown to almost black. In some parts, such as Orkney, it is often called the 'black' seal (as opposed to the 'brown' seals which are grey seals!). The spots are very numerous (Pl. 23) and small, rarely, if ever, fusing into patches, and there is little difference in the ground colour between back and belly, a difference usually very marked in grey seal cows, although not so obvious in grey seal bulls. There are no apparent differences in pelage between bulls and cows.

The molar teeth are quite different to those of the grey seal (Fig. 12) having three distinct cusps almost equally developed.

As mentioned for the species as a whole, it has a preference for coastal and estuarine waters. The usual statement of its preference for sandbanks exposed at low tide is not of such general application as many authorities maintain. In Orkney and Shetland, I have seen, and the Venables have recorded, common seals hauled-out on pebble beaches and on rocky slabs. Indeed if these were not acceptable they would not find many places there which would be, for sandy beaches are rare. What I have noted, however, is that the approaches to these haul-out sites are all gently shelving and they are not found on boulder strewn shores or where the ascent is steep and difficult. It may well be that they are less able to use the digital flexure of their fore-limbs to haul themselves up as the grey seal does. The use of sandbanks would, therefore, be the local expression of their inshore, shallow water, habitat preference. Where only rocks are available rocks have to be used and it is perhaps significant that they often take up a hauled-out position *before* the rock is uncovered and remain there until they are floated off by the rising tide. In Orkney and Shetland I have seen them on many occasions lying in the hauled-out posture apparently in the sea. A quarter of an hour later and they are seen to be on the top of rocky slabs, well above sea-level. This behaviour can also be seen on sandbanks in the Wash. Certainly in the Northern Isles common seals accept much more exposed and rocky situations than they do elsewhere in Britain.

The common seal is fairly generally distributed round the coasts of Great Britain, except for regions where there are extensive cliffs (Figs. 40 and 41). It is undoubtedly commoner on the east coast of England and Scotland, but there are parts of the west where it can be found in some numbers, particularly among the sea-lochs of north-west Scotland. In Ireland it is known to occur in Strangford Lough and Dundrum Bay, but elsewhere there is insufficient evidence as to either its occurrence or abundance. Eire maintains a bounty for common seals as a measure of protection for the salmon fisheries of the west coast and the number of claims is fairly constant, so that there is probably a reasonable population there, using the bays and sea-lochs as in the west of Scotland. It does not appear off the Cornish and Devon coasts but the

Common Seal
Recorded Sightings

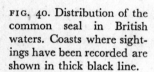

FIG. 40. Distribution of the common seal in British waters. Coasts where sightings have been recorded are shown in thick black line.

occasional report of common seals in the Solent area suggests that there may be a Channel population probably connected with the East Anglian area. Personally I am inclined to think that these are accidental wanderers from the North Sea. Specimens are frequently found in the Thames Estuary and every few years or so one makes its way up the river as far as London. On the other side of the North Sea the whole coast-line from Belgium round to Denmark is admirably suited to its requirements and there existed a large population whose pups were culled commercially each year. There is now no culling permitted in Holland, the local population now being estimated at around 700 only. So far there is no evidence that the Dutch and Wash population mix or come into contact with each other. Orkney and Shetland each have considerable numbers, although recently the Shetland population appears to have declined abruptly, probably as the result of the shooting of adults as well as of pups when the price for pelts rose considerably in the 1960's. The Fair Isle population seems to have disappeared and it is perhaps a mark of the local nature of populations that it has not been re-established from either Orkney to the south or Shetland to the north, each distant only about 25 miles.

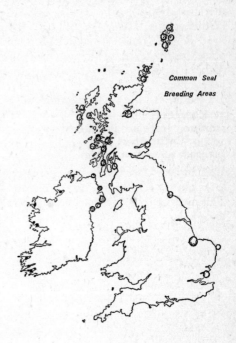

Common Seal Breeding Areas

FIG. 41. Distribution of common seals in British waters. The areas where breeding is known to occur are shown by black circles. On the Irish coast the exact localities are not known but possible sites are indicated by black spots. The size of the circle is not indicative of the numbers of seals involved in breeding.

The yearly cycle of the common seal is comparatively simple or so it would appear at our present state of knowledge. Certainly there is one complication missing compared to the grey, and that is the territorially dominated rookeries on land or shore-line. Perhaps associated with this is the separation of pupping and mating times. Pupping takes place in summer beginning in the latter half of May, through June and the first half of July with slight variations due to latitude. For any given locality the period is quite short: about a fortnight. Suckling of the young continues for about 4 to 6 weeks, that is until August. It is generally believed that moulting then follows and precedes mating which takes place in September. The information is however rather scant and different stories have been told from different parts of the species' world-range. In Britain we have been sadly remiss until recently in attempting to unravel the yearly cycle of this seal. It was not until 1955–56 that Mr and Mrs Venables made observations of a breeding area in Shetland and described the mating behaviour which takes place in the second half of September and which definitely resulted in coition. They had previously described pupping (and some peculiar play 'in pairs' which precedes it in May) which for Shetland is from 14th June to 5th July approximately, and later (1959) elaborated on the vernal mating behaviour. The picture is, therefore, by no means clear even now. Suspended development occurs also in this species, as first shown by Mansfield in Canada, and, according to Prof. R. J. Harrison, renewed development followed by attachment takes place 'before January, but after 1st November'. Active gestation is, therefore, of the order of 7 months with, again very approximately, $2\frac{1}{2}$ months' suspended development.

Feeding is, of course, possible all the year round because there is no attachment to a land-based rookery, but it may be restricted during suckling, moulting and mating. There is no published evidence.

The pup is born already moulted into a dark coat, the white 'puppy' coat having been shed *in utero*. Occasionally pups are found with white coats which are said to be soon shed. The new-born pup has very large hind flippers and looks quite out of proportion to anyone accustomed to other phocid species. This must be considered an adaptation to the aquatic life of the pup, who has to be able to swim actively within a few hours of birth.

CHAPTER 12

THE COMMON SEAL – REPRODUCTION, PUP, MOULTING, FOOD AND NUMBERS

THE common seal is a contrast in almost all respects of behaviour with the grey seal and certainly not least in its reproductive pattern. While the grey seal comes ashore and remains there (more or less) for several weeks (cows) or months (bulls) the common seal remains in the sea, only touching land momentarily for the actual birth, and, of course, for the usual low-water haul-outs.

Only within the past twenty years or so have observations been made on the various phases of reproduction in the four sub-species. Unfortunately the different observers do not agree, particularly on the times of year at which these phases occur. There does not seem to be, at present, any simple solution and comparisons between the results will be postponed until we have surveyed all the phases – mating, gestation, parturition – with the phenomenon of moulting which has to be fitted into the cycle somewhere.

Mating, with which the cycle naturally starts, invariably takes place in the water, probably in the autumn. The Venables have given an excellent account of the proceedings as observed in Shetland; one of the best places in which to make observations. The cliffs, with which the bays are surrounded, allow one to see what is happening in the water. At sea-level, as in the Wash and on the Dutch coast, it is impossible to observe anything that happens below the surface, not only because of the low elevation but also because the water is murky.

In Shetland the last week of August sees aggregations of common seals in certain sheltered bays. These, according to the Venables, are not those used for haul-outs at other times of the year. When the waters of these bays are calm the seals can be seen rolling over and over, sometimes two (a bull and a cow) taking part together in 'aquabatics'. This activity is, however, subdued compared to what follows.

In the first week of September (3rd–4th September) the rolling in pairs becomes intensified, the two seals becoming almost interlocked in their gyrations, hind flippers follow fore flippers and heads in rapid succession; backs and undersides are visible in such rapid sequence that it is sometimes difficult to know whether there are two or three animals involved. Accompanying this rolling there is considerable splashing, one feature of which is very peculiar. From time to time the bull brings a fore flipper down on to the surface of the water flat to produce a real crack which echoes round the bay. Although the common seal is normally a very silent seal, particularly when compared with the grey, it is at this time that snarls and yelps are emitted, the most common being a deep 'woof' very like the tentative bark of a dog. Male and female often swim parallel to each other (not unknown in the grey) but the male on his own indulges in long runs at great speed emerging from the sea in 'salmon leaps' at intervals (Pl. 24). I have seen one run that included five such leaps but two or three are the more usual number. The Venables have seen one run with 38 leaps (pers. communication). The seal comes completely clear of the water, the points of exit and entry may be as much as ten feet apart, and the top of the arched back a good five feet above the surface. This 'salmon leaping' can be seen at other times of the year when the seals become excited by something but are a constant and very dramatic feature of the pre-mating behaviour. The noises of splashing and leaping, snarling and yelping are further added to by 'bubbling'. As we have seen earlier, seals empty their lungs when submerging and with the intense activity of the aquabatics they frequently dive before exhaling, which they complete below water, fountains of bubbles rising to the surface. This seems to be a definite part of courtship.

Coition was first seen by the Venables on 7th September and continued off and on until 9th October. There are thus probably about five weeks during which mating takes place. The male mounts the female at the surface and both sink to the bottom for a few minutes. They then float to the surface and separate. There is a post-coitional period of rest before mating is resumed without a change of partners. In any bay there are numerous bulls and cows and no sign of territorial possession has been observed. However, it cannot be stated definitely that the common seal is monogamous. This would imply that one bull mates with one cow only and *vice versa*, but very careful observation would be necessary to prove this even for one day. Random and continuous promiscuity however is not seen so that if monogamy is not the invariable rule, bulls probably mate with only a few cows and cows only with a few bulls, since more than one copulation appears to be favoured.

Sheltered water is usually selected for mating in Shetland and as storms are not infrequent at that time of year, quite small inlets or parts of bays may be used on some days when sheltered, and not on others when open to swell and wind. R. J. Harrison (pers. communication), who has collected considerable numbers of common seals in the Wash, suggests that coition may take place from July through to September, while Havinga reports August to September for Dutch waters. These observations are all on the sub-species *P. v. vitulina*. Even more variation would appear to occur if other sub-species are considered as well. For *P. v. concolor* off the Nova Scotia and New Brunswick coast of the western north Atlantic, Fisher gives June and early July. For the eastern Pacific form *P. v. richardi* there are three sets of observations; Imber and Sarber give 'the autumn' for the Alaskan coast, Fisher gives September to October for British Columbia and Scheffer and Slipp record

September for Washington State. Finally Sleptzov gives June to July for *P. v. largha* in the Sea of Okhotsk in the western Pacific.

The variations may be more apparent than real for the following reason: the Venables have reported mating behaviour even leading to pseudo-coition *before* pupping in June. This they have termed 'vernal coition'. While similar to the performances before true mating, it is usually more subdued. It appears to be an exhibition of eroticism which is not unknown in other seals as we have seen for the grey seal. Thus it is possible that the earlier June and July dates given by other observers elsewhere may in fact be the vernal and not the true coition. To this may be added slight variation in the dates of the pupping season which could well result in the true mating season being brought forward to August.

However, as with pupping, the adult moult and mating seem to be closely linked in time sequence, it may be that different sub-species show different time relationships. Not until full observations are available for the period from May to October in all sub-species will this part of the puzzle be completely resolved.

Delayed implantation occurs in the common seal as well as in the grey. Here again there are problems of dates. Fisher, who first recorded delay in the common seal, states that implantation occurs in September for *P. v. concolor*. Harrison, who has made an extensive investigation in *P. v. vitulina* from the Wash is not prepared to go farther than to suggest that implantation takes place *before* January, but *after* 1st November. He has found young *corpora lutea* not only in September and October, which fits in with a mating period of August to September, but also in May and has had a spontaneous ovulation in a captive female in August. If we go on to Sleptzov's observations on *P. v. largha* in the Sea of Okhotsk, the picture becomes more confused still. He maintains that mating takes place at the end of June, through July and into the first half of August. Meanwhile, from cows, he obtained a number of early embryos from blastocyst onwards and believes that there is no suspended development but that gestation runs for about $8\frac{1}{2}$ months as, from the literature he quotes, pupping in that region takes place in March and April and in Tartor Bay even in February. This view is confirmed to some extent by Chapsky who 'factually' determined the length of pregnancy as 9 months in the Korsk area. He does not explain what 'factually' means!

The pupping season for British *P. v. vitulina* appear to be the four weeks from approximately mid-June to mid-July. Venables and Venables give 14th June for the first Shetland pup and the end of May for Northern Ireland. Harrison has recorded a first pup on 4th June in the Wash but Sergeant gives 17th June, and Havinga, 14th June for Dutch waters. Until birth rate curves exist for each locality no true comparison between different areas can be made. As with the grey seal 'early' pups occur as well as 'late' ones and isolated records do not really mean much. There seems, however, to be little doubt that the dates given by Fisher for *P. v. concolor*, which are nearly a month earlier, represent a real difference. Recently Boulva gives late May with a thirty-one day spread for Sable Island which agrees well enough. Similarly the dates of Scheffer and Slipp for *P. v. richardi*, all May and June, fit into the cline found by Bigg, which shows a span from March to July along the west coast of North America. Sleptzov, for *P. v. largha*, gives March and April and Naito records the latter half of March which would tie in with the Bering Sea *P. v. richardi*. However *P. v. kurilensis* pups in the latter half of May which presents a problem if it is only a sub-species of *P. vitulina*.

To sum up is rather difficult. A summary of the information available is set out in Table 20. There is little doubt about the pupping dates as these can be easily observed. Consequently the comparative lateness of *vitulina* and earliness of *largha* must be accepted as indicative that the cycles of the different sub-species have different terminal dates. If the mating dates are taken as the starting dates however, the sub-species do not fall into the same order. Moreover in *vitulina* and *concolor* 'delayed implantation' has been proved beyond doubt but the early date of mating in *concolor* proves an obstacle and results in very different periods of total gestation although the periods of active gestation (7 and 8 months respectively) are not too dissimilar. Again the similarity of the gestation periods of *richardi* and *largha* with the others' active gestation periods is misleading because they are based on mating dates and if 'delayed implantation' were eventually shown to occur, they would be very different. Unfortunately only in *richardi* is the period of spermatogenesis known and here it points to a correctness of the mating time. Another missing factor is the absence of moulting dates for *richardi* and *concolor*. There is time for moult between pupping and mating in *richardi*, to conform with the sequence of *vitulina* and *largha*, but not in *concolor*.

(In the Table gestation has been counted from the *mean* dates of mating and implantation to the *mean* dates of parturition. Not all of the authors quoted have done this.)

Parturition is stated by the Venables to be usually just above the water level on gently sloping rock or sandbank, sometimes in the shallow water alongside. The newly born pup is closely guarded by the cow, whether on land or in the sea. The pup has notably large hind flippers which appear to hinder active movement on land, although they assist swimming in the sea, in which they tend to spend more time, floating alongside the mother.

The common seal pup is already moulted at birth into its first grey coat. The initial white coat grown on the foetus is shed *in utero*, towards the end of pregnancy and can be found in the amniotic fluid surrounding the full-term foetus and also in the alimentary canal of the pup. The first faeces always consist of a mat of creamy white 'puppy' fur. Just when this moult takes place is uncertain but it is probably very near to full-term. It is said that some pups are born still in their white coats, almost suggesting that it is touch and go whether they moult before or after birth. White common seal pups do occur, but certainly not nearly as frequently as this suggests. I have asked seal

Table 20. Reproduction in the Common Seal

Author & Sub-Species		D J F M A M J J A S O N D J	Unknown	Length of Gestation
Venables and/or Harrison *P.v. vitulina*	Spermatogenesis Pupping Moult Mating 'Implantation' Gestation		?	9/6 months
Fisher (1954) *P.v. concolor*	Spermatogenesis Pupping Moult Mating 'Implantation' Gestation		? ?	11/8 months
Scheffer and Slipp et aliis (1944–52) *P.v. richardi*	Spermatogenesis Pupping Moult Mating 'Implantation' Gestation		? ?	8 months
Sleptzov (1943) (Chapsky) *P.v. largho*	Spermatogenesis Pupping Moult Mating 'Implantation' Gestation		?	8½ months

hunters how many white pups they have seen and replies indicate that one in a thousand or so would be an over-estimate. One or two of long experience have never seen such a pup at all. Pale, almost white, adults also occur very rarely and while it is possible that some white pups recorded are the young stages of these, there are clear differences to the expert.

The new-born pup must be regarded as a very well developed youngster with large hind quarters, in proportion to the rest of the body, and capable of maintaining itself in the sea. Its size also points to its advanced state. An average length of 33.74 inches is given by the Venables for eleven pups, with weights between 20–25 lbs., measurements very nearly as great as that of the grey seal. Also like the grey seal the milk dentition has already gone and the permanent teeth begin to erupt within the first few days.

Suckling at first takes place in the sea, probably because the pup is so clumsy on land. However the rich milk, as rich as that of the grey seal, soon fills out the pup and its hind-limbs become stronger. After these first two or three days the pup can not only swim and dive quite well, but it can clamber ashore at low water or on an ebbing tide where it will be seen alongside the mother. The attachment of mother and pup appears to be more noticeable in the common seal than in the grey, although in the latter's truly land-based rookeries like Gaskeir and North Rona, there is an approach to the common seal situation. By three weeks the common seal pups have developed considerable ability in the sea. Their aquatic behaviour in fact closely resembles that of the adult as they can float vertically as well as horizontally and the sculling action of the hind flippers becomes more controlled while the paddling action of the fore flippers becomes more limited. I have seen the same progress in the grey seal pups on the more aquatic rookeries of Ramsey Island. At four weeks the pup is well covered in blubber and the teeth have all erupted; lactation appears to cease at this point and the pup begins its independent existence. There is a suggestion, however, that the mother–pup bond may continue for a week or two more. It is not known whether they continue to associate with the mothers or not. That they do is possible for two reasons. In the grey seal the break in mother–pup relations at the end of lactation is reinforced by a moult on the part of the pup and by the onset of oestrus, leading to mating, on the part of the mother. Neither of these occur in the common seal. Nevertheless the Venables record that the mothers do tend to reject the pups at this stage. Suckling a pup with erupted teeth could be painful. The weight has trebled (60–70 lb.) but after weaning a decrease takes place, as in the grey, until the young seal can catch sufficient food on its own.

Exact information about the moult of the adults is not yet available. Certainly both bulls and cows undergo this process after the pupping period in July, through August and into the first week in September. It is suggested by the Venables that the bulls may be the first to moult, the lactation period of the cows delaying its onset in the female. During the moult the common seal, like the grey, tends to haul-out more than usual; more are to be seen on the rocks or sandbanks and fewer disporting in the water.

Nothing is known about dispersal movements of either the young or old based on tagging experiments. From general observations it seems unlikely that there are very considerable movements. Certainly between the onset of pupping in mid-June until the end of mating in early October, the adults appear tied to the breeding areas. The common seal is predominantly an inshore and estuarine animal and does not seem to 'go to sea' to any great extent. As mentioned in the previous chapter, the Fair Isle population does not seem to have been replaced from Orkney or Shetland. There are few even approximate counts of numbers but so far no one has noticed any marked fluctuations according to seasons, like those of the grey seal, which should be fairly obvious if a general dispersal took place after mating in the autumn. As the Venables have said, common seals are 'herders' rather than 'roamers'.

Turning now to the food of the common seal, we find that a great variety of fish and other marine life has been recorded from the stomachs. There has been the same difficulty in obtaining much material as in the grey seal and for the same reasons. However, the following species of fish have been listed: saithe and salmon in the North; in the Wash area herring, flounder, whiting, skate, mackerel, sea-trout, hake, cod and eel; shellfish such as whelks, cockles, mussels, squid, octopus and crustacea such as crabs and prawns. So wide is the diet that one must regard the common seal as an opportunist which will take whatever is available, probably in proportion to its abundance. The pups are said to take shrimps and other small crustacea such as shore crabs for several months after weaning, probably as being easier to catch and the proportion of fish increases with age. From experience with common seals in captivity Prof. Harrison reckons that they need about 10 lbs. of fresh fish daily. His experiments on these captive seals has thrown considerable light on the senses of seals, particularly those necessary for the capture of food. He finds that the brain is well equipped to receive visual, auditory, gravitational and contact stimuli. The sense of smell and taste are not apparently well developed. They can detect salt and apparently prefer to drink salt water rather than fresh.* Their eyes are particularly well adapted for night vision or in muddy water being much more efficient at short distances. They can have an acute appreciation of their orientation even when asleep. He also found that the vibrissae are well innervated and are important sense organs of touch. Most of these senses and their level of development are to be found equally in other seals in all probability since they are adaptations to an aquatic mode of life.

Reference has already been made to the pre-pupping erotic behaviour observed by the Venables in their earlier work. Returning in 1958 for further

---

* Captive seals fed thawed frozen fish are almost always sodium deficient (J. Geraci). This might explain their preference for salt water.

PLATE 17. *above:* A newly born grey seal pup. The skin is loose and shows rolls along the body. These will disappear as blubber is deposited from the fat-rich milk of the cow. (September 1951.)

below: Erupting teeth in a grey seal pup. By the end of the first week the teeth are showing through the gums and can inflict severe wounds. (September 1951.)

PLATE 18. *above:* A grey seal cow identifies her own pup by smell, Ramsey Island. Having been in the water for some time, the cow comes ashore for the pup to suckle and it is necessary for her to find her own pup which may have moved from the place where she left it. 'Nosing' is always used for identification. (*Enlarged from 16 mm colour film.*) (September 1952.)

below: A grey seal cow shaking a pup, Shillay. Here scenting has shown the cow that this pup is not hers although close to it. She attacks it to drive it away from her 'territory' which surrounds her own pup. (*Enlarged from 16 mm colour film.*) (September 1955.)

work covering the period 23rd May to 10th June they were able to confirm and elaborate this. They believe they saw coition on six occasions and quite definitely once. The difficulty of being absolutely certain is because coition takes place under water, but the positioning of the pair, the immobility and general behaviour seemed to indicate a true coition. During this period they saw 'frequent outbursts of sex play' during which the penis was seen to be extruded by one of the pair in the course of the rolling behaviour. Comparing this with the autumn behaviour the Venables note that in the spring there is more sex play and less actual coition than in the later season. As the rolling behaviour could be displayed by one, two or three seals or even two pairs combining there would appear to be a distinct and possibly dominant element of play which however may have an erotic origin. The Venables observed that the cow 'almost always' prevented the bull from inserting his penis by arching her head and they concluded that these cows were not ready for mating, although the bulls might well be. It was further noticed that the full grown and pregnant cows did not take part in this play, nor were any 'yearlings' involved. The conclusion tentatively reached was that the cows involved in this play were virgin ones approaching their first oestrus. This would fit in with Harrison's observations of ovulation in May in a captive common seal. Moreover, the Venables thought that this age restriction also applied to the bulls and in this connection we might compare this method of covering the virgin cows in the common seal with what we suppose happens in the grey seal where again it is the mature, but younger (non-territorial) bulls who, by their behaviour of accosting cows without possessing territory, may be the means of bringing the virgin cows into pregnancy. It is also suggested for the common seal that if conception does take place in May–June the suspense period may be prolonged so that the recommencement and attachment of the embryo takes place normally in November–December. No other explanation could be possible with the pupping season so restricted to a couple of weeks.

Finally, on this subject, it should be remembered that even in the grey seal, where the pattern appears clear and precise for the majority of the British areas, the situation in Pembrokeshire, in the Baltic and in Canada present anomalies which still await resolution.

Before passing on to consider the size of populations and the trend in numbers, it must be emphasised that there is not yet any definite information regarding the age of sexual maturity in either male or female common seals. The suggestion has been made by Sleptzov that maturity is at $2\frac{1}{2}$–3 years. This is symptomatic of the lack of precise knowledge. Maturity as such can only be demonstrated at the breeding season and, therefore, it is only possible to describe the age of maturity in units of a year; a half year is quite meaningless.

The absence of rookeries prevents the comparatively easy counting of pups and the relation of this to the total population. In fact no method other than the direct counting of seals in haul-outs at low water has been used so far. The accuracy of such counts, as estimates of numbers in a given area, depend largely on the speed with which they can be done. If more than one day is involved there can be no guarantee that individuals are not counted twice having moved during the interval into the area counted on later days or vice-versa. For this reason alone aerial survey is imperative and for the low sandbanks and mudflats usually occupied as haul-outs the height thus gained is also almost equally essential (Pl. 24). More important, however, is the need to determine the *relevance* of the counts to the total population. This could be affected by a number of factors such as those found in the grey seal: season of the year, major activity such as pupping, moulting or mating, disturbance by man, sex and weather, conditions such as temperature, wind and rain. Only by long and continued observations taken all the year round, with records of all these factors (and perhaps more) will it be possible to use these counts entirely objectively. We have already seen in the grey seal the very serious errors (which have even led to legislation!) which can arise from 'spot' counts in both rookeries and fishing haul-outs. Meanwhile all figures must be regarded as tentative and must always carry provisos regarding the conditions prevailing at the time of the count. In our present state of knowledge it is very dangerous to draw conclusions from any comparative counts unless at least the major conditioning factors are strictly comparable. However, the *maximum counted* in any one area may be considered as the *minimum population*. There may be more uncounted, there cannot be fewer.

During the past few years Vaughan has made counts of common seals in the Wash. He divided the whole area of sandbanks into recognisable sections, so that it was possible to show the great variation in the choice of favoured haul-outs according to wind and tide etc. On several occasions conditions were generally unfavourable and comparatively small numbers were recorded. One feature was very clear and that was that there were no seasonal fluctuations such as those seen on West Hoyle Bank and the Farne Islands with grey seals. The totals recorded are shown in Table 20a. I have added the two bottom rows. These show that comparable averages can be obtained with only a few counts on favourable occasions and that the maxima recorded give no indication of a decreasing population. These maxima must be regarded as the *least* number of common seals.

He also made three counts over part of the Wash in December 1968, January and February 1969, Table 21b. These dates lie about 6 months after the pupping season of 1968 and show that an average of 12.5% of the population was composed of surviving yearlings, despite the commercial cull of pups. This does not answer the question whether such a survival rate is sufficient to maintain future populations although it disposes of extravagant claims that the year's pups had been 'practically' wiped out. Not until we have a life-table for common seals can we be sure that all is well. However

I have carried out a small exercise which may shed some light. If one assumes that the life-tables of grey and common seals are similar except that that of the common seal bulls is the same as that of the cows, because the sex-ratio is maintained equal throughout life (i.e. it is like the Canadian grey seals) and further take the mortality rate at the end of six months as 40% (which is about right for grey seals) then the expected percentage of yearlings would be 15.5. In a similar calculation for a *normal* grey seal situation with a reduced number of adult bulls it would of course be higher, about 18%. This cannot be tested owing to the wide dispersal of grey seal moulters in their first year. The lower figure however is not far removed from the observed in common seal and suggests that the cull at the present levels is not likely to lead to a sudden or catastrophic decline in the total population. We shall return to consider the ineffectiveness of pup culls in controlling breeding numbers in Chapter 14.

Table 21. Common Seals in the Wash

A

	1968	1969	1970
January	—	508	1464
February	472	1196	—
March	1534	—	—
April	1256	—	1077
May	887	—	—
June	783	1396	—
July	1145	1722	—
August	1468	1473	1662
September	1487	—	—
October	—	—	—
November	1121	—	—
December	1085	—	—
Average	1124	1259	1401
Maximum	1534	1722	1662

B

Date of Count	Total Seals	Yearlings	% age Yearlings
21.12.68	526	69	13.1
18.1.69	267	36	13.5
15.2.69	497	56	11.25
Totals	1290	161	12.50

Estimates of the world population have been given by Scheffer:

	min.	max.	
P. vitulina vitulina	40,000	100,000	
concolor	40,000	100,000	
mellonae	500	1,000	
richardi	50,000	200,000	
largha	20,000	50,000	
	150,500	451,000	1 : 3

In this country the common seal has long been killed for its potential damage to inshore fisheries, and more recently for its pelts, but it has proved very difficult to give firm estimates of the losses sustained. The work of the Seals Research Unit at Lowestoft is proving of great value by introducing new methods of counting. The rights and wrongs of the fisheries' case will be discussed in Chapter 14.

CHAPTER 13

OTHER SPECIES OF PINNIPEDE

To complete the survey of 'British' pinnipedes some reference must be made to four species of phocid, to the walrus and to the Californian sea-lion. The first five have been seen in British waters as naturally occurring stragglers or visitors. None of them breed here, nor do their normal distributions bring them very near to the British Isles. They are, in fact, truly 'arctic' species whose usual movements are confined north of latitude 60° N. except in the western Atlantic where arctic water flows south along the shores of Labrador, Newfoundland and Nova Scotia. Such as appear on our coasts are certainly not the relics of a recent native population, nor is there any likelihood of them becoming established in the warm waters of the temperate eastern Atlantic. The Californian sea-lions are escapes from coastal zoos and are at present in the North Sea.

Descriptions of these pinnipedes will now be given since it is as well to be able to distinguish them should a straggler be seen. As well as the accepted scientific name, others which have been used at one time or another are also included so that if they are come across in older books they will be understood. Pinnipede systematics and nomenclature have been cursed by a superfluity of names and descriptions, often based on quite inadequate material. Allen (1880, quoted in Scheffer 1958) said that in the Phocidae alone there were 'probably nearly four hundred [distinct names] or an average of at least twenty names to each species, with a maximum for some of the species of at least thirty'! Despite the enormous slaughter of almost all species of pinnipede for commercial ends, few of the museums of the world have sufficient material on which to base adequate descriptions of the species, when the variations due to sex and age (and pinnipedes are comparatively long lived) have to be taken into account. Fortunately these species about to be dealt with can be fairly safely separated from each other and from the two already described, by external features. It must be remembered however that the grey seal of British waters was thought to be the bearded seal until 1825.

RINGED SEAL   *Pusa hispida* (Schreber) 1775
                             Phoca hispida Schreber 1775 ⎫
                             Phoca foetida Fabricius 1776 ⎬Other names used
                             Phoca (Pusa) foetida Trouessart 1897 ⎭

This is a small seal, like the common, of about $4\frac{1}{2}$–$5\frac{1}{2}$ ft. in length and 200 lbs. in weight, in which male and female show little difference in size, although, again, the males attain the larger sizes (Fig. 42). In colouration too

the sexes are alike, blackish grey in new pelage tending to become brown in
the autumn. On the upper parts this background colour is dotted all over
with palish (yellowish-white) rings containing a dark centre. Sometimes the
rings may be so numerous as to touch and become confluent. Conversely

Ringed Seal

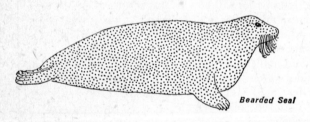

FIG. 42. Rare species of
Pinnipedia in British
waters – 1. ringed, harp
and bearded seals.

Harp Seal

Bearded Seal

along the mid-dorsal line the black centres may be so large as to obliterate or
obscure the paler rings and themselves become confluent. On the under parts
the darker ground colour shades off to a uniform yellowish white. Unfortunately the back of the head, which is the only 'upper part' frequently seen
above water, is without the distinctive rings, and may, therefore, be confused
with the common seal, unless observed when hauled-out. They too have the
rounded head and snub nose of *P. vitulina*. In the young or immatures the
colour differences are less distinct. The pups are white to yellow as in the grey
and they moult at four weeks. A feature only noticeable at close quarters is
that the bulls have a disagreeable odour from which the specific name of
'*foetida*' was derived by Fabricius.

The species is widely distributed around the Arctic and for that reason, and
possibly that reason alone, has been divided into six sub-species, in much the
same way as the common seal (Fig. 43). *P. hispida hispida* is the northern
Atlantic form which does not normally come south of a line from North Cape
(in Norway) to Jan Mayen (north of Iceland), south of Greenland to the

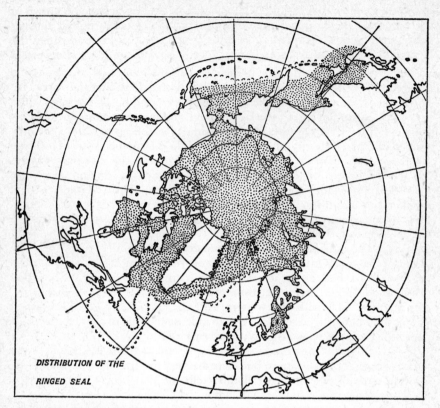

DISTRIBUTION OF THE
RINGED SEAL

FIG. 43. World distribution of ringed seal. A truly circumpolar arctic species.

southern tip of Labrador. *P.h. krascheninikovi* is the form found in the northern Bering Sea, rarely in the Pribilov Islands while *P.h. ochotensis* then takes over and extends westward down the coast of Siberia into the Sea of Okhotsk, southward as far as 35° N. on the Japanese coasts. The remaining three sub-species are all connected with the Baltic Sea, at least historically. *P.h. botnica* occurs in the Gulfs of Bothnia and Finland and as far south as the Pomeranian coast. *P.h. saimensis* and *P.h. ladogensis* are forms occurring in the freshwater lakes of Saimaa and Ladoga respectively.

Throughout its range it is not a seal of the open sea or moving pack ice. In the polar regions it is found in the open water *within* the fast ice and where there is land adjacent in the bays and fjords, as in the coasts of Greenland and Baffin Land. It does not appear to undergo any major seasonal movement and for this reason is rarely seen even in the most northern British waters. Only in the Baltic does it come south of 69° N. in the eastern Atlantic. This is probably for historical reasons, already referred to, having been cut off in the Ancylus Lake along with the grey and common seals after the last glacial period (Fig. 8).

The pups are born in late March to early April, are 25 ins. long and about 10 lbs. in weight. At this time of year the whole area of its distribution is covered in fast ice at least along the coasts and it is here that the young are born, usually in a hollow in the ice or snow covering it. The creamy white pup fur is shed after 2 or 3 weeks, although the mother continues to suckle the pup for nearly 2 months. Mating is similar in timing to that in the grey seal, taking place shortly after pupping, while the mother is still lactating. The main features of the reproductive biology of this seal have been worked out by MacLaren (1958) for the eastern Canadian Arctic and, of course, may not apply exactly to the Pacific or Baltic forms. 'Delayed implantation' occurs for $3\frac{1}{2}$ months so that development does not really begin until August. Cows become sexually mature when six years old although some ovulate too late to be mated the first year of maturity (cf. findings of bull grey seals on page 63). The bulls are not usually sexually mature until a year later. The moult of the adults takes place in June and July during which time they do not feed, but remain on the ice. No rookeries are formed during the breeding period and there is therefore an assumption of monogamy or near monogamy. This matches well with the western Atlantic and Baltic grey seals when noting that these ringed seals can live to at least 43 years of age (cf. grey seals page 66). Their main food is planktonic crustacea and small fish.

It is possibly the commonest seal of the Arctic and provides much of the basic economy of the Eskimos. But there are very few British records, most on the east coast of Scotland. Mr Bonner tells me that he has seen a skin in Shetland in 1970 and was told that another had been taken a few years earlier. No one has attempted to make an estimate of any real precision. Scheffer's 'guesstimate' runs as follows:

	Minimum		Maximum	
P.h. hispida	2,000,000	to	5,000,000	
P.h. ochotensis	200,000	to	500,000	
P.h. krascheninikovi	50,000	to	250,000	
P.h. botnica	10,000	to	50,000	
P.h. ladogensis	5,000	to	10,000	
P.h. saimensis	2,000	to	5,000	
	2,267,000	to	5,815,000	(1 : 2.6)

As he says 'the width of the gaps between minimum and maximum is an indication of the author's confidence in the estimate'! Even at the lower figure it still falls in the top class of pinnipeds as regards numbers. Among the phocids only the harp seal (the next to be described) and the crabeater seal of the Antarctic top the one million mark, and among the otariids only the northern fur-seal (carefully managed by the United States Fish and

PLATE 19. *above:* A grey seal pup suckling. The teats of the cow are normally sunk into pits, but the pup has just transferred to the left teat and the right one is still protruding.

below: A grey seal pup about 12–14 days old, Ghaoidemal, Inner Hebrides. By now well plumped out with blubber, Hebridean pups often splash about in rock pools rather than venture into the rough waters of the sea, as the Pembrokeshire ones do. (October 1956.)

PLATE 20. *above:* A grey seal pup towards the end of its third week, Scroby Sands. The moult has begun in the typical way on fore- and hind-limbs and on the head.
below: A grey seal bull moulter, Ramsey Island. The male pelage pattern is quite distinctive. (October 1959.)

Wildlife Service) comes into this category. Naumov (1933) says that 10,000 *P.h. hispida* are killed in northern Europe plus 50,000 of *P.h. ochotensis* in the Far East. These figures apply to pups and are probably now exceeded.

HARP (OR GREENLAND) SEAL   *Pagophilus groenlandicus* (Erxleben) 1777
                                       Phoca groenlandica Erxleben 1777
                                       Pagophilus g. Gray 1850

This is another smallish seal of about 5–6 ft. in length from head to tail in the bull and less than 5 ft. in the cow. It is unmistakable because of its colour pattern of contrasting yellowish white with dark bands (Fig. 42). The only other seal with such a bright and large pattern is the banded or ribbon seal of the north Pacific Ocean. The male harp seal is yellowish white as a ground colour with a black nose and front of the head, and with a black band running over the shoulders down and back along the sides and meeting again over the rump. Seen from the side the half of this black band, together with the silhouette of the back, is in the shape of a harp, whence its name is derived. The cow is grey along the back and pale yellow below with large dark spots along the line of the male black band. Its alternative name of Greenland seal is due to its use of the Greenland Sea as one of its breeding areas. It is a migratory seal of the open sea and pack ice, in the north Atlantic and Arctic Oceans with a range there almost identical with that of the ringed seal, except that it does not extend quite to the North Pole, nor much farther westward than North Baffin Land and the mouth of the Mackenzie River (Fig. 44). On the European side it only rarely comes south of 60° N. and consequently it has rarely been recorded as British other than in the Northern Isles of Shetland and Orkney. From this wide range the breeding stock collect in four zones in the early part of the year. These areas are:

1. off the north-east coast of Newfoundland
2. the Gulf of St Lawrence,
3. in the Greenland Sea between Iceland and Spitzbergen, off the east coast of Greenland and
4. in the White Sea.

It would be stragglers from this third group which *in summer* might be seen in the north of the British Isles. On an average there are only 1–2 records a decade in the last century, and fewer since.

During breeding in March the bulls stay in open pools near the ice flows on which the cows have pupped. The pups are suckled for about 2 weeks when they enter the water and presumably lose their white puppy coat. Commercially they are exploited at about 3–10 days old while the white fur is still firmly rooted. The cows moult about 4–5 weeks after pupping and mating presumably precedes this. Again commercial exploitation occurs particularly in the immatures in the moulting assemblies, for both oil (blubber) and pelt (as leather). According to the sealers this seal is sexually

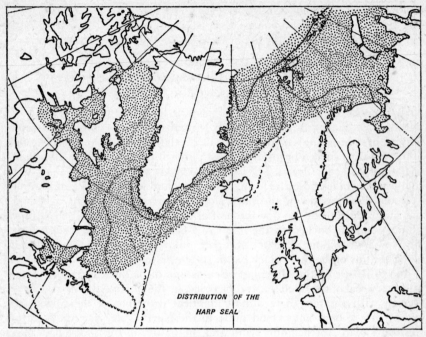

DISTRIBUTION OF THE

HARP SEAL

FIG. 44. World distribution of harp seal. An arctic species confined to the North Atlantic.

mature at the 5th year and this, plus or minus a year, may well be true. The food is said to be mainly fish but also crustaceans and molluscs are taken.

Scheffer has given estimates as follows:

	Minimum	Maximum
White Sea area	1,000,000	1,500,000
Iceland to Spitzbergen area	500,000	1,000,000
Newfoundland area	3,000,000	4,500,000
	4,500,000	7,000,000

The range of estimates (1 : 1.5) is the closest he makes for any species as these figures are based on fairly accurate counts. This seal has been under commercial pressure for many, many years but this has been intensified recently. Estimates of commercial culls are:

White Sea	320,000	Naumov 1933
Newfoundland	229,000	Fisher 1956
World kill	500,000	Bertram 1940

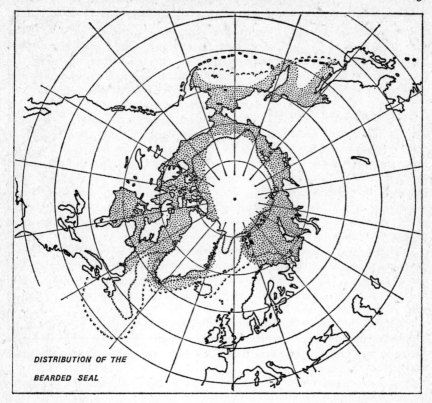

DISTRIBUTION OF THE
BEARDED SEAL

FIG. 45. World distribution of the bearded seal. An almost circumpolar species, not extending to the pole. Note how the distribution of the grey seal bridges the gap in the North Atlantic and thus led to confusion between the two species.

As there was clear evidence of over-exploitation in the two more eastern groups, the sealers have turned their attention to the Newfoundland area. Attempts to control the cull by the Canadian government has only met with partial success. *

BEARDED SEAL   *Erignathus barbatus* (Erxleben) 1777
              Phoca barbata Fabricius 1776

This is a large seal, comparable with the grey although its maximum sizes can exceed those of the grey (Fig. 42). The bulls reach 10–12 ft. and the cows

* The most recent estimate for the Newfoundland stock is only 1,255,000 with a total kill of 236,000.

may be over 7 ft. (usually reached by the grey cow). It is grey and dark coloured, sometimes with spots on the upper side, while on the under it is very pale grey. The similarity, even in the range of variability, to the colouring of the grey and its almost equal size led to confusion between the two species. The distinguishing external feature of the bearded seal is the presence of very long *curved* vibrissae which form a large brush around and below the muzzle. These large hairs are flattened in section.

Their distributions also led to the confusion between the grey seal and this species. The bearded seal is found at the edge of the ice along all the northern coasts of America and Asia as far as the North Cape in Norway (Fig. 45). From there across the north Atlantic to Iceland, and, of course, southward to the British Isles, the grey seal 'takes over' (Fig. 7). The distributions are, therefore, complementary. There does not seem to be any obvious seasonal movement as it appears resident along all the coastal shallow waters and even up estuaries. It also seems to be a solitary species, except during the breeding season when up to 50 have been reported on the ice in one group.

Little is known about the breeding cycle although it is clear that the main breeding is in the 'early' part of the year. Sleptzov gives February for the Sea of Okhotsk. The pups have a dark grey woolly fur which, after a few weeks, is moulted into a bluish grey coat. It is in this stage that the pelt is commercially valuable.

Owing to the ease of confusion with the grey it is usually stated that there is only one undoubted record for Britain, a young male in Norfolk in 1892. There is fossil evidence however that in the last glacial they were to be found in the North Sea area.

It is not a very numerous species, Scheffer giving estimates of 75,000 minimum to 150,000 maximum. There are no good figures for the annual cull, but as it is an important animal for the natives of the far north a total kill of 5,000–10,000 is likely.

HOODED SEAL   *Cystophora cristata* (Erxleben) 1777
                Cystophora borealis Nilsson 1820

This is the last of the phocids recorded for British waters and like the three preceding species is a seal of the Atlantic-Arctic. Another name for it is the bladdernose seal because its distinguishing characteristic is the muscular inflatable bag of skin on the nose of the adult male (Fig. 46). Until recently this has been taken to indicate a close relationship to the elephant seals and it has been placed in the same sub-family, as the northern representative of the antarctic and tropical elephant seals. King has however cast very strong doubts on this relationship, arguing that it is a case of superficial similarity (or 'convergence') and that it is more nearly related to the Phocinae. Certainly there are strong doubts that the hood is homologous with the 'proboscis' of the elephant seals.

The bulls attain a nose to tail length of 9–10 ft. weights over 800 lbs., while

PLATE 21. *above:* Two grey seal bulls meeting at the junction of their territories, North Rona. When territories are well established little fighting takes place, usually only a challenging hiss or snarl. (October 1959.)
below: Grey seal bull and cow in copulation, Farne Islands. In land-based rookeries copulation does not usually occur in water, unless there are deep rock pools.

PLATE 22. *above:* A grey seal cow branded as a moulter in 1960 reappears on Brownsman in the Farne Islands in 1966 when she is 6 years old and sexually mature.
below: A group of grey seals hauled-out on West Hoyle Bank, Wirral Peninsula, Cheshire. The numbers have increased over the past 15 years. (June 1971.)

the cows are slightly smaller. Their colour is greyish in general, lighter below, but consists of two colour tones, occurring in irregular splotches over the whole body, usually dark on light although in the bulls the dark spots may be numerous so that the lighter patches are isolated. (This is not unlike the grey seal.)

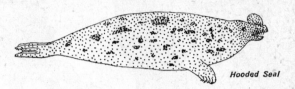

Hooded Seal

FIG. 46. Rare species of Pinnipedia in British waters – 2. hooded seal and walrus.

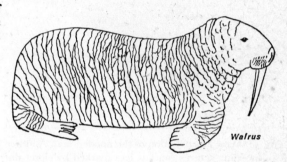

Walrus

Their distribution is even more restricted than that of the last species (Fig. 47). Again it is migratory (like the harp seal) with two breeding areas: 1. off Jan Mayen and 2. between Newfoundland and Greenland which are occupied in the early spring (February). There appears to be a complex series of movements which are not fully understood. Moulting concentrations appear in the Denmark Strait in June to July.

Breeding takes place on the ice floes. The pups have shed their puppy coat before birth, like the common seal pup, and appear in a silvery blue grey pelt which is much valued by the sealers. Pups are suckled for about 2 weeks and mating takes place at about the time of weaning. They appear to be monogamous as family groups of bull, cow and pup are seen during the breeding season.

Scheffer gives the following figures for world population:

minimum 300,000, maximum 500,000

King has estimated the annual catch as 75,000, but as this seal is hunted at the same time and over the same ice area as the harp it is not really possible to separate the returns accurately. It is stated that only about 55% of the take are pups and if this is so the population is being grossly over-exploited.

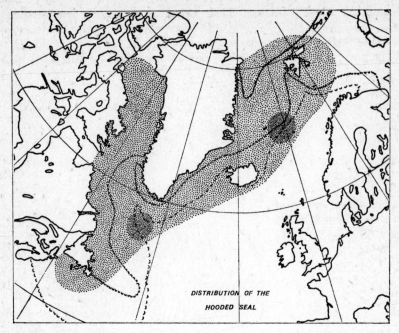

FIG. 47. World distribution of the hooded seal. Another North Atlantic species with two breeding centres (on floe ice) marked by closer dots.

It is unfortunate that so little is known of the biology of this species. There are few British records, most are from Scotland and all of young or adult males. Females would almost certainly have gone unnoticed because of their similarity to grey seals.

WALRUS   *Odobenus rosmarus* (L) 1758
          Phoca rosmarus Linnaeus 1758
          Trichechus rosmarus (Trouessart) 1897

The walrus is placed in a family of its own with two sub-species, the Atlantic and the Pacific. They are large and massive, the males attaining 15 ft., 10–12 ft. being quite usual; the females somewhat smaller at 9–11 ft. (Fig. 46). Their bulk can be judged by the 3,000 lbs. which a 12 ft. male would weigh. Their appearance is quite unmistakable with a thick wrinkled skin on which there are very short and sparse brown-grey hairs; the muzzle bears abundant curved vibrissae and is very broad, to accommodate the tusks which are present in both sexes, although not obvious in the young. These tusks are larger in the males, where they are used for fighting. Relative to the size of the rounded head the eyes are small and 'piggy'.

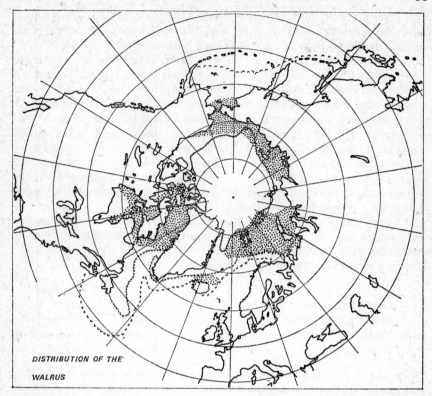

DISTRIBUTION OF THE
WALRUS

FIG. 48. World distribution of the walrus. A restricted and broken distribution probably induced by over-cropping for commercial ends.

It is another arctic species, confined to coastal waters, but there is a slight southward movement during winter. The distribution which is now patchy is shown in Fig. 48. The shallow water habitat is probably dictated by its feeding habits. The principal species preyed on are large bivalve molluscs. It has been stated that the huge tusks are used for grubbing up molluscs as well as in fighting. But it is difficult to see how the young, with very small tusks could do this effectively. Mansfield and Carlton Ray have pointed out that there is no sign of severe wear on the tusks and that the bivalves are sucked out of their shells by the surprisingly mobile lips, the vibrissae being used possibly for locating the prey. This specialised diet has affected the character of the molar teeth which are blunt-ended stubs, quite unlike those of any other pinnipede.

The pups are born in April to May, weighing about 100 lbs. Lactation

takes place for more than a year, somewhat exceptional in the pinnipedes.*
Even after weaning, the young stay with the mother and probably feed on
molluscs disturbed by her, since their own tusks are poorly developed (only
about 1 inch long by the end of the first year). Because of this prolonged
lactation, the females only breed once every two years. The males have the
usual annual cycle and mating takes place in April to May, with a gestation
period of almost a year, without 'delayed implantation', as evidenced by the
finding of embryos about an inch long in mid-June. Walruses appear to be
polygamous but there is no harem formation and perhaps 'promiscuous'
would better describe the sexual relationship. Throughout the year they are
very gregarious, occurring in herds. This may not be true for the young or
immature individuals because it is significant that all those seen on the
British coasts – Northern Isles and the north and west of Scotland – have been
young with a preponderance of males.

Although this species is arctic like the other phocids described and its
world population has been steadily declining, there have been numerous
records for British waters over the past 100 years, the last being in 1954.
Scheffer has estimated the numbers as follows:

	Minimum	Maximum
O. rosmarus rosmarus (Atlantic)	20,000	40,000
O. rosmarus divergens (Pacific)	25,000	50,000
	45,000	90,000

Considerable work has been done in recent years on the walrus, largely
because of its threatened status and revised figures are given as:

	Minimum	Maximum
O. rosmarus rosmarus (N.W. Atlantic)	10,000	20,000
(N.E. Atlantic)	1,000	5,000
O. rosmarus divergens (Pacific)	85,000	160,000
(Laptev)	4,000	4,000
	100,000	189,000

Unfortunately there are two products for which the walrus has been
commercially exploited: the tusks (ivory) and the skin. The latter is
extremely thick and tough, and has been in use for driving belts where
length is required. Consequently only adults are killed. This reduces the
breeding population and, as we have seen, the dependence of the young for
at least two years means that many such young deprived of its parent would
starve to death. Even now probably about 6,000–7,000 are killed every year,
the biggest drain being on the Siberian coasts where the walrus is an

* Lactation in some species of *Arctocephalus* lasts over a year.

important feature of the Eskimo economy. Scheffer regards the species as being insecure.

CALIFORNIAN SEA-LION   *Zalophus californianus* (Lesson) 1828
                        Otaria californianus (Lesson) 1828

It was mentioned at the beginning of this chapter that the presence of Californian sea-lions in British waters was unnatural and due to escapes from zoos. However, as this species represents the third family of pinnipedes and as it is only very recently that any account has been given of its biology and behaviour, something more than a passing reference may be of value, even though it is unlikely that it will ever become a breeding species here; both the individuals known to have escaped are females.

It is, of course, the well known circus and zoo 'seal', easily recognised here because all the other members of the family occur in the Antarctic or Pacific Oceans, and its distinguishing field characters are familial rather than specific. These are:

1. the presence of elongate external ears,
2. the large size of the fore flippers which, on land, are used to support the forepart of the body in a semi-erect posture,
3. the turning forward of the hind-limbs in a more normal foot position,
4. the eminence of the 'hip' which, again on land, produces a distinct hump or kink in the dorsal silhouette,
5. the presence of an undercoat of fur, not, however, so thick as in the fur-seals,
6. the testes are contained in a scrotal sac, just in front of the tail,
7. the nails on the fore flippers are vestigial.

Most of these characters are visible in the drawing in Fig. 1.

The Californian sea-lion is a medium-sized pinnipede, the bull being about 6½–8 ft. and weighing 4–6 cwt., while the much smaller female is only 5–6½ ft. and weighs 1–2 cwt. Much of the additional weight in the bulls lies in the massive shoulder and neck region. There are three separate natural populations now, one off the Californian coast, one around the Galapagos Islands and one in the Sea of Japan. Very little difference can be detected between them. It is the Californian group which has been recently studied in detail by Peterson and Bartholomew and these workers have shown that the cows and young tend to remain the year round near the breeding rookeries, but that the bulls tend to move farther northward. Their principal food is squid and cuttlefish, but fish are taken in nature (as well as in zoos!).

Breeding takes place in June and July when the cows gather to pup along the coast-line, forming dense rookeries. The bulls maintain a line of territories in the seaward side, but these are held only for about two weeks at the most, so that there is a succession of males. As in the grey seal, the females pay no attention to the territories of the bulls, i.e. there are no harems. Again like the grey seal, the females are aggressive after their pups are born and seem to become almost territorial. Mating takes place about 2 weeks after parturition, apparently only once and it may take place on land or in the sea. At about this time the pups tend to collect in pods of their own. Suckling procedure and duration are very different to anything so far described in this book. Only during the first two or three weeks will a pup suckle on more than one occasion during a day, usually there is only one period and later on the intervals may be prolonged so that in one *week* there may be only one such period. The suckling periods are, however, long when compared to those of the grey seal. Peterson and Bartholomew give 33 minutes as the mean with 48 minutes as the maximum observed. Suckling at infrequent and irregular times continues *through the first year of life*, the pup continuing to associate with the mother. No cow was ever observed to suckle any pup other than her own. While in the later stages there is mutual recognition, during the first couple of months or so it is the mother who identifies her pup partly by vocalisation and partly by smell.

Scheffer gives the following estimates for world population:

	Minimum	Maximum
Zalophus californianus californianus	50,000	100,000
Zalophus californianus japonicus	200	500
Zalophus californianus wollebaeki	20,000	50,000
	70,200	150,500

Peterson and Bartholomew do not make any such estimates and their observations on San Nicholas Island, California, show considerable changes in numbers even in the breeding season and these are accentuated in the non-breeding season. As in the grey seal, at no time and at no place are all categories of the population gathered together to present a reasonable sample. Counts on land, therefore, can be thoroughly misleading, as they have been of the grey seal in the past. Scheffer's figures must therefore remain 'guesstimates'. Peterson and Bartholomew do, however, regard the increasing human pressures in California as a menace to the species.

CHAPTER 14

CONSERVATION OF BRITISH SEALS

IT was mentioned at the beginning that the work of British zoologists in the Antarctic had resulted in the protection of the seals and fur-seals there, and so had led to a steady increase in the population. It could similarly have been shown that the protection afforded by the United States Government to the northern fur-seals, breeding in the Pribilov Islands, had allowed the population to increase from an all-time low of about 215,000 animals in 1911–12 to about 1½ million by 1935. This was achieved by an International Agreement to prohibit pelagic sealing in the north Pacific (except for aborigines) and some degree of management of the land-take by the United States Bureau of Fisheries. The pelagic take was cut from over 200,000 to 20,000 per decade and since this type of sealing is non-selective and included numbers of pregnant cows, the breeding stock had been seriously affected. On the other hand, the cull of surplus young bulls in a highly polygamous species has had little effect. Continuous monitoring of numbers has enabled observers to build up a very good picture of what can happen under these conditions of conservation. By 1922, a method of estimating the increasing population had been devised and the potential cull of young bulls could be predicted. In the late 1930's it became evident however that the predicted numbers were not available. This was not because the population was decreasing, but because the expected increase had not taken place. This suggested that the population was reaching its optimum and was levelling off and that the method of calculating the population was not able to take this into account.

In 1940 the Bureau of Fisheries was succeeded by the Fish and Wildlife Service which has continued researches from then until the present time, with the exception of the war years. These workers, by establishing methods of age determination, annual counts of pups and harem bulls etc., were able to build up all the necessary parameters for the construction of life-tables for both cows and bulls. Thereafter the cull has been precisely regulated and the total herd (population) stabilised at around the 1½ million mark. The annual land-take is between 60 and 70 thousand (average 66,000) young bulls (bachelors) measuring 41–45 ins. in length. About two-thirds of these are 3-year-olds, the rest 4-year-olds, with few 2-year-olds (1%) and 5-year-olds (2%). Some cows have been culled from time to time to prevent the population from becoming excessive and causing depredations on the valuable Pacific salmon fisheries of Alaska, British Columbia and Washington State.

This example shows how conservation of a species can be obtained while the 'natural resource' is still used. Protection by itself can only be a first aid measure or as a means to help in stabilising a complex situation. As Kenyon, Scheffer and Chapman pointed out, if pelagic sealing were again permitted using modern equipment the Pribilov seal herd would be in jeopardy within a few years. By continuing the prohibition the herd can be managed at its land bases using the accumulated knowledge of many years.

In Great Britain we have been slow to appreciate the need to adopt logical attitudes to our treatment of wild animals. Historically it is possible to trace man's attitude to animals starting from a purely egocentric position; animals existed for man's use and convenience: if they were useful they were culled and if necessary protected; if they were detrimental as pests or in any other way they were destroyed to the point of extinction if possible. In certain spheres these attitudes still persist, albeit modified, as in fisheries and other 'natural resources' which are culled for food and in pest control where control rather than extermination is now recognised as a practical aim. A third approach also has considerable antiquity – the use of animals for sport. This could cut across both of the other approaches as in the preserving of game for the benefit of the landlord's sport at the expense of the tenant's agricultural economy. Only very recently has an entirely different approach been strongly voiced namely that animals exist in their own right and that man as the dominant and rational species should admit some responsibility for the continuance of other species whose habitats he has been disrupting for many thousands of years.

Out of this modern approach has grown the concept of 'conservation' involving the use of all available knowledge as to habits and ecology in order to 'manage' the species at a level of 'peaceful coexistence', to borrow a political phrase. Previously any management of animal populations consisted largely in preventing them from being killed by the wrong people; only rarely as in venery was there also an attempt to manage the habitat to the animal's advantage. In any case the motive was wrong and thus it could not lead to a permanent relationship. These motives, stemming from ego-centricity, are hard to eradicate so that it is not surprising that those who first attempted to stem the tide of slaughter did so by promoting 'protection' and protection alone to ensure the continuance of species of animal for the enjoyment of future generations. Very praiseworthy no doubt, but still very egocentric. That protection alone could lead to a violent state of affairs, since it paid no attention to changed habitats, did not enter the minds of the promoters.

To modern thinking protection is a weapon to be used primarily to ensure that a population does not drop below a viable minimum, in the same way that we accept culling as a method to maintain numbers below the un-acceptable maximum. Conservation management should be such that neither that minimum nor this maximum are exceeded, preferably are not too nearly approached.

The history of man's treatment of seals, in fact of pinnipedes generally, discloses all these approaches. We know that neolithic man caught seals because their bones have been found in the middens of that age. Probably the meat was eaten, the blubber used for lighting or heating oil and the pelts for clothing or thongs. This trend has persisted in one place or another in the world right down to the present day, not only among primitive races like the Eskimos whose economy is still very dependent on certain species of seal, but even among the most sophisticated where the wearing of seal skin coats made from the northern fur-seal pelts is a status symbol of wealth. Until paraffin became a cheap source of light and fuel, seal oil was used in most peasant communities of north-west Europe, particularly in the Hebrides.

With the growth of sea-fisheries, particularly in the shallow seas, seals were seen as competitors with man for the stocks of edible fish. The truth of this belief is difficult either to prove or to disprove. As will have been noted in previous chapters, our knowledge of the feeding habits of both our resident species of seal is sadly deficient and there are considerable difficulties in the way of making it more precise and accurate. Without such precision in measureable terms it is impossible to form a firm opinion as to whether the seal populations above a certain level constitute a menace to our inshore fisheries. Nevertheless in some parts seals have been and are still being killed whenever possible on these grounds. I have met a fisherman of the Isles of Scilly who firmly believed that his fishing was seriously affected by the presence of seals and always shot them if possible. Here a slightly different argument was used in that it was suggested that the shoals of pilchard and herring were dispersed by the presence of seals hunting them. Akin to this argument is the more demonstrable one used on the east coast of Scotland and on the west coast of Ireland: that seals make use of the salmon runs towards the rivers to gain easy prey. This they certainly do and the damage the seals do at the standing nets of the fisherman, both in loss of catch and in torn nets, can be recognised and, to some extent, accurately determined. As the shooting of these seals is selective, in that it culls those who have adopted this method of feeding leaving the others alone, it has much to be said for it as a method of control, although it may be expensive in time and man-power.

More recently still the seals of Britain have been convicted of another offence, that of carrying a parasite which in its immature stages infests members of the cod family, whence it derives its name of cod-worm. The adult is found in the gut of both species of seal and while it has been known from fish caught outside the North Sea for many years, it is only with the considerable rise in the population of North Sea seals that it has spread widely through the fish there too. This cod-worm cannot infect man, but its presence in the flesh of the fish makes it unacceptable for open sale and infected fish have to be rejected for the market and turned into fishmeal for fertiliser at a much reduced price. Here is a much stronger case, well documented on the increasing percentages of infected fish and financial loss. Elimination of the cod-worm could only follow elimination of the seals, but the rate of infection and consequent monetary loss could be reduced to an acceptable level with a proper management of the seal populations.

'Sport' has never been concerned with seals possibly because their distribution does not lend itself to exploitation and seal-hunting has always been considered a 'peasant' occupation. Nevertheless in very recent years some individuals have taken to taking pot-shots from the land at seals just offshore in what they apparently regard as sport. The weapons used were shot guns, for which no Firearms Certificate was required, only a licence purchasable over the counter of a Post Office*. Such shooting could only inflict wounds, possibly to the extent of blinding the animal or preventing it from closing the nostrils so that it would die eventually from starvation. It is difficult to imagine the mentality of the 'sportsmen' who indulged in this activity. German tour operators advertise seal shooting tours to Ireland.

In the pre-1914-war period it was feared that the grey seal was in danger of extinction in the British Isles. In certain regions there is no doubt that its numbers had been much reduced both for pelts and as a protection for inshore fisheries. As the result of pressure based on estimates of the population remaining, the Grey Seals Protection Act of 1914 was passed prohibiting the killing, wounding or taking of any grey seals between 1st October and 15th November. This 'close season' was too short and did not cover the very considerable breeding which occurs on the west coasts in September nor the late breeding extending into December on the Farne Islands. This fault was corrected in the 1932 Act which extended the close season to the four months, 1st September to 31st December. It is of interest that this bill was piloted through the House of Lords by Lord Strathcona and Mount Royal, then Joint Parliamentary Under-Secretary of the Ministry of Agriculture and Fisheries, himself the owner of Colonsay, Oronsay and neighbouring islands, the centre of the Inner Hebridean breeding grounds of the grey seal, to which he had given all-the-year-round protection so far as it lay within his power.

Protection on the breeding rookeries themselves could always be given by the landowner if he so wished and could enforce it. The National Trust, which had adopted the policy of complete protection on all its properties, so protected the Farne Islands sites. Almost certainly the passing of this Act was for the time being a good thing since it gave time for some of the breeding groups to recover. Nevertheless, its provisions laid down that any relaxation in the protection under an Order, by the Minister of Agriculture and Fisheries for England and Wales and by the Secretary of State for Scotland, had to be taken before Parliament and was, therefore, subject to debate. This

* This is no longer true.

safeguard was probably quite justifiable in the 1930's, but in the atmosphere of the 1950's onwards it provided an opportunity for lobbying on emotional grounds which led to serious delays in attempting to establish reasonable management of the populations.

Trouble began in the 1950's when the salmon fishing interests, both the coastal commercial and the riverine sporting, made representations that the grey seal populations of the east coast should be reduced owing to their increasing depredations. As a result a Joint Committee on 'Grey Seals and Fisheries' was set up with representatives from the Ministry of Agriculture, Fisheries and Food, from the Nature Conservancy and from independent sources such as the universities and learned societies. For a time information was collected by officers of the Ministry and Conservancy and some research work was carried out in the universities. However, it soon became apparent that it was necessary to have a full-time worker under the direction of the Committee and Mr E. A. Smith was appointed to this post in 1960. He was able, much more speedily than before, to gather information as to the effects of seal depredations on the fisheries and to collect seal material so that our knowledge of the biology of the seal could grow rapidly in the right direction. One of the first results of his activity was the discovery that the Orcadian population of grey seals was a massive one and not of the order of a hundred or so, as previously thought. It proved a useful source of material without any real detriment to the population. In October 1960 the first cull was carried out in Orkney. This was experimental to the extent that it was not yet certain which means of culling was practicable. On this occasion bulls, cows and pups were shot on two small islands, Wartholm and Little Greenholm. This provided the first adult material from a breeding colony and gave a picture of the age distribution which has been little altered by subsequent information. This cull was expeditiously and humanely carried out by expert marksmen and a veterinary officer under the direction of the Home Department of the Scottish Office. It showed, however, the limitations of adult culling under the conditions of transport then available and subsequent culls were confined to moulters.

The previous year a cull of moulters had been carried out successfully on the Farne Islands, but adverse (and largely misinformed) publicity had resulted in the National Trust refusing permission for further culls. Moulter culls were, however, operated in Orkney, the number to be taken being determined by the Joint Committee. Over several years the number was maintained, although it varied from year to year depending on weather conditions. Meanwhile Mr Smith continued to monitor the total number of pups born. There was clear indication after some four or five years that the breeding population had decreased, but this was not due to moulter culls since the year-groups affected had not yet entered the breeding population to any extent. The drop could be accounted for partly by the cows and bulls shot for research purposes and partly by increased activity of local sealers.

The value of adult pelts had risen sharply over this period, but a subsequent decline greatly decreased this loss in the population.

The following years, when the effect of the culls should have appeared, did not produce conclusive evidence that they had materially affected the breeding population. Meanwhile on the Farne Islands the numbers of pups born had been increasing annually (Fig. 49) at a high rate. Between 1956 and 1966 the breeding population of cows had more than doubled.

At about this time some concern was being shown publicly about the status of the common seal in the Wash area and reports were coming in that in Shetland the breeding population had also dropped markedly. The killing of common seal pups (and of adults in Shetland) was also connected with the high price paid for pelts. There were also requests for permission to take grey seal pups and moulters in the Hebrides where numbers were certainly no fewer than before, although precise figures were difficult to obtain. Mr Smith moved to another post at about this time. As a result a Seals Research Unit was set up combining both grey and common seal investigations, with increased manpower and facilities, with a remit which included all aspects of seal biology and not only those affecting fisheries. It came under the administration of the Natural Environmental Research Council and had its headquarters at the Fisheries Laboratory at Lowestoft with Mr Nigel Bonner at its head. The Joint Committee was turned into an Advisory Sub-Committee* of N.E.R.C.'s Marine Biology Committee.

The work of this Unit has now been proceeding for some years and several new aspects of seal research have been developed. With the increase in personnel, monitoring of numbers of seals, both common and grey, has been much more widely based, and the methods of counting particularly of the common have been made more accurate by the use of air survey and high speed boats.

Contributing to the knowledge about grey seals, the Scottish section of the Nature Conservancy cannot be omitted. North Rona is a National Nature Reserve not only on account of its magnificent sea-bird populations in the spring and summer, but also because it has had for many years a large population of breeding grey seals in the autumn. After Fraser Darling's visit in 1938, interrupted for several weeks by the Munich crisis, no scientist interested in seals had visited the island until 1959 when an expedition of four remained there from 1st October until 26th October. From then onwards an annual visit has been made (with only one exception due to appalling weather) and an immense body of information has been collected and published. Marking, first with rings or tags and later by branding, has also brought in knowledge of the spread of the young seals and of the date of their first appearances as breeders. The leader in this work has been Dr J. Morton Boyd, for long the N.W. Scotland Regional Officer and now Scottish

* This has now been disbanded and another Advisory Committee has been appointed under a new Act.

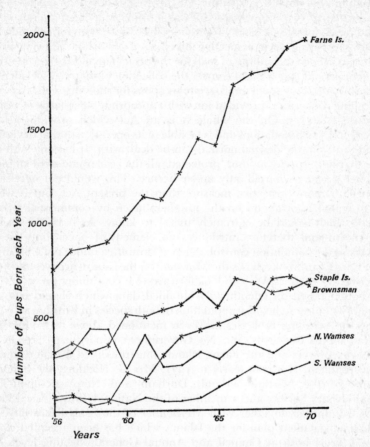

FIG. 49. Numbers of pups born in the Farne Islands, and in its constituent rookeries, 1956-1970. The astonishing increase in the numbers of grey seals in the Farne Islands is well shown in the graph for the total. In constituent rookeries the growth in the numbers born on Brownsman is the most notable feature.

Director, ably assisted by Niall Campbell, one of his colleagues. Throughout they have co-operated first with the Seals Officer and later the Seals Research Unit.

In the late 1960's it was becoming clear that the old Grey Seals Protection Act was not the best of instruments and that something should be done about common seals as well. Lord Cranbrook, then President of the Mammal Society, prepared and introduced a Bill for the Conservation of Seals, into the House of Lords. It was in fact defeated on the Second Reading, but it had made so successful an impression that Lord Shackleton, spokesman for the

Government, offered official facilities for the preparation of an amended Bill. Consequently in 1970 this revised Bill was introduced as a private member's Bill and finally passed. Basically it provides for close seasons for common and grey seals covering their respective breeding times while allowing under Ministerial licence the culling of seals for the protection of fisheries' interests, some commercial take and, of course, the collection of material for scientific purposes. It also lays down appropriate weapons for shooting seals. Access to all breeding rookeries is provided for with appropriate safeguards in respect of Nature Reserves. On the whole it is an Act which provides for the *management* of seal populations and is flexible in its operation so that deviations up or down from the desired normal can be dealt with. It has one fault and that is that both species are not 'protected' all the year round with killing at any time of year permitted only under licence. This would not necessarily have been a more protective measure than the present Act, but it would have provided information on the numbers taken by commercial culling, a figure which would be extremely useful to know. As it is, this will be an unknown and therefore introduces an element of uncertainty in any calculations for population control. A new Committee under the Chairmanship of Lord Cranbrook advises the Minister* on the issue of licences and other administrative matters. We can look forward to a continuing process of seal conservation based on scientifically obtained data which should ensure a reasonably stable and healthy population of both species in British waters.

Access to breeding rookeries has been mentioned above as having been provided for in the Seals Act. No Government department likes to use compulsory powers and the Farne Islands thus presented a major administrative problem. However, early in 1971, Mrs G. Hickling, the honorary secretary of the Northumberland, Durham and Newcastle-upon-Tyne Natural History Society and a member of the National Trusts' Local Farne Islands Committee, together with Mr Bonner of the Seals Research Unit, issued a management plan for the Islands which has been accepted by the National Trust both at Council and Annual General Meeting level. The complete and continued protection of the grey seal on the Islands has resulted not only in a great increase in the breeding population, but has begun to destroy the habitat features of the islands to the detriment of the bird populations. Moreover the breeding rookeries have become so overcrowded that pup mortality has risen to a high level. The islands no longer can be regarded as a 'show-piece' during the annual breeding season of seals not only because of the stench of decomposing bodies and the pitiful appearance of starveling and wounded pups, but because this overcrowding has produced a high degree of aggressiveness in the cows. (This frequent aggression was noted on North Rona, many of whose rookeries were as densely crowded, with high mortalities, as on the Farne Islands.)

The Management Plan proposes a reduction of the *breeding* population to

* Secretary of State for Home Affairs.

1,000 from the present one of just on 2,000 by shooting off adult cows over 3 years, most being killed in the first year, none in the second and the remainder in the third. This is now believed to be practicable. Many other minor proposals are made both to maintain control and to restore the damaged habitat. From any point of view the main proposal is a drastic one, but only drastic measures are now available. It is an excellent example of what happens when a policy of protection is allowed to continue beyond its period of usefulness to permit a small population to increase to a viable level.

Something must now be said about the *methods* of control. When dealing with an amphibious animal which is found on land only in somewhat remote islands, difficult of access in all but fairly calm weather, the practicality of the method may tend to outweigh the efficiency based on scientific data. In the earlier culls it was clear that the culling of pups or moulters was easier than the shooting of adults. The provisional life-table gave data which allowed a calculation of the proportion of young to be culled in order to reduce the breeding population to an agreed level within 5–10 years' time. The Joint Committee therefore advised this moulter cull to take place and in Orkney it has been carried out for a sufficient number of years for results to be visible if it was successful. Actually the reduction due to cull is hard to discern. The commercial and research cull of adults complicates the picture particularly as the size of the former is unknown, but no significant reduction, mathematically speaking, can be seen due to the cull alone. But if about a quarter of the young are culled, how can this fail to affect the numbers of adults in later years?

Now there is a growing body of evidence that mortality rates due to different causes are not necessarily cumulative. In other words one type of mortality may result in an increased probability of survival of the remaining individuals. Alternatively it may be argued that those dying from one cause may well have died from another had the first not taken effect. In the grey seals, for example, if a pup cull was made at random, 60% of those culled would have died anyway within the first year from 'natural causes'. But even if the cull is postponed until after the full pup mortality has taken effect and only well nourished moulters are taken the same is true for perhaps 30%. Here there is obviously a considerable degree of 'replacement' or 'substitute' mortality, but it probably goes further than this. In very carefully controlled populations, such as those of the game birds, it has been shown that the annual shoot (or cull) can be increased very considerably, up to nearly 50%, without affecting the breeding population of birds the following year to any significant degree. The exact mechanism involved here is not fully understood, but there is little doubt that the principle of 'substitute mortality' is a very real phenomenon.

It would seem, therefore, that scientifically speaking the direct culling of *adults* is the most efficient method of population control when dealing with long-lived animals such as seals. It has been suggested that the culling of territorial bulls might very materially reduce the pregnancy percentage, but the presence of many sexually mature bulls, who have failed to gain a territory at the beginning of the season, makes this impracticable. Dr Backhouse and I tried this on a very small scale on the Orkney island of Ruskholm. Within a very short time, under the hour, the shot bull had been replaced by another. Towards the end of the season this might not have occurred, but not only would this require very exact timing, but there would have already been sufficient matings to ensure a high pregnancy rate, if not quite as high as normal.

The culling of cows is, therefore, the most effective, and modern transport makes this a practical proposition. On the Farne Islands the growth of aggression among the cows will add to the ease of cull since they remain ashore alongside their pups instead of taking to the sea. The pups can thus be identified and culled and so prevent their dying from starvation. This will ensure as humane a procedure as possible.

North Rona, as a National Nature Reserve, will probably continue to be an untouched breeding area, except for observational work. The visiting of rookeries undoubtedly has some effect, but this is being kept constantly under review not only at North Rona, but also by the Seals Research Unit. Human disturbance can lead to the desertion of pups by cows and even a reluctance to breed there in subsequent years. It is also a contributory factor to the growth of aggression although overcrowding is the dominant one.

Elsewhere, in the Hebrides and in west Wales, some control measures may become necessary, but not enough is yet known as to the exact status of the populations of grey seals in those areas. They may have reached a maximum, but the establishment of a breeding rookery on St Kilda suggests that new sites might be selected to accommodate a further overall increase.

The situation of the common seal is somewhat different to that of the grey. This is because its numbers are much less certainly known and popular opinion as to the effect of the commercial cull has led to conclusions for which there is little real evidence. Thus when the commercial cull in the Wash area rises to round about 900 it is widely announced that very few can have survived. This is based on the assumption that the total born is about 1,000 and for this there is no justification. A survey made by the Seals Research Unit in the Wash shortly after the end of the breeding season (and after the cull) showed that there were *at least* a number of pups surviving equal to those killed. Pups can easily be distinguished by their size in haul-outs on sandbanks. Even if they have taken to the water before being counted, their tracks on the sand are so much narrower that they can be identified without difficulty. The use of helicopter or light aircraft enables the counts to be made over a wide area within the limits of one low water, so that the possibility of counting seals twice or not at all is eliminated. Since the degree of protection and management under the 1969 Seals Act is the same for common seals as

PLATE 23. *above:* A common seal cow and her pup, showing the typical pellage pattern of small spots and the rounded head. (The Wash.)
below: A closer view of the head of the common seal. The round head, depressed profile and closely set V nostrils, leaving only a very narrow groove between the moustachial pads, is well seen in both.

PLATE 24. *above:* An aerial view of a sandbank in the Wash with common seals hauled-out. The movements of the seals can be seen in the tracks. They can thus be counted even if they flee into the sea on the approach of the plane.
below: A series of nine consecutive frames enlarged from a 16 mm colour film showing the 'salmon leap' activity of common seal bulls during the mating season. (West Loch, Mousa, Shetland; September 1963.)

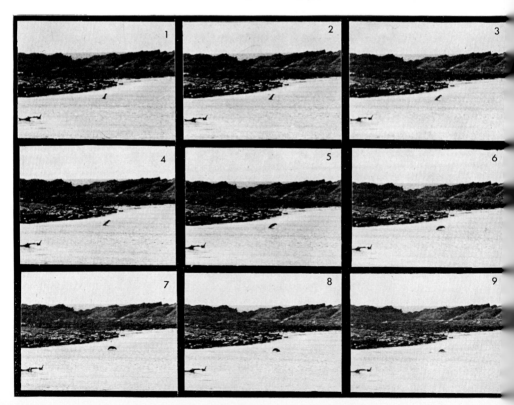

for grey, there is a reasonable hope that, given the increasing knowledge of the common seal, this species will survive as successfully as the grey.

Throughout this book I have tried to emphasise the importance of accurate knowledge in attempting to understand the complicated dynamics of any animal. It is true that some knowledge is better than none, but the limits of the deductions to be drawn from it must be recognised and action must always be conservative and not irreversible. Although there is still a very great deal to be learnt about both species, there is no doubt that present action is much more surely based than when the earlier Seals Acts were passed, and that we can look forward to well managed populations of these most interesting animals.

APPENDICES

CLASSIFICATION OF PINNIPEDIA

Super-family	Family	Sub-family	Tribe	Genus	Species	Number of sub-species
OTARIOIDEA	OTARIIDAE	Otariinae		Otaria	flavescens	
				Eumetopias	jubatus	
				Zalophus	californianus	3 ssp.
		Arctocephalinae		Neophoca	cinerea	
				Phocarctos	hookeri	
				Arctocephalus	pusillus	
				,,	forsteri	
				,,	doriferus*	
				,,	tasmanicus*	
				,,	gazella	2 ssp.
				,,	australis	3 ssp.
				,,	philippii	2 ssp.
				Callorhinus	ursinus	
	ODOBAENIDAE			Odobenus	rosmarus	2 ssp.
PHOCOIDEA	PHOCIDAE	Phocinae		Phoca	vitulina	5 ssp.
				Pusa	hispida	6 ssp.
				,,	sibirica	
				,,	caspica	
			Phocini	Histriophoca	fasciata	
				Pagophilus	groenlandicus	
				Halichoerus	grypus	
			Erignathini	Erignathus	barbatus	2 ssp.
		Monachinae	Monachini	Monachus	monachus	
				,,	tropicalis	
				,,	schauinslandi	
			Lobodontini	Lobodon	carcinophagus	
				Ommatophoca	rossi	
				Hydrurga	leptonyx	
				Leptonychotes	weddelli	
		Cystophorinae		Cystophora	cristata	
				Mirounga	leonina	
				,,	angustirostris	

* *A. tasmanicus* is sometimes treated as a synonym of *A. doriferus*, sometimes as a sub-species and sometimes as a species. There is not sufficient material to reach a definite conclusion.

Common Name	Distribution	Alternative specific names
South American sea-lion	East and west coast of South America, south of 10°S	*byronia*
Steller's sea-lion	Coastal waters of north Pacific Ocean	*jubata*
Californian sea-lion	Coastal waters of California and Gulf of C., Galapagos Islands	
Australian sea-lion	Coastal waters of South-West Australia	
New Zealand sea-lion	Seas south of New Zealand	
South African fur-seal	Coastal waters of South Africa	
New Zealand fur-seal	Seas south-east and west of New Zealand	
Australian fur-seal	Coastal waters of S.W. Australia and Tasmania	
Tasmanian fur-seal	Seas round Tasmania	
Kerguelen fur-seal	Seas around islands of south Atlantic & south Pacific Oceans	*tropicalis*
South American fur-seal	E. and W. coasts of S. America, south of 30°S, Galapagos Islands	
Philippi fur-seal	Seas off coasts of Chile and California	Guadalupe fur-seal
Northern fur-seal	North Pacific Ocean, Bering Sea	
Walrus	Arctic seas, north of 65°N	
Common (Harbor) seal	Coastal waters of sub-arctic and temperate N. Atlantic and W. Pacific Oceans	
Ringed seal	Arctic seas (circumpolar) and N. Pacific Ocean	
Baikal seal	Lake Baikal (Central Asia)	
Caspian seal	Caspian Sea	
Ribbon seal	Arctic and sub-arctic seas of N. Pacific Ocean	
Harp seal	Arctic and sub-arctic seas of N. Atlantic Ocean	Greenland seal
Grey seal	Seas of N.W. Europe, S. Baltic, Iceland, Newfoundland & Nova Scotia	
Bearded seal	Arctic and sub-arctic seas, except N.W. Europe	
Mediterranean monk seal	Mediterranean and Black Seas	
Caribbean monk seal	Caribbean Sea	
Hawaian monk seal	Seas round Hawaiian Islands	
Crabeater seal	Arctic seas (circumpolar) of southern oceans (pack ice)	
Ross seal	Arctic seas (circumpolar) of southern oceans (pack ice)	
Leopard seal	Arctic and sub-arctic seas (circumpolar) of southern oceans (fast ice)	
Weddell seal	Arctic and sub-arctic seas (circumpolar) of southern oceans (fast ice)	
Hooded seal (bladdernose seal)	Arctic and sub-arctic seas of north-west Atlantic Ocean	
Southern elephant seal	Circumpolar on sub-arctic islands of southern oceans	
Northern elephant seal	Seas and islands of Californian coast	

An alternative classification based on the view that the hooded seal (*C. cristata*) is *not* closely related to the elephant seals (*Mirounga*) but *is* to the bearded seal (*E. barbatus*).

The Erignathini remain in the Phocinae and the Lobodontini in the Monachinae. The subfamily Cystophorinae is suppressed.

Tribe	Genus	Species	Common Name
Erigna-thini	*Erignathus*	*barbatus*	Bearded seal
	Cystophora	*cristata*	Hooded seal
Lobodontini	*Lobodon*	*carcinophagus*	Crabeater seal
	Ommatophoca	*rossi*	Ross seal
	Hydrurga	*leptonyx*	Leopard seal
	Leptonychotes	*weddelli*	Weddell seal
	Mirounga	*leonina*	Southern elephant seal
	,,	*angustirostris*	Northern elephant seal

APPENDIX B

BREEDING ROOKERIES OF GREY SEALS

and haul-out sites in the non-breeding period.

EAST COAST

Farne Islands Staple Island
     Brownsman
     N. Wamses
     S. Wamses
Scroby Sands Southern end
Isle of May

NORTHERN ISLES

North Rona Fianuis peninsula
     Escarpment
     Sceapull
Shetland Lady Holm
     Fitful Head gen.
     Moussa ?
     Yell   ?
     Unst   ?
Orkney   Muckle Greenholm
     Little Greenholm
     Holm of Fara
     Ruskholm (N.E.
      side)
     Wartholm
     Little Linga
     Gairsay (small
      beaches)
     South Ronaldsay
      (small beaches)
     Holms of Spurness

HEBRIDES

Gaskeir   All over top
Shillay   Eastern side
Coppay   Eastern side
Monarch Isles
St Kilda
Summer Isles
Treshnish Isles Linga
Oronsay   Eilean nan Ron
     Ghaoidmeal
     Eilean an Eoin

WEST WALES

Cardiganshire coast Isolated bays and
      islands
Strumble Head area Caves and small bays
Ramsey Island Caves and small bays
Skomer

IRELAND

Lambay Island Caves
Saltee Islands Caves and small
      beaches
West Kerry coast (No details)
Clare Island Caves and small
      beaches

Haul-out Sites in the Non-breeding Period, (January–August) of Grey Seals
Several groups have not been investigated sufficiently for such sites to be listed. In others, such as the Farne Islands, all-the-year-round visits have resulted in very complete information. In Orkney and Shetland the list is compiled from the known origin of material collected for research and the months for which information is available are added in brackets. Those known to be moulting haul-outs, often of considerable size, are marked with an asterisk. Haul-outs are smaller and much more variable in location from March to August.

Farne Islands: See Appendix D, p. 219 for details of islands and months

Shetland
* Horse Holm (Jan., Feb., Apr.–Aug.)
  Lady Holm (Jan., Feb., May, July, Aug.)
* Ve Skerries (Jan., Feb., Aug.)
  Moussa (Jan., Feb.)
  Fitful Head (Feb.–June, Aug.)
  Wick of Shunni (Apr., May)
  Black Skerry (April)
  The Ords (June)
  Siggar Ness (June)
  Pierie Holm (June)
  Whales Wick (June, August)
  Noness Head (August)
  Swarta Skerry (August)

Haul-outs distant from Breeding Rookeries
  West Hoyle Bank, Wirral, Cheshire
  Donna Nook, Lincolnshire
  Abertay Sands, East Scotland
  Scroby Sands, Norfolk

Orkney
* Ruskholm (Feb., Apr., May)
* Boray Holm (Jan., Feb., Apr.)
  Little Greenholm (January)
  Wyre (Jan., May, Aug.)
  Damsay (Jan., July)
* Barrel of Butter (Feb.–Apr.)
  Holms of Spurness (February)
  Eynhollow (March, April)
  Burray (March, June)
  Switha (March, June)
  Swona (March, May)
  Auskerry (March)
  Sandwick Bay (March)
  Calf of Flotta (March)
  Deerness (April)
  Taing Skerry (April, August)
  Pentland Skerries (May–July)
  Brough Ness (June)
  Grassholm (August)
  Gairsay (August)

A.   A LIFE TABLE FOR GREY SEAL COWS

Year	Number at beginning of year	Percentage Mortality	Numbers and Groups
0	1,000	60	1,000 Pups →Moulters
1	400	30	
2	277	12	1,362 non-breeding cows
3	244	6.7	(1,149 are immature)
4	228	6.7	
5	213	6.7	(Capable of conception)
6	199	6.7	(Capable of bearing pups)
7	185	6.7	
8	173	6.7	868
9	161	6.7	
10	150	6.7	
11	140	6.7	
12	131	6.7	
13	122	6.7	613
14	114	6.7	
15	106	6.7	
16	99	6.7	
17	92	6.7	
18	86	6.7	432
19	80	6.7	
20	75	6.7	
21	70	6.7	
22	65	6.7	
23	61	6.7	306
24	57	6.7	
25	53	6.7	
26	49	6.7	
27	46	6.7	
28	43	6.7	215
29	40	6.7	
30	37	6.7	
31–34	66	?	66

2,500 cows of breeding age at 80% pregnancy give 2,000 pups

B.   A LIFE TABLE FOR GREY SEAL BULLS

Year	Number at beginning of year	Percentage Mortality	Numbers and Groups
0	1,000	60	1,000 pups →moulters
1	400	30	⎫
2	277	12	
3	244	6.7	⎬ 1,362 immature bulls
4	228	6.7	
5	213	6.7	⎭
6	199	6.7	⎫
7	185	10	691 mature bulls almost all without
8	166	15	⎬ territories
9	141	25	
10	106	40	⎭
11	64	40	⎫
12	38	40	
13	23	40	
14	14	40	
15	8	40	⎬ 265 territorial bulls
16	5	40	
17	3	40	
18	2	40	
19	1	40	⎭
20	1	40	⎫
21	1	?	
22	1	?	⎬ 2 idle or senile bulls?
23	0	?	
24	0	?	⎭

FARNE ISLANDS SEAL COUNTS,
1956–1968

It has been said earlier that, in the non-breeding part of the year, the grey seals haul out on sites which may differ widely from those used as rookeries. In the North Sea the availability of such sites is limited compared with the countless skerries and islands of the north and west coasts of Britain. The grey seal population of the Farne Islands has therefore to depend on those islands for both breeding and other haul-outs; Donna Nook, Lincs., and Scroby Sands, Norfolk, being the only other sites regularly used. Mrs Grace Hickling and her colleagues have made a long series of counts (123 between April 1956 and July 1968) which has produced a unique record, since the sample represented by the haul-out on the Farne Islands must be a very high one in view of the absence of alternatives. The non-rookery islands are all within a very short distance of the breeding islands and thus preferences can be clearly and markedly displayed, if they exist. By an analysis of the counts we can perhaps answer the question 'How *much* do the seals avoid their rookeries in the non-breeding period of the year?' with some mathematical precision.

This is not the place to discuss the methods I have used, so I will detail only the results and the sort of conclusions that can be drawn from them. Fig. 50 shows the maximum counts recorded each year as well as the number of pups born (as a criterion of the increasing population). The two lines have been fitted by eye and are nearly parallel. Thus there is evidence that the numbers hauled-out have increased over the years in about the same proportion as the population. Thus from the point of view of the increasing population, we need not regard the counts as more biased at one end of the series than at the other.

Next I must run ahead of the data as now presented and state that for meaningful figures to be obtained, the islands must be divided into four groups thus:

Group 1 (Breeding Islands)	*Group 2*
Staple Island	Big and Little Harcars
Brownsman	Blue Caps
S. Wamses	Nameless, Roddam and Green
N. Wamses	Northern Hares
Group 3	*Group 4* (Inner Farne Islands)
Longstone End	Megstone and S. Goldstone
Longstone	Inner Farne
Knivestone	Wideopens
Crumstone	The Scarcars
Callers	The Bush

Groups 2 and 3 comprise Outer Farne Islands other than the breeding islands. The reason for the separation into the two groups will become apparent when the numbers of seals in haul-outs is examined but their geographical distribution is shown in Fig. 51 and is not without interest by itself.

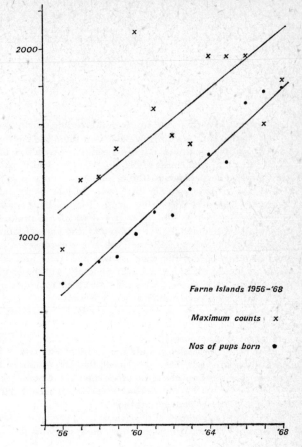

FIG. 50. Maximum counts
and numbers of pups born,
Farne Islands 1956-68.

The average percentage haul-out for these four groups of islands over the whole
period is seen in Table 22, col. 1. Over half the number are found on the islands of
Group 3, the outermost and most isolated of the Outer Farne Islands. Indeed about
40 of the 57% is provided by counts on the Knivestone and Crumstone alone. The
breeding islands (Group 1) and Group 2 each account for about one-sixth of the total,
while Group 4 (Inner Farne Is.) only provide about one-tenth.

But before accepting averages as being the only or best criterion it is necessary to
look at the individual records closely. One very startling feature emerges: that many
of the haul-outs on the breeding islands are as large as those on the much favoured
Knivestone and Crumstone of Group 3. In col. 2 of Table 22 is shown the number of
haul-outs when more than 100 seals were counted on an island (large haul-outs).
In brackets alongside are shown the percentages which seem to indicate at first sight
that these figures are in much the same proportions as those in col. 1. But col. 3, in

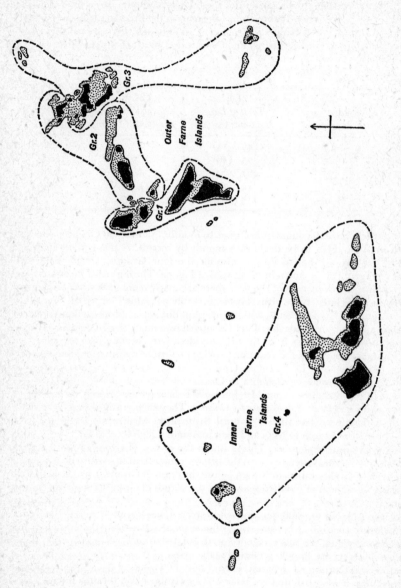

FIG. 51. The Farne Islands.

which are the numbers of haul-outs with more than 500 seals (very large haul-outs), suggests a very different picture. If we express col. 3 as percentages of col. 2, shown in col. 4, we can see that the proportion of these large haul-outs (over 100) which are very large (over 500) is nearly three times as great on the Breeding Islands (Group 1) as in either Group 2 or 3. Group 4 has none at all although there are nearly as many over 100 as in Group 1. Some further analysis is called for to account for this.

Table 22

	Col. 1 Average %age Haul-out	Col. 2 Total of Large Haul-outs (>100)	Col. 3 No. of Very Large Haul-outs (>500)	Col. 4 Col. 3 as %age of Col. 2
Group 1	15	47 (11)	13	28.3
Group 2	17	65 (16)	7	10.8
Group 3	57	261 (63)	26	10.0
Group 4	11	42 (10)	nil	0.0
	(100)	415 (100)		

Now as there are 123 counts spread over 10 months (January to October) there are enough to allow them to be dealt with month by month. If this is done both as a monthly total for all the islands and also for the four Groups, a very remarkable picture emerges. This is shown in the graphs of Fig. 52. The curve for the totals shows that in the first three months of the year there are many more seals (over 60% more) hauling-out than later in the year. This is probably accounted for by the moult, first of the cows and then of the bulls, with an overlap. But again this overall picture is too simple because the curves for the island Groups show a much more complex situation.

Group 4 we can dismiss from further consideration; the numbers are small and fairly constant throughout the year and provide no further information than what has already been obtained (i.e. ±10%). Groups 1 and 2 however are almost identical except for slight increase in Group 2 in October, which is probably associated with the onset of the breeding season. In January, February and March they maintain constant figures, *twice as high as those for Group 3*. They then crash, through April and May, and remain at less than 1% until September. Meanwhile the numbers in Group 3 rise from March to May and then maintain a high level at 80%–90% of the monthly totals until September. This is almost the reverse of Groups 1 and 2 but not quite, because there is a steady rise in the first four months of the year which accounts for the peak in total numbers in March before the crash of Groups 1 and 2. Is this due to a steady movement of moulted seals from the islands of Groups 1 and 2 to those of Group 3?

One answer to our original question is now seen to be: 'From March to September the seals neglect (avoid?) the breeding islands totally, but from January to March they prefer them to the more exposed and isolated islands. Neighbouring islands (Group 2) however are equally preferred to the breeding islands over this period.'

The high proportion of very large haul-outs in Group 1 islands has not been explained even if we attribute the preference for Group 1 and 2 to the moult. Can it be a question of the size of the islands? This does not seem likely since very large haul-outs occur in both Groups 2 and 3 on quite small islands and skerries. No ready

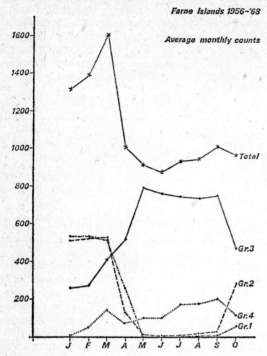

FIG. 52. Average monthly counts, Farne Islands, 1956-68, in total and in groups.

answer occurs to me but it would be interesting to know something more about the composition of those haul-outs bearing in mind that the sexes differ in their time of moult. We have also seen in Orkney that there is a difference in behaviour between pregnant and non-pregnant cows and that young cows appear to predominate in these early months of the year. It is quite clear that the month of March is a critical time for changes in behaviour.

Probably some observations which will help to answer these problems are already available in the field notes at the time of many of the counts, but more will certainly be necessary. We can now pinpoint the differences of behaviour in both time and space. What this preliminary analysis has shown, I hope, is the importance of prolonged and accurate observations. Such work is almost impossible for the professional, but the amateur can, in this way, make most valuable contributions to our knowledge.

RESEARCH AND WORLD CONSERVATION
OF SEALS

From the accounts of the grey and common seals in this book, it will be apparent that our two British seals are in many ways by no means typical of phocids generally, and more especially of phocines. A glance at the world distribution map (Fig. 53) of the true seals (Phocidae) will show that the majority of the Sub-family Phocinae prefer colder arctic waters and are ice-breeders rather than land-breeders, while the Monachinae similarly are confined to antarctic seas and pack ice with the exception of the monk seals and the elephant seals which are found in warmer waters and are land-breeders. The grey seal, a phocine, is a land-breeder in Great Britain, an ice-breeder in the Baltic and something halfway in Canada.

Of the other two Families of pinnipedes, the walruses (Odobaenidae) are likewise arctic but the Otariidae (sea-lions and fur-seals) are found in sub-polar and temperate seas even penetrating the tropical waters of the Pacific Ocean (Fig 54). Like the monk seals and elephant seals they are land-breeders with complicated social systems established in the breeding rookeries.

In considering the relationships between the pinnipedes and man two principal factors have been involved. First, the majority of the animals are to be found in regions of the world with small human populations. Secondly, the animals themselves are relatively inaccessible whether ice- or land-breeders. Until about 250 years ago seals were predated upon only by small local populations. For example seals formed a significant part of the eskimo's way of life—meat and blubber to eat, blubber for heat and light and the pelts for clothing. Similarly in the north-west of Europe and in the Mediterranean, seals were hunted for the same products. In north America ice-based seals were hunted, in Europe land-based ones. It is probable that in neither case did man's depredations have any significant effect on the seal populations. It is possible however that in the more densely inhabited Mediterranean the monk seal was being slowly but steadily reduced in numbers.

The great change came in the years of world exploration and exploitation so that from the late 18th century onwards it was possible for the seal populations in all parts of the world to be attacked primarily for their blubber but also, in the fur-seals, for their pelts. We thus find that the main onslaught was made on land-based breeding pinnipedes in both northern and southern hemispheres. This was so intense that by the end of the 19th

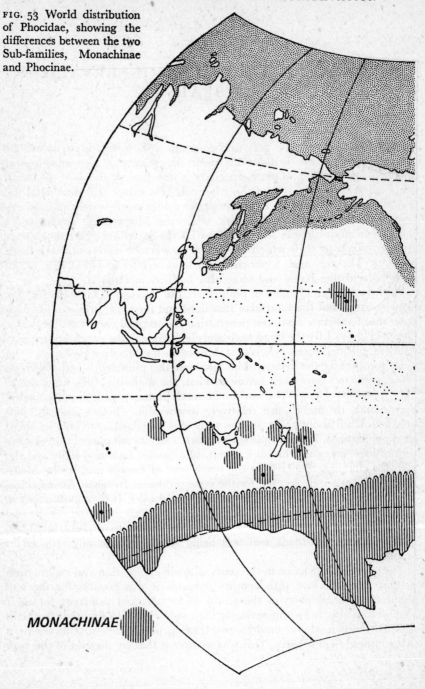

FIG. 53 World distribution of Phocidae, showing the differences between the two Sub-families, Monachinae and Phocinae.

MONACHINAE

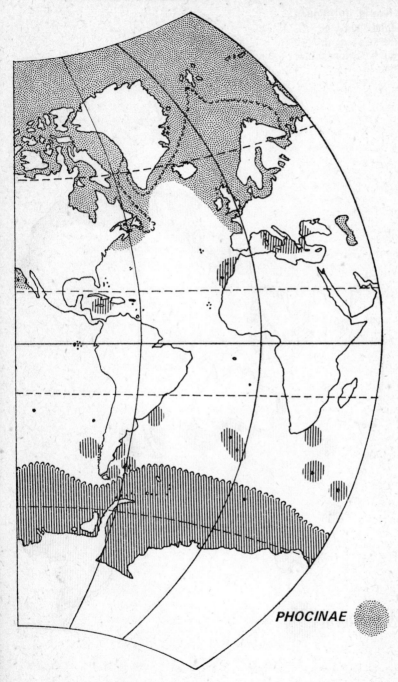

PHOCINAE

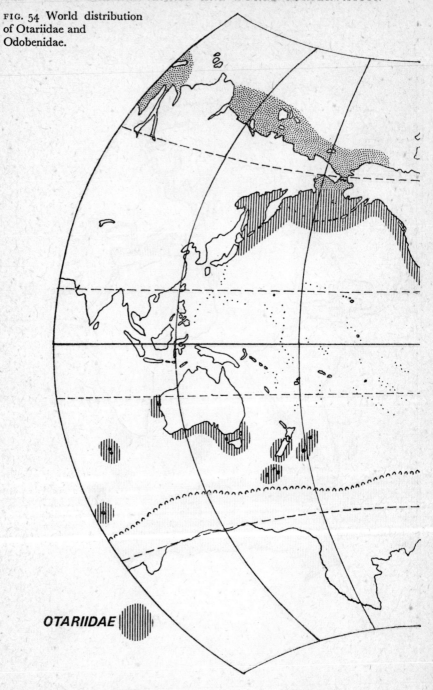

FIG. 54 World distribution of Otariidae and Odobenidae.

OTARIIDAE

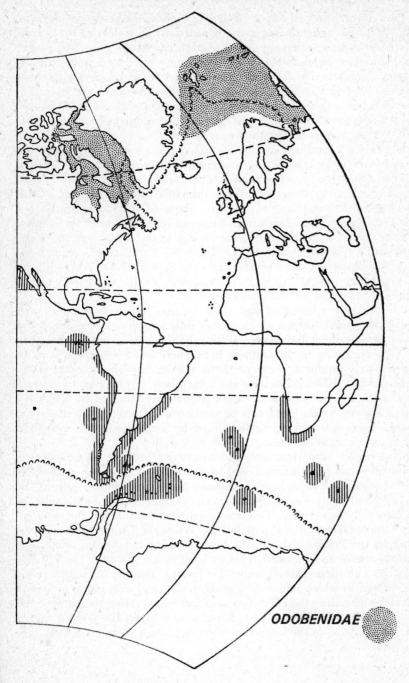

ODOBENIDAE

century many of the species involved were brought to the verge of extinction. In the Antarctic, where many of the populations were isolated on islands, whole rookeries were wiped out and only gradually have some of them come to be used again. Much of the slaughter must be attributed to the rapidly increasing populations of America and western Europe, coupled with rising standards of living. Part of this pressure still exists today in some countries. The introduction of paraffin oil and wax as sources of heat and light possibly did as much to save the remnants of the pinnipede populations as the effect of diminishing returns on lengthy voyages.

Now land-based animals can be conserved (i.e. managed) provided the country to which the land belongs exercises its sovereignty but this was not done until almost too late. The control of the fur-seals in the Pribilov Islands by the United States Government was probably the first instance of this happening but it took place only in 1911, about 40 years after the United States had acquired the islands from Russia in 1868. Great Britain followed suit in the Antarctic in the 1920's, associating, as the Americans had done, control with a research operation, the 'Discovery Expeditions', which dealt with pinnipedes as well as cetaceans. Since the Second World War, with the increasing interest in Antarctica, other countries with a territorial stake in that part of the world have also taken action.

If we turn to the ice-based and more oceanic pinnipedes of the north Atlantic and Pacific Oceans an altogether different picture emerges. Some intensive seal hunting has been traditional in this area but, with severe restrictions on sealing in the southern hemisphere and a demand still maintained for seal products, these northern species have been attacked by modern methods with an intensity not known before. This type of hunting takes place in international waters and cannot be controlled by unilateral action of any one country unless it be to control the activities of their own nationals. Even this can be circumvented by landing catches elsewhere, where restrictions do not exist.

Thus it can be seen that, although the major commercial exploitation of pinnipedes has been international in character, it has been possible to control it where the animals are essentially land-based. But as soon as the exploitation moves into international waters, the high seas, international action alone can really be effective. This was clearly demonstrated in the management of the northern fur-seal populations. When the United States limited hunting on the Pribilov Islands, the fur-seals using the Asiatic islands off Siberia continued to be hunted. This by itself would not affect the Pribilov population but there existed a pelagic sealing industry over the north Pacific Ocean in which nationals from both east and west coasts took part and this would reduce the effectiveness of any conservation measures in the Pribilov Islands. The international agreement between the United States, Russia and Japan, as the countries whose nationals were concerned, was the answer.

International agreements can be arrived at only when all parties are convinced of the rightness of the measures proposed. Inevitably one or more of the parties are going to be, at least temporarily, worse off and consequently it is they who have to be converted by hard facts that, in the long run, restrictions now will ultimately be profitable.

These hard facts can only be obtained by research and good ecological research at that. Pinnipede research cannot be carried out cheaply. The conditions are difficult and only by use of modern sophisticated methods can substantial and reliable results be obtained within a reasonable space of time when dealing with animals so amphibious and wide ranging. Only five countries, the United States, Great Britain, Canada, Australia and the Soviet Union have anything like the sort of co-ordinated research teams necessary. Let us take a look at what each of them is doing.

In the **United States** the Fish and Wildlife Service has, since the 1920's, maintained a programme of research, starting with the northern fur-seal, for obvious reasons. This has been expanded to deal with: the northern elephant seal, the harbour, ribbon and bearded seals, the Hawaiian monk seal, Steller's and the Californian sea-lions and the Pacific walrus. In many instances the work has been continued in the University of California (Los Angeles) and in the Alaska Department of Fish and Game. Among the best known of the researchers have been: G. A. Bartholomew, J. L. Buckley, F. H. Fay, K. W. Kenyon, R. S. Peterson, Carleton Ray, Dale W. Rice, Victor B. Scheffer, and Ford Wilke. The area covered by them extends from the Bering Sea (Pribilov Islands) to the Mexican border (Guadalupe and San Nicholas Islands) and includes the Hawaiian Islands (Leeward group), and even to the Sea of Okhotsk at Hokkaido. Thus all of the north Pacific Ocean pinnipedes are being dealt with from field work to systematics. A truly impressive record.

It is difficult to evaluate in numerical terms the result of their work but one set of data will indicate something of what has been achieved in one species. Table 21 is taken from Kenyon, Scheffer and Chapman (1954), where the recorded kills are used to show the fluctuations in the total populations. All the figures prior to 1911 are substantially defective in being too low. Nevertheless up to that date they may be used comparatively over 3 or 4 decades. We can see that over-exploitation produced two minima, one in the decade 1831-40 and the other in the decade 1911-20, before the results of protection could become wholly effective. The two corresponding maxima of 1811-20 and 1881-90 were probably of the same order since the earlier figures are the more defective. The relaxation of hunting effort consequent upon a considerable reduction of the population, gradually permitted a return of higher yields. The yield of 60-70,000 young males, reached in 1941, has been maintained with little effect upon the breeding reserve. The major result observed was that males became territory holders at 9 years of age instead of 10. The mean *reported* annual take over 164 years

Table 21. The Kill in Decades of Northern Fur-seal

Decades	St Paul and St George	Pelagic	Totals
1786–1790*	208,879		
1791–1800	420,099		
1801–1810	422,440		
1811–1820	428,460		
1821–1830	271,860		
1831–1840	104,615		
1841–1850	130,814		
1851–1860	186,087		
1861–1870	624,766	17,486	642,249
1871–1880	1,042,520	71,926	1,114,446
1881–1890	939,103	238,484	1,177,587
1891–1900	165,252	421,300	586,552
1901–1910	163,111	208,611	371,722
1911–1920	197,411	20,834	218,245
1921–1930	268,576	39,401	307,977
1931–1940	555,900	11,698	567,598
1941–1950	664,036	1,106	665,142

*Five years only

is 47,712, which is admitted well below the actual but doubling the figures for the first 100 years would only raise this to 75,000 or so. Thus the present system of management produces approximately the same number of skins at a *constant* rate and is therefore a better economic proposition than the original 'go-stop'. It also maintains the population at a reasonably high and viable level with no risk of any catastrophic variations. This has been achieved by a thorough understanding of the ecology of the species and adjustments of the management control as new fact came to light.

On the eastern seaboard of North America is the Arctic Unit of the Fisheries Research Board of **Canada** which has carried out pinnipede work. Harbour, grey, harp, ringed, hooded and bearded seals have all received attention and the Atlantic walrus too has not been neglected. The leader has been A. W. Mansfield, ably assisted by H. D. Fisher, I. A. MacLaren, E. Mitchell, D. E. Sergeant, T. G. Smith, F. H. C. Taylor and others. Again it can be seen that all the available species have been worked on.

Continuing in the northern hemisphere we find that the **Soviet Union,** besides work on their own Baikal and Caspian seals, have concentrated largely on the eastern coast around the Sea of Okhotsk where the harbour (common), ribbon, ringed and bearded seals have all been investigated. The northern fur-seal on the Asiatic islands and the walrus on the northern coasts have also come in for attention. Two institutes are involved: the Laboratory of Ecological Morphology of Sea Mammals at the Severtsov Institute of Animal Morphology and the Pacific Ocean Research Institute of Sea Fish Husbandry and Oceanography. Among the researchers are: V. M. Byel'kovich, S. E. Kleinberg, K. K. Chapsky, G. A. Klevezel, M. N. Sleptzov and E. A. Tikhomirov.

The contribution in the north-eastern Atlantic by **Great Britain** has been the subject of this book and little further need be said. However mention may be made of the 1972 expedition to North Rona which took place too late to be used in the main text of this book. It was organised jointly by the Seals Research Unit and the Nature Conservancy (Scotland) and lasted from September 5 to December 6, covering the whole of the breeding season. The full results are not yet published but a preliminary account shows its great value. In general it has confirmed the tentative (and extrapolated) findings of the 1959 season and has added a great deal of detail to what was previously known or suspected only in broad outline. One of the major deficiences of the 1959 expedition lay in the field of pup mortality on the rookeries. The data then collected has always seemed to me to be on the low side in view of later data from the Farne Islands. In the 1972 expedition a new much improved technique was used to count dead pups and the overall average mortality for the island was found to be 35% with the highest percentage (61%) in the gullies of Fianuis, where, in 1959 the highest figure (29%) was also obtained. The extremely accurate count of pups born was the lowest recorded since 1959 but confirmed the method of estimate used in the intervening years. On the whole the figures so far suggest that the North Rona population is 'saturated' and that a naturally stable population of grey seals may have fluctuations which are not negligible as a result of density dependent factors. They also suggest that the mortality rate for pups of about 25% now reached on the Farne Islands indicates that the numbers there have by no means reached their 'natural' maximum and further justify the management plan referred to in Chapter 14.

Previously the main effort of British zoologists interested in pinnipedes has been in the southern hemisphere where the pioneer work of the Discovery Expedition was followed up by the Falkland Islands Dependencies Survey and now the British Antarctic Survey. C. Bertram, J. E. Hamilton and L. H. Matthews studied Weddell, crabeater and southern elephant seals and the southern fur-seal. Later workers like R. M. Laws, W. N. Bonner, R. J. F. Taylor and others have continued the work and leopard seal and Kerguelen fur-seal have also received attention. The only antarctic species which has so far not been investigated is the Ross seal because of its extreme rarity. Recently a larger population has been found and something may now be possible. The area covered has necessarily been largely confined to the Falkland Islands, South Georgia, South Orkney, South Shetland,

Grahamsland and small islands like Signy Island lying in the British sector of Antarctica.

Australia has, during the last ten years or so, carried out an intensive series of investigations through the Division of Wildlife Research, C.S.I.R.O., Canberra, the Antarctic Division of External Affairs, Melbourne and the Australian National Antarctic Research Expeditions. In this they have covered southern elephant, Weddell, crabeater and leopard seals, Kerguelen, Australian, New Zealand and South American fur-seals, working on Macquarie and Heard Islands and on the mainland of Antarctica and Australia. R. Carrick, S. E. Csordas, Susan Ingham, J. K. Ling and many others have been producing a long series of papers covering a wide range of aspects of pinnipede research which has supplemented, in the Indo-Pacific longitudes, the British work in the Pacifico-Atlantic.

The characteristic common to all the work here mentioned is that the main objective is the thorough understanding of the population dynamics of the species in question and of the ecological and behavioural requirements. This has necessitated the careful co-ordination of field work and laboratory studies, involving personnel in other disciplines where necessary. Elsewhere in the world there are many individual workers, such as R. W. Rand and J. A. J. Nel in the Union of South Africa, A. G. Johnels and L. Eckerblom in Sweden, A. C. V. van Bemmel and E. F. Jacobi in Holland, R. vaz Ferreira in Uruguay and others in New Zealand, Japan and France, all of whom are doing good work limited largely by resources and a failure to receive sufficient governmental support to form properly co-ordinated teams. Fortunately Norway, one of the nations whose members have benefited enormously from the exploitation of pinnipedes, has recently shown signs of organised research at the Institute of Marine Research. T. Oritsland and others are tackling the harp and hooded seals in the north and the Kerguelen and South American fur-seal in the south.

Much more remains to be done to enable us to understand the bionomics of the many species of pinnipede and to arrive at positive conclusions and recommendations for their proper conservation. There is apparent however a growing awareness of the need for this, particularly in those countries which have in the past, and still do, profit most from the exploitation of pinnipedes. It is to be hoped that some truly international conventions will be possible within the next few years to save the north Atlantic seals from the fate of their southern relatives a century ago.

ACKNOWLEDGEMENTS

Acknowledgement is made for the following figures which have been redrawn and based in whole or in part on the originals indicated:

FIG. 5 Irving, L., Scholander, P. F. and Grinnell, S. W. (1942). J. cell. and comp. Physiol., **17**, Fig. 15, p. 166.

FIG. 6 Harrison, R. J. and Tomlinson, J. D. W. (1956). Proc. zool. Soc. Lond., **126**, Plate 1.

FIG. 8 Davies, J. L. (1957). J. Mammal., **38**, Figs. 3-7, p. 304.

FIG. 14 Hewer, H. R. (1964). Proc. zool. Soc. Lond., **142**, Fig. 11, p. 613.

FIG. 21 Hewer, H. R. and Backhouse, K. M. (1968). J. Zool. Lond., **155**, Fig. 8, p. 522.

FIG. 22 Craggs, J. D. and Ellison, N. F. (1960). Proc. zool. Soc. Lond., **135**, Fig. 5, p. 384.

FIGS. 24, 29 and 35 Hewer, H. R. (1957). Proc. zool. Soc. Lond., **128**, Figs. 2 and 7, pp. 25 and 35.

FIG. 27 Davies, J. L. (1949). Proc. zool. Soc. Lond., **119**, Map 2, p. 677.

FIG. 28 Hewer, H. R. and Backhouse, K. M. (1960). Proc. zool. Soc. Lond., **134**, Fig. 1, p. 158.

FIGS. 30 and 34 Boyd, J. M., Lockie, J. D. and Hewer H.R. (1962). Proc. zool. Soc. Lond., **138**, Figs. 1 and 4, pp. 259 and 264.

FIG. 33 Hewer, H. R. (1960). Mammalia, **24**, Fig. 1, pp. 402-3.

FIG. 38 Coulson, J. C. and Hickling, G. (1960). Trans. nat. Hist. Soc. Northumb., **13**, Fig. 3(a), p. 166.

FIG. 4: Bonner, W. N. and Hickling, G. (1971). Trans. nat. Hist. Soc. Northumb., **17**, Figs. 3 and 4, pp. 147-8.

Acknowledgement is made for permission to use again the author's photographs, previously published by the Zoological Society of London as under:

PLATE 2 (bottom)   Proc. zool. Soc. Lond., **134**, Pl. 2A.

PLATE 3 (top)   Proc. zool. Soc. Lond., **128**, Pl. 2, fig. 3.

PLATE 6 (bottom)   Proc. zool. Soc. Lond., **138**, Pl. 2, fig. 4.

PLATE 10 (bottom, right) J. Zool. Lond., **155**, Pl. V, fig. 27.

PLATE 12 (top, left)   J. Zool. Lond., **155**, Pl. I, fig. 1.

  (top, right)   Pl. IV, fig. 17.

  (bottom)   Pl. V, fig. 18.

236   ACKNOWLEDGEMENTS

PLATE 13 (top)   J. Zool. Lond., **155**, Pl. IV, fig. 19.
       (middle)   Pl. IV, fig. 21.
PLATE 16 (top)   J. Zool. Lond., **128**, Plate II, fig. 4.

BIBLIOGRAPHY

AMOROSO, E. C. and MATTHEWS, J. H. (1951). *The Growth of the Grey Seal* (Halichoerus grypus) *from birth to weaning.* J. Anat., **85,** 427.

AMOROSO, E. C., BOURNE, G. H., HARRISON, R. J., MATTHEWS, L. H., ROWLANDS, I. W. and SLOPER, J. C. (1965). *Reproductive and endocrine organs of foetal, newborn and adult seals.* J. Zool. Lond. **147,** 430–86.

ANON (1955–6). *Seal Marking.* Nature in Wales, **1,** 56; **2,** 269–70.

ATKINSON, R. (1949). *Island Going.* London: Collins.

BACKHOUSE, K. M. (1954). *The Grey Seal.* Univ. Durh. Sch. Med., Gaz., 1954.

BACKHOUSE, K. M. (1960). *The Grey Seal* (Halichoerus grypus) *outside the breeding season. A preliminary report.* Mammalia, **24,** 307–12.

BACKHOUSE, K. M. (1960). *Locomotion of Seals with particular reference to the fore-limb.* Symp. zool. Soc. Lond., No. **5,** 59–75.

BACKHOUSE, K. M. and HEWER, H. R. (1956). *Delayed implantation in the Grey Seal.* Halichoerus grypus. Nature, Lond., **178,** 550.

BACKHOUSE, K. M. and HEWER, H. R. (1957). *A note on Spring Pupping in the Grey Seal,* Proc. zool. Soc. Lond., **128,** 593–4.

BACKHOUSE, K. M. and HEWER, H. R. (1958). *Behaviour in the Grey Seal in the Spring.* Proc. zool. Soc. Lond., **129,** 450.

BACKHOUSE, K. M. and HEWER, H. R. (1960). *Unusual Colouring in the Grey Seal,* Halichoerus grypus. Proc. zool. Soc. Lond., **134,** 497–9.

BACKHOUSE, K. M. and HEWER, H. R. (1964). *Features of Reproduction in the Grey Seal.* Med. biol. Illust., **14,** 144–50.

BARNES, R. M. (1960). *The Grey Seal* (Halichoerus grypus) *in Norfolk.* Trans. Norfolk Norwich Nat. Soc., **19,** 73.

BARRETT-HAMILTON, G. E. H. (1911–15). In *Clare Island Survey, Pt. 17.* Proc. R. Ir. Acad., **31.**

BEMMEL, A. C. V. van (1956). *Zeehonden in Nederland.* Levende Nat., **59,** 1–12.

BEMMEL, A. C. V. van (1956). *Alle Zeehonden werden geteld.* Wekelijkse Studiereeks Stichting IV10, **12.**

BEMMEL, A. C. V. van (1956). *Planning a census of the harbour seal* (Phoca vitulina *L.*) *on the coasts of the Netherlands.* Beaufortia, **5,** 121–32.

BERRY, R. J. (1969). *Non-metrical variation in two Scottish colonies of the Grey Seal.* J. Zool. Lond., **157,** 11–18.

BIGG, M. A. (1969). *Clines in the pupping season of the Harbor Seal* Phoca vitulina. J. Fish. Res. Bd. Can., **26,** 449–55.

BIGG, M. A. (1969). *The Harbor Seal in British Columbia.* Bull. Fish. Res. Bd. Can., **172,** 1–33.

BONNER, W. N. (1970). *Seal deaths in Cornwall, autumn 1969.* N.E.R.C. Pub. Ser. C., **1.**

BONNER, W. N. (1970). *Humane Killing of Seals.* Seals Res. Unit, N.E.R.C., Occ. Pub., **1.**

BONNER, W. N. (1971). *An aged Grey Seal* (Halichoerus grypus). J. Zool., **164,** 261–2.

BONNER, W. N. and HICKLING, G. (1971). *Grey Seals at the Farne Islands – a management plan.* (Privately circulated.)

BONNER, W. N. and HICKLING, G. (1971). *The Grey Seals of the Farne Islands; Report for the period October 1969 to July 1971.* Trans. nat. Hist. Soc. Northumb., **17,** 141–62.

BOYD, J. MORTON (1957). *Aerial Studies of a breeding colony of grey seals,* Halichoerus grypus *(Fab.) at Gaskeir, Outer Hebrides in 1955 and 1956.* Proc. zool. Soc. Lond., **129,** 333–42.

BOYD, J. MORTON (1962). *Seasonal occurrence and movements of seals in North-West Britain.* Proc. zool. Soc. Lond., **138,** 385–404.

BOYD, J. MORTON (1963). *The Grey Seal in the Outer Hebrides in October.* Proc. zool. Soc. Lond., **141,** 635–62.

BOYD, J. MORTON (1967). *Grey Seal Studies on North Rona.* Oryx, **9,** 19–24.

BOYD, J. MORTON and CAMPBELL, R. NIALL (1971). *The Grey Seal* (Halichoerus grypus) *at North Rona, 1959–1968.* J. Zool., **164,** 469–512.

BOYD, J. MORTON and LAWS, R. M. (1962). *Observations of the Grey Seal at North Rona in 1960.* Proc. zool. Soc. Lond., **139,** 249–60.

BOYD, J. MORTON, LOCKIE, J. D. and HEWER, H. R. (1962). *The breeding colony of Grey Seals on North Rona, 1959.* Proc. zool. Soc. Lond., **138,** 257–77.

CAMERON, AUSTIN W. (1967). *Breeding behaviour in a colony of Western Atlantic Gray Seals.* Can. J. Zool., **45,** 161–73.

CAMERON, AUSTIN W. (1969). *The behaviour of adult gray seals* (Halichoerus grypus) *in the early stages of the breeding season.* Can. J. Zool., **47,** 229–33.

CAMERON, AUSTIN W. (1970). *Seasonal movements and diurnal activity rhythms of the Grey Seal* (Halichoerus grypus). J. Zool., **161,** 15–23.

CAMPBELL, R. NIALL (1966). *Grey Seal marking at North Rona.* Scott. Fish. Bull. No. **25** (July), 14–16.

CAMPBELL, R. NIALL (1967). *The recapture of marked seals.* Scott. Fish. Bull. **28,** 29.

CHAPMAN, D. G. (1961). *Population dynamics of the Alaska fur-seal herd.* Trans. 26th N. Amer. Wildlife Conf., 356–69.

CHAPSKY, K. K. and KOVALEV, K. (1938). *Game mammalia of the Barents and Kara Seas* (Erignathus barbatus *and* Delphinapterus leucas). Trurty arkt. nauchno-issled Inst. (Trans. arctic Inst. Lenningrad) 1938, 1–70. (In Russian.)

CLARK, J. G. D. (1946). *Seal hunting in the Stone Age of North-Western Europe, a study in economic pre-history.* Proc. prehist. Soc., n.s. **12,** 12–48.

COLLET, R. (1881). *On* Halichoerus grypus *and its breeding on the Fro Islands off Throndhjemsfjord in Norway.* Proc. zool. Soc. Lond., 1881, 380–7.

CORBET, G. B. (1971). *Provisional distribution maps of British mammals.* Mammal Review, **1,** 95–142 (seals 136–7).

COULSON, J. C. (1959). *Growth of Grey Seal calves on the Farne Islands, Northumberland.* Trans. nat. Hist. Soc. Northumb., **13,** 86–100.

COULSON, J. C. and HICKLING, G. (1960). *Grey Seals of the Farne Islands, 1958-59.* Trans. nat. Hist. Soc. Northumb., **13,** 151–78.

COULSON, J. C. and HICKLING, G. (1960). *The Grey Seals of the Farne Islands. An interim report dealing mainly with the 1959 breeding season.* Trans. nat. Hist. Soc. Northumb., **13,** 196–214.

COULSON, J. C. and HICKLING, G. (1961). *Variation in the Secondary Sex-ratio of the Grey Seal,* Halichoerus grypus *(Fab.) during the breeding season.* Nature, Lond., **190,** 281.

COULSON, J. C. and HICKLING, G. (1962). *The Grey Seals of the Farne Islands: a report on observations made between 1st July, 1960 and September 1961.* Trans. nat. Hist. Soc. Northumb., **14,** 90–100.

COULSON, J. C. and HICKLING, G. (1963). *The Grey Seals of the Farne Islands.* Trans. nat. Hist. Soc. Northumb., **14,** 170–83.

COULSON, J. C. and HICKLING, G. (1964). *The breeding biology of the grey seal,* Halichoerus grypus *(Fab.), on the Farne Islands, Northumberland.* J. Anim. Ecol., **33,** 485–512.

COULSON, J. C. and HICKLING, G. (1965). *The grey seals of the Farne Islands: report for the period 1st May, 1963 to 31st March, 1965.* Trans. nat. Hist. Soc. Northumb., **15,** 121–39.

COULSON, J. C. and HICKLING, G. (1969). *The grey seals of the Farne Islands: report for the period 1st April 1965 to 1st September 1968.* Trans. nat. Hist. Soc. Northumb., **17,** 29–46.

CRAGGS, J. D. and ELLISON, N. F. (1960). *Observations on the Seals of the (Welsh) Dee Estuary.* Proc. zool. Soc. Lond., **135,** 375–85.

CURLE, A. O. (1933). *An account of further excavations at Jarlshop, Sumburgh, Shetland, in 1932 and 1933, on behalf of H.M. Office of Works.* Proc. Soc. Antiq. Scot., **8,** 224–319.

CURRY-LINDAHL, K. (1970). *Breeding biology of the Baltic grey seal,* (Halichoerus grypus). Der Zoologische Garten, **38,** 16–29.

DARLING, F. F. (1939). *A Naturalist on Rona.* Oxford.

DARLING, F. F. (1947). *Natural History of the Highlands and Islands.* London, Collins (p. 222 et seq).

DARLING, F. F. (1952). *The Atlantic grey seal.* Animal Kingdom, **55,** 122.

DARLING, F. F. and BOYD, J. M. (1964). *Natural History of the Highlands and Islands.* 2nd Ed. London, Collins.

DAVIES, J. L. (1949). *Observations on the grey seal* (Halichoerus grypus) *at Ramsey Island, Pembrokeshire.* Proc. zool. Soc. Lond., **119,** 673.

DAVIES, J. L. (1953). *Colony size and reproduction in the Grey Seal.* Proc. zool. Soc. Lond., **123,** 327.

DAVIES, J. L. (1956). *The Grey Seal at the Isles of Scilly.* Proc. zool. Soc. Lond., **127,** 161–6.

DAVIES, J. L. (1957). *The Geography of the Gray Seal.* J. Mammal., **38,** 297–310.

DAVIES, J. L. (1958). *The Pinnipedia: an essay in zoogeography.* Geogrl. Rev., **48,** 474–93.

DAVIES, J. L. (1958). *Pleistocene geography and the distribution of northern pinnipedes.* Ecology, **36,** 97–113.

DEGERBOL, M. (1933). *Danmarks Pattedyr i Fortiden.* Copenhagen.

DUNCAN, A. (1952). *A small colony of grey seals* (Halichoerus grypus *Fab.) in the south of the Isle of Man.* Rep. mar. biol. Stn. Port Erin, **64,** 22.

DUNCAN, A. (1956). *Some notes on the food and parasites of two Grey Seals* (Halichoerus grypus *Fab.) from the Isle of Man.* Proc. zool. Soc. Lond., **129,** 635–44.

FISHER, H. D. (1952). *The Status of the harbour seal in British Columbia, with particular reference to the Skeena River.* Bull. Fish. Res. Bd. Can., No. **93.**

FISHER, H. D. (1952). *Harp seals of the north-west Atlantic.* Fish. Res. Bd. Can. Atlantic Biol. Station. General Series Circular, No. **20.**

FISHER, H. D. (1954). *Delayed implantation in the Harbour Seal* Phoca vitulina *L.* Nature, Lond., **173,** 879.

FISHER, H. D. (1954). *Studies in reproduction in the Harp Seal,* Phoca groenlandica *Erxleben, in the north-west Atlantic.* Fish. Res. Bd. Can., Rep. Biol. Station, No. **588.**

FISHER, H. D. and MACKENZIE, B. A. (1955). *Food habits of seals in the Maritimes.* Fish. Res. Bd. Can., **61,** 5–9.

FISHER, J. (1948). *'Rockall' and 'Seal flights', 1947.* Notes Rec. roy. Soc. London, **6,** 12–17.

FLINT, R. F. (1947). *Glacial geology and the Pleistocene epoch.* Wiley: New York.

FOGDEN, S. C. L. (1968). *Suckling behaviour in the Grey Seal* (Halichoerus grypus) *and the Northern Elephant Seal* (Mirounga angustirostris). J. Zool., **154,** 415–20.

FOGDEN, S. C. L. (1971). *Mother–young behaviour at Grey Seal breeding beaches.* J. Zool., **164,** 61–92.

GALLACHER, J. B. and WATERS, W. E. (1964). *Pneumonia in Grey Seal pups at St Kilda.* Proc. zool. Soc. Lond., **142,** 177–80.

GORDON, SETON (1946). *Atlantic Seals – Island colonies off the Outer Hebrides.* Scotsman, 2nd November.

GORDON, SETON (1950). *Among the Seals.* Spectator, No. 6387, 541–2.

GORDON, SETON (1951). *Haunts of the Atlantic Seal.* Country Life, **109,** 777–8.

GRINNELL, S. W., IRVING, L. and SCHOLANDER, P. F. (1942). *Experiments on the relation between blood flow and heart rate in the diving seal.* J. cell. and comp. Physiol., **19,** 341–51.

HAMILTON, J. R. C. (1952). *Iron Age Settlement in the Shetlands.* Archeol. Newsletter, **4,** 159–60.

HARRISON, R. J. (1951). *Changes in the reproductive tract of foetal and adult seals.* J. Anat., **85,** 428.

HARRISON, R. J. (1960). *Reproduction and reproductive organs in common seals* (Phoca vitulina) *in the Wash, East Anglia.* Mammalia, **24,** 372–85.

HARRISON, R. J., MATTHEWS, L. H. and ROBERTS, J. M. (1952). *Reproduction in some Pinnipedia.* Trans. zool. Soc. Lond., **27,** 437–540.

HARRISON, R. J. and TOMLINSON, J. D. W. (1956). *Observations on the venous system in certain Pinnipedia and Cetacea.* Proc. zool. Soc. Lond., **126,** 205–33.

HARRISON, R. J. and TOMLINSON, J. D. W. (1960). *Normal and experimental diving in the common seal* (Phoco vitulina). Mammalia, **24,** 386–99.

HARRISON, R. J., TOMLINSON, J. D. W. and BERNSTEIN, L. (1954). *The caval sphincter in Phoca vitulina L.* Nature, Lond., **173,** 86.

HARRISSON, T. H. (1932). *Numbers of the grey seal* (Halichoerus grypus) *on St Kilda and North Rona.* J. Anim. Ecol., **1,** 83.

HARVIE-BROWN, J. A. and BUCKLEY, T. E. (1888). *A vertebrate fauna of the Outer Hebrides.* Edinburgh: Douglas.

HAVINGA, B. (1933). *Der Seehund* (Phoca vitulina *L.*) *in den Holländisden Gewässen.* Tijdschr. ned. dierk. Vereen, **3,** 79–111.

HAY, I. (1934). *Grey Seal in the Firth of Forth.* Scott. Nat., **205,** 39.

HEPBURN, D. (1896). *The grey seal* (Halichoerus grypus). *Observations on its external appearances and visceral anatomy.* J. Anat., **30,** 413–88.

HEWER, H. R. (1955). *Notes on the marking of Atlantic Seals in Pembrokeshire.* Proc. zool. Soc. Lond., **125,** 87–93.

HEWER, H. R. (1957). *A Hebridean Colony of the Grey Seal,* (Halichoerus grypus *Fab.*) *with comparative notes on the Grey Seals of Ramsey Island, Pembrokeshire.* Proc. zool. Soc. Lond., **128,** 23–66.

HEWER, H. R. (1957). *Reports of Ringing and Returns of Grey Seals: No. 1. September 1954– August 1956.* Proc. zool. Soc. Lond., **128,** 594–6.

HEWER, H. R. (1960). *Behaviour of the Grey Seal* (Halichoerus grypus *Fab.*) *in the Breeding Season.* Mammalia, **24,** 400–21.

HEWER, H. R. (1960). *The Grey Seal on North Rona.* New Scient., **6,** 1058–9.

HEWER, H. R. (1960). *Age Determination of Seals.* Nature, Lond., **187,** 959–60.

HEWER, H. R. (1962). *Grey Seals.* Sunday Times. Animals of Britain, No. 7.

HEWER, H. R. (1962). *Populations of the Grey Seal.* Times Science Review (Autumn), 10–12.

HEWER, H. R. (1963). *Provisional Grey Seal Life Table.* In *Grey Seals and Fisheries,* Report of the Consultative Committee on Grey Seals and Fisheries – 27–8. London, H.M.S.O.

HEWER, H. R. (1964). *The determination of age, sexual maturity, longevity and a life-table in the grey seal* (Halichoerus grypus). Proc. zool. Soc. Lond., **142,** 593–624.

HEWER, H. R. and BACKHOUSE, K. M. (1959). *Field Identification of Bulls and Cows of the Grey Seal,* Halichoerus grypus *Fab.* Proc. zool. Soc. Lond., **132,** 641–5.

HEWER, H. R. and BACKHOUSE, K. M. (1960). *A preliminary account of a colony of grey seals,* Halichoerus grypus *Fab. in the Southern Inner Hebrides.* Proc. zool. Soc. Lond., **134,** 157–95.

HEWER, H. R. and BACKHOUSE, K. M. (1961). *'Headless' grey seal pups.* Proc. zool. Soc. Lond., **137,** 630–1.

HEWER, H. R. and BACKHOUSE, K. M. (1968). *Embryology and Foetal Growth Rate in the Grey Seal,* (Halichoerus grypus). J. Zool., **155,** 507–33.

HICKLING, G. (1957). *The Grey Seals of the Farne Islands.* Trans. nat. Hist. Soc. Northumb., **12,** 93–133.

HICKLING, G. (1959). *The Grey Seals of the Farne Islands.* Trans. nat. Hist. Soc. Northumb., **13,** 33–64.

HICKLING, G. (1959). *The Grey Seals of the Farne Islands.* Oryx, **5,** 7–15.

HICKLING, G., JONES, A. W. and TELFER, I. M. (1955). *The Grey Seals of the Farne Islands.* Trans. nat. Hist. Soc. Northumb., **9,** 153–63.

HICKLING, G., JONES, A. W. and TELFER, I. M. (1956). *The Grey Seals of the Farne Islands.* Trans. nat. Hist. Soc. Northumb., **9,** 230–44.

HICKLING, G., RASMUSSEN, B. and SMITH, E. A. (1962). Innvandring fra Storbritannia til Norge av havert (Halichoerus grypus). Fisken Hav. No. 2 (1962), 199–205 Saertrykk av *Fiskets Gang* No. **13,** 1–7.

HOBSON, E. S. (1966). *Visual orientation and feeding in seals and sea-lions.* Nature, Lond., **210,** 326–7.

HOOK, O. (1960). *Some observations on the dates of pupping, and the incidence of partial rust and orange coloration in grey seal cows.* Halichoerus grypus (*Fabricius*), *on Linga, Treshnish Isles, Argyll.* Proc. zool. Soc. Lond., **134,** 495–7.

HOOK, O. (1964). *The distribution and breeding of the grey seal in the Baltic.* In *A Seals Symposium.* Mimeographed Proceedings Edinburgh: Nature Conservancy.

HOOK, O. and JOHNELS, A. G. (1972). *The breeding and distribution of the Grey seal*

(Halichoerus grypus *Fab.*) *in the Baltic Sea with observations on other seals of the area.* Proc. R. Soc. Lond. B **182,** 37–58.

HUMPHRY, J. M. (1868). *The myology of* Phoca communis. J. Anat., **2,** 290.

IRVING, L. and HART, J. S. (1957). *The metabolism and insulation of seals as bare-skinned mammals in cold water.* Can. J. Zool., **35,** 497–511.

IRVING, L., SCHOLANDER, P. F. and GRINNELL, S. W. (1942). *The regulation of arterial blood pressure in the seal during diving.* Amer. J. Physiol., **135,** 557–66.

IRVING, L., SCHOLANDER P. F. and GRINNELL, S. W. (1942). *Significance of the heart rate to the diving ability of seals.* J. cell. and comp. Physiol., **18,** 283.

JOHNSON, A. L. (1956, 1957, 1959, 1961, 1962). *Seal marking and recoveries.* Nature in Wales, **2,** 267–9, **3,** 377–81, **5,** 717–24, **7,** 83–4, **8,** 53–5.

KENYON, K. W., SCHEFFER, V. B. and CHAPMAN, D. G. (1954). *A population study of the Alaska Fur-seal Herd.* U.S. Dept. of Int., Fish and Wildlife Survey, Sp. Sci. Rep. Wildlife. No. **12.**

KING, C. J. (1936). *Grey or Atlantic Seals.* The Field, January 25.

KING, JUDITH E. (1964). *Seals of the World.* Brit. Mus. (Nat. Hist.) London.

KING, JUDITH E. (1966). *Relationships of the Hooded and Elephant Seals (genera Cystophora and Mirounga).* J. Zool., **148,** 385–98.

LAWS, R. M. (1953). *A new method of age determination in mammals with special reference to the Elephant Seal* (Mirounga leonina *L.*). Falkland Islands Dep. Survey, Sci. Rep. No. **2.**

LEGENDRE, R. (1947). *Notes biologiques sur les pinnipèdes. A propos d'un* Halichoerus grypus (*Fabricius*) *observé vivant à Concarneau.* Bull. Inst. oceanogr. Monaco, **44** No. 907.

LING, J. K. (1965). *Functional significance of sweat glands and sebaceous glands in Seals.* Nature. Lond., **208,** 560–2.

LOCKLEY, R. M. (1954). *The Atlantic Grey Seal.* Oryx, **2,** 384–7.

LOCKLEY, R. M. (1955, 1958, 1966). *Seal marking and recoveries.* Nature in Wales, **1,** 15–16, **4,** 537–43, **10,** 59–64.

LOCKLEY, R. M. (1966). *The distribution of grey and common seals on the coasts of Ireland.* Ir. Nat. J., **15,** 136–43.

LOCKLEY, R. M. (1966). *Grey Seal, Common Seal.* London: Andre Deutsch.

LOUGHREY, A. G. (1959). *Preliminary investigation of the Atlantic Walrus* Odobenus rosmarus rosmarus (*Linnaeus*). Canada Wildlife Service: Wildlife Mgt. Bull. ser. 1, No. **14.**

MACINTYRE, D. (1948). *Grey Seals at Shetland.* The Field, Jan. 10.

MANSFIELD, A. W. (1964). *The influence of Pinnipeds on the Fisheries of Eastern Canada.* In *A Seals Symposium.* Mimeographed Proceedings, Edinburgh: Nature Conservancy.

MANSFIELD, A. W. (1966). *The Grey Seal in Eastern Canadian Waters.* Can. Audubon Mag., (1966), 161–6.

MANSFIELD, A. W. (1967). *The Mammals of Sable Island.* Can. Fld. Nat., **81,** 40–9.

MANSFIELD, A. W. (1967). *Seals of Arctic and Eastern Canada.* Bull. Fish. Res. Bd. Can. No. **137.**

MANSFIELD, A. W. (1967). *The Walrus in Canada's Arctic.* Stud. Stns. Fish Res. Bd. Can. 1966 (2), 603–24.

MANSFIELD, A. W. (1967). *Distribution of the harbor seal* Phoca vitulina *Lin. in Canadian Arctic waters.* J. Mammal. **48,** 249–57.

MANSFIELD, A. W. and FISHER, H. D. (1960). *Age Determination in the Harbour Seal,* Phoca vitulina *L.* Nature, Lond., **186,** 92.

MARTIN, MARTIN (1703). *Description of the Western Isles of Scotland.* London.

MATHESON, C. (1950). *Longevity in the Grey Seal.* Nature, Lond., **166,** 73.

MATTHEWS, L. H. (1950). *The natural history of the Grey Seal, including lactation.* Proc. zool. Soc. Lond., **120,** 763.

MATTHEWS, L. H. (1952). *British Mammals,* 254–79. London: Collins.

MCLAREN, I. A. (1958). *Some aspects of growth and reproduction of the bearded seal,* Erignathus barbatus *(Erxleben).* J. Fish. Res. Bd. Can., **15,** 219–27.

MCLAREN, I. A. (1958). *The biology of the ringed seal* (Phoca hispida *Schreber) in the Eastern Canadian Arctic.* Bull. Fish. Res. Bd. Can. No. **118.**

MCLAREN, I. A. (1960). *Are the Pinnipedia Biphyletic?* Syst. Zool., **9,** 18–28.

MCLAREN, I. A. (1966). *Taxonomy of harbor seals of the western North Pacific and evolution of certain other hair seals.* J. Mammal. **47,** 466–75.

MILLAIS, J. G. (1904). *The Mammals of Great Britain and Ireland.* Vol. 1, 240–365. London: Longmans Green.

MITCHELL, E. (1967). *Controversy over Diphyly in Pinnipeds.* Syst. Zool., **16,** 350–1.

MIVART, G. (1885). *Notes on the Pinnipedia.* Proc. zool. Soc. Lond., 1885, 484–500.

MOHR, E. (1935). *Stockholms Zoo auf Skansen.* Zool. Gart. Lpz., (N.F.) **8,** 16–24.

MOHR, E. (1942). *Tragzeit verhältnisse der Robben.* Zool. Anz., **89,** 176–83.

MOHR, E. (1952). *Die Robben der europäischen Gewässer.* Monog. Wildsäugetiere, No. **12,** 1–283, Frankfurt-am-Main.

MOHR, E. (1955). *Der Seehund.* Neue Brehm Büch, **145.** Wittenburg Lutherstadt. ver. A. Ziemsen.

NAUMOV, S. P. (1933). *The seals of the U.S.S.R. The raw material of the marine mammal fishery.* Series: Econ. exploited animals of U.S.S.R. Moscow. (In Russian.)

NEAL, M. and RANKIN, D. H. (1941). *Breeding of Common Seal in Strangford Lough.* Ir. Nat. J., **7,** 329.

OGILVIE, A. G. (1959). *Morbidity in the Farne Island Grey Seal Nursery in 1957.* Trans. nat. Hist. Soc. Northumb., **13,** 83–5.

O'GORMAN, F. (1963). *Observations on terrestrial locomotion in antarctic seals.* Proc. zool. Soc. Lond. **141,** 837–850.

OLDS, J. M. (1950). *Notes on the hooded seal* (Cristophora cristata). J. Mammal., **31,** 450–2.

ØYNES, P. (1964). *Sel pa norskekysten fra Fuinmark til Møre.* Fisken Hav. No. 5 (1964), 694–707. Saertrykk av *Fiskets Gang* No. **48,** 1–14.

PAGE, F. J. T. (1962). *Norfolk Mammal Report.* Trans. Norfolk Norwich Nat. Soc., **19,** 416–34.

PETERSON, R. S. and BARTHOLOMEW, G. A. (1967). *The Natural History and Behavior of the Californian Sea-lion.* Spec. Pub. No. **1.** The American Society of Mammalogists

PLEHANOFF, P. (1933). *The determination of the age in Seals.* Sb. nauchno-issled. Inst. Zool. mosk. gos. Univ.: Abstr. Works. Zool. Inst. Moscow Univ. (1933), 88–91.

RAE, BENNET B. (1960). *Seals and Scottish Fisheries.* Dept. Agric. Fish. Scot. Mar. Res., 1960, No. 2, H.M.S.O.

RAE, BENNET B. (1963). *The incidence of larvae of* Porrocaecum decipiens *in the flesh of cod.* Dept. Agric. and Fish. Scot.: Mar. Res., 1963, No. 2, H.M.S.O.

RAE, BENNET B. (1963). *The food of grey seals.* In *Grey Seals and Fisheries,* Report of the Consultative Committee on Grey Seals and Fisheries, 28–33. London: H.M.S.O.

RAE, BENNET B. (1968). *The Food of Seals in Scottish Waters.* Dept. Agric. Fish. Scot.: Mar. Res., 1968, No. 2, H.M.S.O.

RAE, BENNET B. (1969). *Twin Seals in Scotland.* J. Zool., **158,** 243–5.

RAE, B. B. and SHEARER, W. M. (1965). *Seal Damage to Salmon Fisheries.* Dept. Agric. Fish. Scot.: Mar. Res., 1965, No. 2, H.M.S.O.

REVELSTOKE, Lord (1907). *Seals on Lambay Island.* Ir. Nat., **16,** 20–1.

RICE, DALE W. and SCHEFFER, VICTOR B. (1968). *A List of the Marine Mammals of the World.* United States Fish and Wildlife Service: Special Scientific Report – Fisheries, No. **579.**

RITCHIE, J. (1930). *The protection of the Grey Seal.* Scott. Nat., **181,** 33–6.

ROUX, F. (1957). *Sur la présence de Phoques à l'île d'Ouessant.* Penn ar Bed., **11,** 13–18.

SALMON, H. M. (1935). *Seals on the West Coast.* Trans. Cardiff Nat. Soc., **48,** 13–36.

SANDMAN, J. A. (1912). *Die Verteilung der Seehunde in Finnland.* Rapp. Cons. Explor. Mar., **14,** 124.

SARICH, VINCENT M. (1969). *Pinniped origins and the rate of evolution of carnivore albumins.* Syst. Zool., **18,** 286–95.

SAUNDBY, R. P. (1960). *Observations on the Grey Seals at St Kilda in winter.* Proc. zool. Soc. Lond., **133,** 487–90.

SCHEFFER, T. H. and SLIPP, J. W. (1944). *The Harbor Seal in Washington State.* Am. Midl. Nat., **32,** 373–416.

SCHEFFER, VICTOR B. (1950). *Growth layers on the teeth of Pinnipedia as an indication of age.* Science, **112,** 309–11.

SCHEFFER, V. B. (1958). *Seals, sea-lions and walruses. A review of the Pinnipedia.* Stanford Univ. Press.

SCHEFFER, VICTOR B. and RICE, DALE W. (1963). *A list of the Marine Mammals of the World.* United States Fish and Wildlife Service: Special Scientific Report – Fisheries No. **431.**

SCHOLANDER, P. F., IRVING, L. and GRINNELL, S. W. (1942). *On the temperature and metabolism of the seal during diving.* J. cell and comp. Physiol., **19,** 67–78.

SEGERSTRÅLE, S. G. (1956). *The Distribution of Glacial Relicts in Finland and Adjacent Russian Areas.* Commentat. biol. (Helsingfors), **15** (18), 1–35.

SELBY, P. J. (1841). *Observations on the great seal of the Farne Islands, showing it to be the Halichoerus grisens Nills and not the* Phoca barbata. Ann. Mag. Nat. Hist., **6,** 462.

SELOUS, E. (1915). *Observations on the Grey Seal.* Naturalist, Hull (1915), 217–21, 253–7, 281–4, 358–62.

SERGEANT, D. E. (1951). *The status of the common seal* (Phoca vitulina L.) *on the East Anglian coast.* J. mar. biol. Ass. U.K., **29,** 707.

SIVERSTEN, E. (1941). *On the biology of the harp seal* (phoca groenlandica Erxl.). Hvalråd. Skr., **26.**

SLEPTZOV, M. N. (1943). *On the biology of reproduction of Pinnipedia of the Far East.* Zool. Zh. Moscow, **22,** 109–28.

SMITH, E. A. (1963). *The population of grey seals.* In *Grey Seals and Fisheries*, Report of the Consultative Committee on Grey Seals and Fisheries, 15–17. London: H.M.S.O.

SMITH, E. A. (1963). *Results of Marking/Recovery Experiments, 1951–61.* In *Grey Seals and Fisheries*, Report of the Consultative Committee on Grey Seals and Fisheries, 18–22. London, H.M.S.O.

SMITH, E. A. (Ed.) (1964). *A Seals Symposium.* Mimeographed Proceedings, Edinburgh: Nature Conservancy.

SMITH, E. A. (1966). *A review of the world's grey seal population.* J. Zool. Lond. **150**, 463–89.

SMITH, E. A. (1966). *Nomenclature for seal research in Britain.* J. Zool. Lond. **150**, 457–62.

SMITH, E. A. (1966). *A note on evidence for the onset of sexual activity in male grey seals.* J. Zool. Lond. **150**, 509–11.

SMITH, E. A. (1968). *Adoptive Suckling in the Grey Seal.* Nature, Lond., **217**, 762–3.

SOUTHERN, H. N. (Ed.) (1964). *The Handbook of British Mammals*, 390–400. Oxford: Blackwell's Sci. Pub.

STEVENS, G. A. (1934). *A short investigation into the habits, abundance and species of seals on the North Cornish coast.* J. mar. biol. Ass. U.K., **19**, 489.

STEVENS, G. A. (1936). *Seals (Halichoerus grypus) of Cornwall coasts.* J. mar. biol. Asso. U.K., **20**, 493.

STEWART, M. (1933). *Ronay.* London: Oxford Univ. Press.

TELFER, I. M. and WATT, G. (1953). *The Grey Seal of the Farne Islands.* Trans. nat. Hist. Soc. Northumb., **10**, 165–82.

TURNER, W. (1870). *Note on the capture of the Grey Seal,* Halichoerus grypus, *on the coasts of Fife and Forfar.* J. Anat., **4**, 270–1.

TURNER, W. (1870). *On the species of Seal found in Scotland in Beds of Glacial Clay.* J. Anat., **4**, 260–70.

VAUGHAN, R. W. (1971). *Aerial Survey of Seals in the Wash.* Seals Research Unit, N.E.R.C.: Occ. Pub. no. **2**.

VENABLES, U. M. and VENABLES, L. S. V. (1955). *Observations on a breeding colony of the seal* Phoca vitulina *in Shetland.* Proc. zool. Soc. Lond., **125**, 521–32.

VENABLES, U. M. and VENABLES, L. S. V. (1957). *Mating Behaviour of the Seal* Phoca vitulina *in Shetland.* Proc. zool. Soc. Lond., **128**, 387–96.

VENABLES, U. M. and VENABLES, L. S. V. (1959). *Vernal Coition of the seal* Phoca vitulina *in Shetland.* Proc. zool. Soc. Lond., **132**, 665–9.

VENABLES, U. M. and VENABLES, L. S. V. (1960). *A seal survey of Northern Ireland 1956–1957.* Proc. zool. Soc. Lond., **133**, 490–4.

WATERS, W. E. (1965). *Grey seal haul-outs at St Kilda.* Proc. zool. Soc. Lond., **145** 150–60.

WATT, G. (1951). *The Farne Islands.* London.

WATT, G. (1952). *An experiment on marking the grey seal* Halichoerus grypus. Natur e Lond., **169**, 883.

WILKE, F., NIGGOL, K. and FISCUS, C. H. (1958). *Pelagic fur-seal investigation California, Oregon, Washington and Alaska.* Rep. Bur. Comm. Fish. Seattle, 1–96.

WRIGHT, F. S. (1916). *Mammalian fauna of North Cardiganshire.* Zoologist, **20**, 321.

INDEX